Stephen Johnson studied  Manchester, and went on to study composition with Alexander Goehr at Leeds University. After a brief period working for BBC Radio 3 he moved into musical journalism. Since then he was broadcast frequently for BBC Radio 3, Radio 4 and the World Service, with major projects including fourteen programmes about the music of Bruckner for the centenary of the composer's death (1996). He has written regularly for the Independent, the *Guardian*, *BBC Music Magazine* and *Gramophone*, and is the author of several books including *Bruckner Remembered* (Faber, 1998), and *How Shostakovich Changed My Mind* (Notting Hill Editions, 2018). In 2003, Johnson was voted Amazon.com Classical Music Writer of the Year. His radio documentary, *Shostakovich: Journey into Light*, was nominated for a Sony Award in 2007, and in 2009 his documentary *Vaughan Williams: Valiant for Truth* won a Sony Gold Award.

Further praise for *The Eighth*:

'There have been many books on [Mahler] but Stephen Johnson's new volume is unique, concentrating on the composer's mighty Eighth Symphony (the 'Symphony of a Thousand'), setting the piece and Mahler's work in general within the context of the world and society he lived in. This is a book written with both passion and scholarship that will send listeners to the composer afresh.' Barry Forshaw, *Classical CD Choice*

STEPHEN JOHNSON

THE EIGHTH

Mahler and the World in 1910

faber

First published in 2020
by Faber & Faber Limited
Bloomsbury House
74–77 Great Russell Street
London WC1B 3DA
This paperback edition first published in 2021

Typeset by Faber & Faber Limited
Printed and bound by CPI Group (UK) Ltd, Croydon, CR0 4YY

A CIP record for this book
is available from the British Library

ISBN 978–0–571–36752–8

Contents

Foreword

The Eighth Symphony was going to be different from anything Mahler had ever done before. He'd done with subjective tragedy, or so he told a friend and influential literary spokesman. The intensely personal dramas of his earlier symphonies were a thing of the past – or rather, they were now to be seen as preludes to this new, culminating symphonic statement: he was quite sure it was the greatest thing he had ever written. The first seven symphonies were all, in their very different ways, acts of private confession, the unburdening of a hypersensitive soul, struggling to make sense of its own existence and of the thrilling and terrifying world in which it found itself. The Eighth would speak in different tones, and of a different kind of experience. It would be a bringer of joy. Beethoven had held out the hope of joy in the choral finale of his Ninth Symphony, a hope to be realised when democracy dawned and 'all men became brothers'. But for Mahler it was achievable now: his music would bring it about, perhaps only for as long as the performance lasted, but that in itself might leave a lasting image, an icon of possibility. It was to be his religious rite, his High Mass, but conceived and expressed in terms that were both mystical and humanist. Like a religious rite it was about collective experience, a sense of belonging to something higher than the self, something that both absorbed and transcended the personal. And that something was more than abstract – God, or the mysterious *Ewig-Weibliche*, the 'Eternal Feminine' hymned in the symphony's oceanic final chorus. As to what that something higher might be, Mahler hinted at this

1

when he said that the Eighth Symphony was also a gift, his gift to the nation, by which he clearly meant the German nation; though whether that meant the geographical German nation, forcibly unified into a Prussia-dominated state in 1871, or a notional Greater Germany, a spiritual unity drawing together all German-speaking peoples (including Jews like Mahler himself) and truly embodied in its greatest artistic and philosophical works, he did not specify.

As it turned out, the Eighth Symphony's premiere was itself very different from anything Mahler, or indeed the city of Munich, had ever experienced. Mahler had enjoyed many triumphs as a conductor, especially in the opera house, but even moderate success as a composer had been rare and fleeting, and usually some way from home. For many sophisticates, especially in his adopted city of Vienna, Mahler was known largely as a great conductor. His music was widely treated as an object of ridicule, or worse, of indifference, cherished only by a few questionable zealots. The Eighth Symphony's first performance – or rather performances (the four-thousand-seat hall was sold out twice) – changed all that, sensationally. Thanks in part to a brilliant publicity campaign staged by the impresario Emil Gutmann, the anticipatory tremors soon built to a high pitch of excitement – so high that Mahler's mere arrival on the stage at the start of the concert was enough to set the audience cheering wildly. But the performance itself – Mahler himself directing with the brilliance and theatrical flair of a master illusionist or a glam rock star – drew an almost frenzied response. The press, even those who dissented on musical grounds, agreed that Munich had seen nothing like it. As for the artistic experience itself, there were plenty of big names from the musical and intellectual worlds to testify that it had been life-changing. The novelist Thomas Mann was so stirred and challenged by what he heard, and saw, that he gave the tragic hero of his novel *Death in Venice* Mahler's own physiognomy. His spiritual character too? That's another question entirely, but if there was a definite moment of conception for Mann, it was surely at that heaven-storming premiere in Munich in September 1910.

For Mahler's staunch champions it was a vindication, but for Mahler himself too much had changed in the four years between the Eighth Symphony's dazzlingly rapid composition in 1906 and its triumphant emergence onto the world stage. In 1907, the year of his strained departure from the Vienna Court Opera, he had discovered a weakness of the heart, which may or may not have posed a serious threat to his energetic public and private life, though his response to it was bafflingly inconsistent. Then there was the death, that same year, of his adored daughter Maria ('Putzi'). For Alma, writing years later, those were the 'three hammer-blows of fate' that eventually felled Mahler; but how much truth is there in that account, and might Alma have had reasons of her own for wanting to present those events in such a light? Mahler's next two works, the song-symphony *Das Lied von der Erde* ('The Song of the Earth') and the Ninth Symphony, are charged with images of death and loss, and haunted by a sense of the exquisite fragility of life. But whose life? Many at the time thought these works were eerily prophetic of Mahler's own agonisingly premature death, less than a year after the Eighth Symphony's premiere. But how much did hindsight come into play, and are we still guilty of misrepresenting – and at the same time underestimating – Mahler's spiritual progress in those last four years? Had Mahler lived to complete his Tenth Symphony, fully sketched in 1910, would the Mahler legend, and even the story of classical music's development in the twentieth century, look very different to us today?

Whilst working on the Tenth Symphony, during the summer of 1910, Mahler famously discovered that his wife Alma, his own *Ewig-Weibliche*, had been unfaithful to him. This precipitated what was probably the most agonising crisis of his life. Desperate to win her back, he showered her with love poetry, extravagant presents, soul-searing entreaties; he also broke the habit of a lifetime and offered her the dedication of the Eighth Symphony – he'd never inscribed a score to anyone before. By the time the long-planned Munich premiere came about, the need to re-conquer Alma's heart had taken precedence over everything: the thunderous applause, the ecstatic reviews, the long-yearned-for acknowledgement that Mahler was a great composer, a great *German* composer, how much did all that mean now if even the faintest possibility remained that his mother-goddess might desert him? Did it in fact work – did Mahler win back Alma's heart? The evidence is contradictory, but it makes for a fascinating story.

But then the story of Mahler's artistic and personal fate in 1910 is fascinating from so many angles. From both points of view this was perhaps the most extreme year of Mahler's life, during which he swung repeatedly between ecstasy and triumph and the profoundest dread and depression. Is this perhaps a story of tragic reversal? Does the abyss opened out in the Tenth Symphony's finale negate the Eighth's thunderous affirmation? Were the harrowing events of 1907 and 1910 a punishment prepared by Nemesis for the heaven-storming Hubris that had driven Mahler to create the Eighth? Or is the Eighth Symphony in fact a much more complex, multi-faceted statement than many of its critics have been prepared to admit? Of all Mahler's symphonies, this – the one he thought his supreme achievement – is the one that most divides audiences. How can that be: was Mahler simply mistaken?

Or have most interpretations of the work been over-simplistic? Can a deeper understanding of the texts he set, of Mahler's reasons for choosing them, and of how the music colours and even transforms their meaning, help the modern listener? It has certainly helped me. It is my hope in writing this book that the new understanding I have found might be helpful to others approaching this extraordinary symphony, either as performers or listeners. It still amazes me how many people who protest love or hatred for Mahler's Eighth seem to have given very little consideration to the words, to what they mean, and above all what they meant for Mahler himself.

For some time it has been a habit amongst commentators to look for answers in Mahler's individual psychology. There is nothing wrong with that, in theory at least. Sigmund Freud's famous encounter with Mahler, and his attempt to make sense of Mahler's alleged obsessional neurosis by drawing out details of a reported traumatic childhood experience, has been examined at some length. So too has the suggestion by Professor Kay Redfield Jamison, the world's leading expert on bipolar disorder, that Mahler himself suffered from this condition. I should at this stage point out that I have particular experience of, and personal interest in, this aspect of Mahler's biography. As a member of the Musical Brain charitable trust I have worked with neurologists, clinical psychiatrists, psychologists, psychotherapists and interested musicians on the relationship between so-called mental disorder and creativity, especially musical creativity. I am also a sufferer from bipolar disorder, and have sometimes felt that the intense love – and sometimes the equally intense difficulty – I have experienced in my own relationship with Mahler might have some connection with this. There is a huge danger in over-identification with a subject, and I hope the reader will note my caution in jumping to categorical conclusions.

The really important point however is that Mahler was not a disconnected 'psyche', floating freely and independently amid the cultural and political currents of his time. He was very much a man of his time and place, however complex his relationship to time and place might have been. Indeed he could justly be categorised among that creative type, identified by his philosophical hero Friedrich Nietzsche, that bears the imprint of his time like an open wound. This is where I hope this book will be most illuminating – not perhaps for specialists, but for those listeners who love Mahler but remain baffled by certain aspects of his towering yet sometimes seemingly contradictory achievement. Placing Mahler within his world – in particular the German-speaking world – in 1910, re-assessing his thoughts in the context of the prevailing thought of his age, has been fascinating for me, full of the kind of experiences modern Germans call *Aha Erlebnisse* – 'aha moments'. These have come not only in relation to the artistic and intellectual movements of the time, but through consideration of political climate and historical background, and on into science, medicine, technology, mass entertainment, and even the development of modern PR. The broader currents will all be considered, especially those leading to two world wars, the ending of the Habsburg Imperial dynasty and the transformation beyond all recognition of Mahler's world; many of the elements of that future world were emerging even in 1910, and Mahler might have been well placed to embrace some of them had he lived just a little longer. But other 'aha moments' have come through the examination of apparently trivial, everyday details of Mahler's world. In an age of e-communication, and in which something as simple as the addressing of an envelope is far less formal, less socially stratified, might Mahler have remained ignorant of Alma's affair?

In the end, for me, came the realisation that Mahler's Eighth and Tenth symphonies are part of a story, not only of an awe-inspiringly original mind and its creations, but also of the times that gave birth to him and them. Far from narrowing down the interpretative options, this realisation flings them even wider, showing (I hope) how pointless and limiting it is to attempt one definitive reading of either of these works. Literary and philosophical critics have long accepted that this is the case for the masterpieces of Mahler's idols, Dostoyevsky and Nietzsche; why should it not be true of Mahler too? A more recent philosopher, Bertrand Russell, said that while philosophy cannot provide any answers, it can at least help us ask better questions. Researching and writing this book has definitely done that for me, and it is my sincere hope that it might do the same for others. And even if it doesn't, the story of Gustav Mahler's fortunes in 1910 is a very compelling one. If I have related it half as well as it deserves, the reader's time will not be completely wasted.

Introduction:

The Arrival of the Queen of Heaven

On the evening of 6 September 1910, Alma Mahler arrived with her mother, Anna Moll, at the Hotel Continental, Munich, and was shown to the suite of rooms her husband Gustav had booked for them. Given the tone of Gustav Mahler's communications to her over the previous few days, Alma was no doubt preparing herself – perhaps even bracing herself – for some kind of lavish symbolic welcome. Only the previous day, Mahler had somehow found time amid his busy rehearsal schedule to send her two telegrams and three long letters, including at least one freshly composed love poem. Even so, what Alma found when she entered her suite must have made her pause in her tracks. Every room was filled with roses. On her dressing table, Alma found a copy of the newly printed score of the Eighth Symphony, with its dedicatory inscription on proud display: *Meiner lieben Frau Alma Maria* – 'To my beloved wife Alma Maria'. There was more to come: Anna Moll then found on her bedside table a copy of the piano score of the Eighth Symphony with a somewhat longer inscription, 'To our dear mother, who has been everything to us and who gave me Alma – from Gustav in undying gratitude.'[1]

All of this would have been remarkable enough if Alma and Gustav Mahler had been a couple of excited young newlyweds. But they'd already been married for eight years: eight very testing years, especially for Alma, an intellectually lively, highly creative woman who, despite her husband's obvious devotion to her, had largely found herself forced into the position of the classic 'work widow'. Sidelined by Mahler's demanding workload as conductor, first in Vienna, later in New York, she was on the whole expected to preserve a discreet distance during their shared summer holidays as Mahler worked energetically on the sketch of his latest composition, or in the spare moments during work periods he usually devoted to filling out and elaborating the full score. Motherhood had brought only limited consolations, and when the Mahlers' elder daughter, Maria, had died of scarlet fever and diphtheria in July 1907, Alma's feelings of grief had been, by her own admission, more complicated than those of her husband. Up till now Mahler seems to have been more or less oblivious to the effect all this was having on Alma. His state of being when absorbed in his own creative process is probably best reflected in the words of the poem by Friedrich Rückert he'd set in his exquisite song 'Ich bin der Welt abhanden gekommen' (I am lost to the world): 'I live alone, in my heaven, in my love, in my song.' And there he might have remained if a bizarre accidental discovery hadn't awoken him to the perilous truth during the Mahlers' most recent holiday, in the Alpine village of Toblach, in the summer of 1910. The shock precipitated the greatest emotional crisis of Mahler's life. Was it really possible he might be about to lose his adored 'Almschi' – his habitual pet name for her – his irreplaceable 'Saitenspiel', his 'lyre'? 'Almschili,' he wrote to her in one of those long letters of 5 September, 'if you had left me at the time, I would simply have been snuffed out, like a candle starved of air.' Without doubt, he meant it.

When Alma arrived at Munich's Central Station that same September evening, Gustav was there to meet her, 'looking ill and run down', as she noted later in her memoirs, *Memories and Letters*. As well he might: the rehearsal schedule for the world premiere of the Eighth Symphony, six days later, had been hugely demanding, and others had noticed that, while Mahler had thrown himself into directing rehearsals with all his usual volcanic energy, the strain was beginning to tell physically. But it wasn't just the effort involved in co-ordinating and urging on the massive vocal and orchestral forces demanded by the Eighth Symphony that was draining his physical and emotional resources. Behind it all was a desperate desire that Alma herself should understand and love the work he had explicitly dedicated to her, and to whom he had 'addressed every note' of the score – as he had told her in one of those effusive letters of 5 September. None of Mahler's earlier symphonies had carried personal dedications, and there had been no talk of one when the sketch score of the Eighth had been completed back in 1906. But soon after the crisis had broken at Toblach, Alma experienced a sudden dramatic visitation. Like most prosperous married couples at that time, Alma and Gustav Mahler slept in separate bedrooms. But one night, Alma tells us, she awoke to find Mahler standing, ghostlike, by her bed, in the darkness. Would it give her any pleasure, he asked, if he dedicated the Eighth Symphony to her? For reasons that aren't clear in her narrative, she begged him not to, pointing out that he had never dedicated anything to anyone before. He might regret it, she warned him. It was too late, Mahler replied: he had already written to his publisher, Emil Hertzka – 'by the light of dawn'.[2]

It was Hertzka whom Mahler had entrusted with bringing out the score of the Eighth Symphony in time for the premiere. Mahler's letter to him is relatively businesslike, but the sense of urgency still shines through:

Dear Herr Director!

May I kindly ask you to print a separate sheet with just these words: 'To my dear wife Alma Maria'. Please send me a proof of this as quickly as possible. It is most important to me that this sheet is included in the copies [of the score] when they become available for sale in Munich.[3]

In other words, the world must see these words and, presumably, Alma must know that the world sees them. One can imagine Mahler scribbling it, 'by the light of dawn' as he says, in a frantic effort to save both his marriage and his sanity: the writing is barely legible in places, but Mahler has clearly made an effort to steady his hand when it comes to the words of the dedication. Alma's response to Mahler's surprise nocturnal revelation had been to tell him that he might come to regret it. Was that a warning, or an expression of compassion – or possibly a form of self-protection? All three are possible. It is also possible that Alma recalled what Mahler had written to her after completing this colossal symphony: his talk of Plato and Jesus Christ, of Socrates and of that philosopher's imaginary conversation with the priestess Diotima, of Goethe's 'eternal feminine', of the 'sublimation' of the sexual urge in creativity and of the role of Eros in the creation of the world – all rather abstract, otherworldly, compared to what he was telling her now: that the Eighth Symphony was addressed to her, the real flesh-and-blood woman, and to her alone. Mahler had never shrunk from expressing his feelings for Alma in his private communications to her, but recently the heat had been turned up several degrees. In one of those long letters written on 5 September, the first day of rehearsals for the symphony's first performance, Mahler had written to Alma to tell her how, every time he broke

off during the morning session, he had scanned the empty auditorium – how wonderful it would be if his goddess were sitting in
the hall, drinking it all in! A mere sight of her dear little face, he
insists, would make everything – all the effort, all the complicated
logistics – utterly worthwhile.

Only the day before Alma had received this outpouring, veering
precariously between faith and desperation. She was always the
light and the central point of his life and work, he insists, and now
what torment and what pain it is to him that she can no longer
return his love:

But as surely as love must wake to love, and faith find faith again,
and so long as Eros is the ruler of men and gods, so surely will I
make a fresh conquest of all, of the heart which once was mine and
can only in unison with mine find its way to God and blessedness.[4]

'Jungfrau, Mutter, Königin, Göttin, bleibe gnädig!' (Virgin,
Mother, Queen, Goddess, be merciful!), implores the tenor in the
final solo section of the Eighth Symphony's culminating Part II. A
Catholic by upbringing, Alma may well have initially presumed
– as many apparently still do on encountering this symphony for
the first time – that the personage being entreated here with such
surging fervour is the Virgin Mary, Mother of Jesus Christ, the
Queen of Heaven. Did she understand that Goethe's conception
of Heaven, as portrayed in the final scene of his great verse drama
Faust Part II, was some way removed from any kind of orthodox
Christian version? Mahler had been at great pains to tell her so
in the letters to her about the Eighth Symphony, before the crisis
of 1910 had called the foundations of their marriage into question; but following even an edited selection of Mahler's ecstatic

outpourings to Alma on this subject can leave the reader feeling spiritually punch-drunk. If she did sense that she herself was being addressed in those words, can anyone blame her for drawing back? 'You might regret it' – so might any male who enthrones his lover as a 'goddess'. Woody Allen once quipped that he had always tended to put his wives under a pedestal. Did Alma feel elevated by all this devotion, or crushed by it? Reading *Memories and Letters* carefully one can intuit that her feelings were mixed, to say the least.

On one level, Alma clearly enjoyed her status, as the wife of the famous composer-conductor, and as the dedicatee of what was already being heralded as his *magnum opus*. She also seems to have sensed the power Mahler's anguished neediness gave her. Now, she tells us with evident pride, 'he was ready to take offence at the slightest sign that I was not being paid enough honour or not received with enough warmth'. At this stage in *Memories and Letters* there are ugly hints that Alma was working to distance her husband from his family, and from at least some of his closer allies. Mahler, she tells us, was understandably eager to hear what his friends thought of the Eighth Symphony, the work he was convinced was the greatest thing he had ever composed. Instead, he found himself alone, neglected by even trusted confidantes, who were now revealed as heartless self-seekers, interested only in the reflected glory of being intimate with a great artist. Alma reserves special scorn for Mahler's sister Justine ('Justi') who, she tells us with barely concealed satisfaction, was driven away with the words 'Alma has no time for you'.[5] Justine Mahler was a sensitive, sympathetic woman to whom her brother clearly felt very close. The suggestion that her attachment to him was little more than parasitic rings decidedly hollow. Note too that reported

'Alma has no time for you' – not 'I have no time for you'. One of the things that makes *Memories and Letters* such fascinating reading is that in moments like this Alma is sometimes more candid than she apparently realises. As for those other friends, keeping silent, leaving Mahler alone, it is hardly possible that Mahler's feelings were simply of no account to them; on the contrary it is much more likely that, painfully aware of what was taking place, they were exercising an extreme form of delicacy. At least some of them would have known what had occurred during the summer of 1910, and one can hardly blame them if they felt unsure of how best to help their friend.

In any case, even the best informed of them was probably unaware of one salient fact: in a room in a nearby hotel, the Regina Palast, Alma's handsome young lover, the architect Walter Gropius, was eagerly awaiting her next communication.

1

Setting the Stage

The forces required for the Eighth Symphony are huge – bigger than for any other work by Mahler. Apart from the eight vocal soloists, the two large mixed choirs and boys' choir, the score demands twenty-two woodwinds, seventeen brass, plus an offstage brass band of four trumpets and three trombones (so twenty-four brass in total), nine percussion instruments, celeste, piano, harmonium *and* organ, two harps, mandolin and a full string section – which for reasons of sheer practicality would need to be significantly bigger than the kind of string section normally employed in, say, a Brahms or a Tchaikovsky symphony, where the total number of woodwinds stipulated would never be more than nine, or the brass more than ten. However Mahler also recommends that there should be several players per part on harps and mandolin, and adds a note stipulating that 'when large choirs of voices and strings are used' (and it's hard to imagine a performance without them), 'doubling of the principal woodwind parts is recommended'. Mahler was an immensely practical musician, a professional conductor with three decades' experience of orchestras of very different sizes and abilities, and what may look on paper like musical megalomania often makes excellent sense when it comes to realising the kind of sounds and textures he had in mind.

One of Mahler's reasons for choosing Munich, rather than his previously adopted home city of Vienna, as the location for the Eighth Symphony's premiere was that the city had recently erected a magnificent new Musik Festhalle (Music Festival Hall), with

3,200 seats and a large stage. Space was a vital consideration, not just to accommodate the players and the anticipated large audience, but for acoustic reasons too. I still remember vividly how, when hearing Klaus Tennstedt's magnificent 1991 performance of the Eighth in London's Royal Festival Hall (hardly a small venue), the effect when the offstage brass entered at the ending of each part was rather like sitting between two huge distorting loudspeakers – and that was in a good seat in the stalls. Even so, it was still thrilling.

The logistics involved were formidable. Extra singers and players had to be brought in from various parts of the German-speaking world, and then there was the need to assemble a first-class team of eight soloists, who would need to be there for almost the entire rehearsal schedule. Unlike Beethoven's 'Choral' Symphony, no. 9, and unlike Mahler's two previous choral symphonies, nos. 2 and 3, the Eighth Symphony requires all the singers, solo* and choral, to be present throughout the work's eighty-minute timespan, and to be active for long stretches of each of the two parts. Accordingly Mahler and his impresario Emil Gutmann arranged an awe-inspiring rehearsal timetable covering an entire week, from Monday 5 September to Sunday 11 September. The soloists, most of whom one imagines had demanding work schedules of their own, were expected to be present from the afternoon of day two right through to the two performances booked for 12 and 13 September. Gutmann had gambled on the PR stir he had created being effective enough to fill the Musik Festhalle twice over – and the gamble paid off. Total and energetic commitment was therefore required from the entire army of performers for a full eight days (nine for the orchestral musicians). One has to remember

* Except for the third soprano, who sings Mater Gloriosa in Part II only.

that at this time the long-established system of 'deputies' was causing nightmares for conductors all over Europe. In London, for
instance, the conductor Henry Wood (who would give the British
premiere of the Eighth Symphony in 1930) had only just begun
to win his hard-fought battle against the deputy system: up till
then orchestral players were able, if offered more lucrative work
somewhere else, to send a substitute to a rehearsal for which they
had been booked, or even for the concert itself. According to the
treasurer of London's Royal Philharmonic Society at this time, the
substitution process became so extended and complicated that a
conductor could regularly expect to see as many as three different
musicians in the same seat during the rehearsal process, and yet
another musician in the same place for the concert.

Mahler would have none of that, and in his years conducting
orchestras and directing opera houses in Budapest, Hamburg
and Vienna he had developed the firm resolution and political
skill necessary to ensure full and committed attendance from his
musical troops. 'Those who saw iron discipline exercised down
to the smallest detail at the [Vienna] Opera House under Gustav
Mahler, and energy combined with meticulous accuracy taken for
granted by the Philharmonic, can rarely be entirely satisfied with
theatrical or musical performances today,' remembered the novelist Stefan Zweig three decades later.[1] 'He was by far and away the
finest conductor I ever knew,' recalled the English composer Ethel
Smyth, but working with him 'was like handling a bomb cased in
razor-edges' (and Smyth could be pretty robust when it came to
dealing with powerful men).[2] Nevertheless there was one decidedly awkward moment that nearly destroyed the *esprit de corps*.
For some time Mahler had had reservations about the competence
of the leader of the Munich orchestra, the Konzertverein, and he

wrote to Gutmann in June 1910 offering a solution: he would ask Arnold Rosé, much-admired leader of the Vienna Philharmonic (and coincidentally also Mahler's brother-in-law), to step in and remedy the situation. Unfortunately Gutmann doesn't appear to have communicated this to the orchestra, and an embarrassing incident occurred during the first full rehearsal. According to Alma, Mahler had asked Gutmann to made his decision known to the musicians, but for some reason Gutmann was nervous about doing so – which sounds unlikely, given what one knows of this normally bold and resourceful man. Mahler however telegraphed to Rosé, who promptly came over to Munich from Vienna. On the morning of the first full rehearsal the two men entered the hall together and Rosé went to take his place at the head of the orchestra – at which, Alma tells us, the entire orchestra rose up and walked off the platform, to Mahler's utter astonishment and dismay. For his part Rosé got up slowly and, after gallantly trying to comfort Mahler, left the platform, violin tucked under his arm, and made his way solemnly to the back of the hall.

It all sounds acutely embarrassing. An anonymous contemporary report, however, gives a slightly different take on the event. According to the author of *Anekdoten zu den Proben zur Uraufführung der VIII. Symph. in München* ('Anecdotes from the rehearsal for the premiere of the Eighth Symphony in Munich'), rather than walking off the stage, the musicians began to hiss as soon as Rosé appeared on the platform, and the gentleman who had thought he was to lead the orchestra got up and delivered an impromptu speech, in which he made clear his anger at finding himself supplanted in such a cavalier manner. Mahler listened in dignified silence, then told the speaker that his manner was better suited to a pontificating privy counsellor than an artist. On this point however it seems Mahler was forced to yield and accept the resident Munich leader. Who does one believe? Either way, it makes what Mahler achieved in those rehearsals, and in the subsequent public performances, still more impressive. Several eyewitnesses noted, as Alma had on meeting her husband at the station on 6 September, that initially Mahler looked drawn and pale. But as soon as he got to work it was as though he was suddenly plugged into a hidden energy supply. The *Neues Wiener Journal* reported that Mahler had an armchair placed in front of the music stand, and that he sometimes remained seated even after beginning to beat time – but not for long: soon he was on his feet, directing every bar with typical precision. Mahler's biographer Paul Stefan noted how often the visibly ailing composer seemed worn out both by the rehearsal process and by his own intense commitment to the music; and yet, almost miraculously, he still managed to carry everyone along with him, so that one could gradually see the whole artistic edifice come into being. How much these accounts of Mahler's personal struggle were influenced by hindsight – by knowledge of what was to happen in the months following the Eighth Symphony's premiere – is hard to tell, but clearly Mahler was able to rise magnificently to the occasion.

As the rehearsals proceeded, more and more people assembled to hear and watch. Some, like the Dutch composer Alphons Diepenbrock, came with serious doubts about the whole thing, only to find themselves converted. Diepenbrock had received an advance copy of the vocal score, and on first inspection he had come to the conclusion that the whole thing was a disaster: the treatment of Goethe's text in Part II was hopeless, he wrote to a friend, while the melodic writing suggested to him that Mahler's powers of invention were on the wane. For such an impassioned admirer of Mahler it was all dreadfully disappointing. But after hearing one rehearsal Diepenbrock reported delightedly to his wife that he'd been utterly wrong about it all. In fact hearing the music live reduced him to tears. That same day Diepenbrock fired off a postcard to another friend back in Amsterdam: the whole thing was a fabulous miracle – it was nothing less than divine! Meanwhile anecdotes began to circulate rapidly about Mahler's colourful behaviour and comments during these rehearsals. He may not have intended to provide Gutmann with publicity material, but when it came to stoking up curiosity, all such accounts – genuine, exaggerated or simply fabricated – were invaluable. There was Mahler's response to a recalcitrant trumpeter: 'You, my dear sir, are an excellent trumpeter. You shall have the last note, but I shall have the last word.' The first harpist tried a different approach, responding to Mahler's every remark with oily deference. 'Flattery!' cried Mahler. 'You're from Vienna, and you don't know how to flatter properly!' Several commentators noted how much he seemed to enjoy working with the children. (Despite the instruction in the score, it seems girls were also included in the 'boys' choir'.) 'If you succeed in giving more than you have, then you will be richer than before,' he apparently told them – a remark that does sound authentically Mahlerian. In one particularly complicated passage in Part II the children were having difficulty in making themselves heard distinctly enough: Mahler told them to sing so loudly that 'the angels in heaven' could hear them. Mahler was so moved by the result, we are told, that a moment or two later he had to take out his pocket handkerchief to wipe away the tears of happiness and gratitude that streamed down his cheeks. Another observer nicknamed him *Ewiger Wonnebrand* ('eternal flame of joy'), from the baritone's first words in Part II.

It wasn't quite everlasting joy and good humour. In his days
at the Vienna Opera Mahler had perfected the art of the caustic
put-down. To the orchestra: 'Gentlemen, are you playing at all?
It's the *rests* you're best at.' To the organist, clearly having trouble
finding the right colour combinations: 'It's no better than a fair-
ground organ, I've never heard anything so appalling in all my life.
It would do for a beer festival . . .' To the ladies of the chorus, who
insisted on talking when they should have been listening: 'This
symphony is meant to be *sung*. My next one will include spoken
parts. If you insist on talking, kindly go to Australia' – in other
words, the obscure nether regions of the world. But there were
also times when the imagery was wonderfully memorable: 'Here I
want my orchestra to be nothing but a large guitar!'; 'My children's
choir must enter here like a knife through butter'; 'Children, you
must imagine that your G will deliver a slap!'; and to the choral
basses, in the hushed first section of Part II: 'No music without
soul . . . Not so characterless, gentlemen, imagine you're playing
the cello.'[3]

The young conductor Otto Klemperer, however, took away a
rather different impression: less colourful perhaps, but of more
enduring significance. Until then, despite working as Mahler's
right-hand man on several occasions, he had apparently remained
doubtful about, or at least underwhelmed by, certain aspects of his
music. Hearing the Eighth Symphony in rehearsal (Klemperer was
unable to stay for the public performances) changed all that. It was
not until then, Klemperer confessed later, that he really began to
understand Mahler's music and to grasp what a great composer he
was. One of Mahler's remarks remained with him for life. Klemperer
noted how the composer always wanted more clarity, more depth
and power of sound, and more dynamic contrast. At one point in

the rehearsals Mahler turned to Klemperer and his fellow assistant conductor Bruno Walter and said, 'If, after my death, something doesn't sound right, then change it. You have not only a right but a duty to do so.'[4] I once saw the autograph score of the Fourth Symphony which Mahler had used when conducting some of its earlier performances. It shows how he put his own principle into practice: strengthening a line here, thinning out another there, perhaps even adding a new instrumental colour. Should conductors do the same when performing Mahler's works today? Leopold Stokowski, who directed the Eighth Symphony's sensational American premiere in 1916, certainly did. But fascinatingly, Klemperer – on whom Mahler's remark made such a lasting impression – remained largely faithful to the letter of his scores. Clearly for Klemperer, Mahler's scores – like those of Beethoven and Bach – were too close to holy writ to be tinkered with lightly.

By all accounts, the final rehearsal went exceptionally well, but then it must have seemed that all Munich was willing it to succeed. Even the drivers of the city's trams had been instructed to slow down as they passed the hall, and on no account to ring their bells. The critic Julius Korngold, father of the dazzling young composer prodigy Erich Wolfgang Korngold, was there representing Vienna's influential *Neue Freie Presse*. Korngold had been one of the very few Viennese critics who had consistently championed Mahler as a composer, often going very much against the grain of received opinion. For most of his career Mahler was, for the majority of musical Viennese, a great conductor who also composed – unfortunately, a good many of them would have added. One of those was Alma's own stepfather, the painter Carl Moll, who bluntly restated the received opinion that Mahler's music wasn't worth taking seriously. But Korngold, reporting back to a still largely disbelieving Vienna, was magisterially defiant. If only his detractors could see him on the podium at Munich – they would be forced to swallow their own words raw. Even from the moment Mahler began tuning the orchestra one could see how the force and magnetism of his personality worked upon everyone present. And the moment he began conducting it was as though flames could be seen leaping from his tiny frame as he steered his thousand-strong forces in any direction he willed, throwing up huge waves of sound one moment, then subsiding into incredible delicacy, focusing on the minutest details, the next. And how gloriously *melodic* it all was! Even the audience's reaction had something altogether extraordinary about it. After the symphony's gigantic closing crescendo had reached its peak, applause erupted from every part of the huge auditorium. It was like a roaring tidal wave of sound, welling up again and again, drawing Mahler back time after time to the podium to acknowledge this intense, almost religious adulation. Reading Korngold's enthralled reaction, it's easy to forget that what he is describing was just the final rehearsal. Was it possible that the official first public performance could reach still greater heights?

*

One person working determinedly to make sure that it would was Mahler's impresario, Emil Gutmann. Gutmann was one of the leading concert organisers and artists' representatives in the German-speaking world, with offices in Munich and Berlin. A contemporary flyer listing just his best-known clients makes impressive reading: the list of pianists alone includes Wilhelm Backhaus, Ferruccio Busoni, Harold Bauer, Alfred Cortot, Marie Dubois, Ignaz Friedman, Wanda Landowska, Moritz Rosenthal and Artur Schnabel – to take only the most stellar names. It was Gutmann who had organised an orchestral tour for Mahler in 1908, during which he'd given several performances of his recently premiered Seventh Symphony, and Mahler was evidently impressed enough by Gutmann's efforts to engage him for the work he now considered his *magnum opus*, the Eighth.

Gutmann threw himself into the task of attracting the largest possible audience for the Eighth Symphony's two Munich performances. Of course this wasn't simply a high-minded demonstration of faith in a grand artistic project; it was also driven by sheer financial necessity – the cost of mounting and co-ordinating the performances and rehearsals had been greater than even the practical Gutmann had anticipated. What Gutmann contrived looks more like a modern PR exercise than anything even Mahler had previously experienced in his own field. Gutmann's approach in Munich alone was close to saturation bombing. Mahler's colleague from his Vienna days, the painter and graphic- and set-designer Alfred Roller, created two arresting posters: the larger of the two was crowned by Mahler's initials, 'G. M.', and the number 'VIII' transformed into a version of one of Mahler's most characteristic conducting poses – the head low, the arms widely outstretched; the smaller one contains text alone, but in dramatic Jugendstil Gothic type, crossed by parallel lines that seem barely able to contain the words. Gutmann had the larger posters plastered over every street kiosk and advertising hoarding he could find, while the smaller ones filled the city's trams and trains. Shop windows displayed portraits of Mahler, photographs or copies of the bust of the composer by Auguste Rodin, along with engravings, silhouettes – anything with Mahler's face or profile on it. Bookshops were filled with copies of Paul Stefan's new biography of Mahler and other smaller published tributes, and with copies of the newly published 'pocket score' – though given the amount of information condensed into those minutely crammed pages, one would have needed capacious pockets to contain it. (The number of staves on the final page of Part I is just short of forty, nearly double the number required for the ending of Beethoven's Ninth.) Copies of the score were also discreetly 'left' in strategically chosen public places: for example, the tables of cafés where musical connoisseurs and critics were known to congregate.

Meanwhile Gutmann had charmed, strong-armed, possibly even bribed, an impressive number of newspapers and music journals right across Germany into previewing the premiere, publishing analyses of the music alongside, of course, plenty of sensational gossip about this colossal new work and the various dramas involved in putting it on. How truthful some of these stories were, at least in details, is hard to gauge, but at the very least they are symptomatic, and offer insights into wider thoughts and feelings. For example, a newspaper in Bremen – nearly five hundred miles from Munich – gleefully reported an incident on a train headed for the Bavarian capital, in which a fight had broken out between two Frenchmen, a Berliner and a Viennese when the Frenchmen had impertinently questioned Mahler's artistic worth. Even if it isn't true, the fact that this was published at all tells us something about Franco-German artistic and political relations in 1910, and the sensitive nerves that were touched by news of Mahler's symphony.

As is usual when a powerful and sophisticated hype engine goes into overdrive, there were reactions against all this. And every now and again the kind of antisemitic prejudice (more often implied than directly stated) that had plagued Mahler in Vienna reared its head again, as it did, bizarrely, in a largely complimentary article about Mahler by the Swiss critic, William Ritter. Ritter had started out as a confirmed anti-Mahlerian, but was in the process of changing his mind – the experience of hearing the Eighth Symphony was evidently crucial. He later became a determined and influential Mahler champion. But the person who seems to have been most horrified by it all was Mahler himself. Arriving in Munich for the rehearsals, he was stunned by the sheer quantity of publicity material – it seemed there was nowhere he could turn without encountering his own face staring back at him. The Viennese journalist Julius Stern, writing two decades later, recalled one cringe-inducing moment just after Mahler had set out for the Musik Festhalle. Stern was with Mahler as he drove to the Exhibition Hall, along with Alma and Mahler's young friend and protegé, the conductor Bruno Walter. Suddenly Mahler noticed the posters advertising the performance on the city's trams, with his own name proudly emblazoned in huge letters. A vainer man might have found it all deliciously self-affirming. Mahler's reaction, however, was to shrink back in his seat, bury his head in his hands and groan with shame.

But there was worse to come. Looking at CD covers or concert billings today, you will often find Mahler's Eighth Symphony furnished with a supplementary title: 'Symphony of a Thousand'. There have certainly been performances where the total number of singers and instrumentalists has been close to a thousand, and given what the composer himself recommends in the score one can imagine him nodding approval. But as a rule Mahler didn't like to give his symphonies titles: the name 'Titan', under which the First Symphony made its debut, was soon withdrawn; its successor, Symphony no. 2, was never officially the 'Resurrection' Symphony, though that is the name of the ode by Friedrich Klopstock that

Mahler sets in the closing stages of the finale. Thoughts of calling the Third Symphony 'Pan', or 'The Joyful Science' (after one of Friedrich Nietzsche's philosophical works), were discarded when the music was still in sketch. But those at least had something to say about the nature of the music and its message. It was Gutmann who came up with the nickname 'Symphony of a Thousand' (*Symfonie der Tausend*), quite without Mahler's permission. The first time Mahler saw the name in print he was horrified. This was about sensation, not about art. The whole thing, he moaned, was turning into 'a catastrophic Barnum and Bailey show'.[5]

Mahler knew better than most Europeans at that time what the names Barnum and Bailey signified. The hugely successful travelling circus company had been particularly active on America's east coast during Mahler's recent stay in New York, where he conducted the city's Metropolitan Opera and Philharmonic Orchestras. He would have seen their posters, loudly trumpeting 'The Greatest Show on Earth' – wasn't what Gutmann was doing horribly similar? Mahler must have winced at some of Barnum and Bailey's imagery, which so often seemed to feature a conductor-like figure (classical music references were far more common in popular culture then than they are now), perhaps dressed in clown's hat, baton in hand, urging on 'Wonderful Performing Geese and Roosters and Musical Donkey', or (worse still) in full evening dress, directing a 'Troupe of Very Remarkable Trained Pigs', each equipped with its own xylophone, 'Performing Numerous Difficult, Clever and Wonderful Tricks & Animals Showing Almost Human Intelligence and Reason'. For Mahler the ironist, the mordant self-satirist – the composer who had included a black, sardonic funeral march for woodland animals in his own First Symphony – the ouch-factor must have been acute.

But it wasn't just the potential loss of dignity that hurt: that was a side issue. What bothered Mahler most, or so Bruno Walter tells us, was that people would come for him, for the sensation, and not for the music itself. Separating the composer, as a living human being, from the music he created is harder with Mahler than it is with most other composers. Even so there is a difference, one of which Mahler was well aware, however much he struggled to make sense of it. Writing about his First Symphony to his friend Max Marschalk in March 1896, Mahler admitted that the painful ending of a love affair had left a deep imprint on the music. Even so, he continued, the symphony's significance as a work of art went way beyond autobiography. The affair may have stimulated Mahler to write the symphony, and may well have influenced its character, but it was not the *explanation* of the music. The real meaning, he wrote, was in some other world, the more mysterious world of music, in which considerations of time and space were irrelevant. Inventing a literary programme to fit a completed work was, he insisted, a sterile, pointless activity.

As we shall see, this is all highly relevant to the Eighth Symphony. One thing was quite clear to Mahler, however: if literary programmes were useless when it came to opening up the true meaning of a piece of music, the putatively scientific approach of musical analysis had nothing better to offer. When Mahler's publisher Hertzka proposed printing an analytical programme note for the premiere of the Eighth Symphony, Mahler reacted in horror. It was, he insisted (in a letter full of underlinings), his firm conviction, born of long experience as a composer and a conductor, that they were of no artistic or practical value for anyone. Describing a musical work in terms of themes and developments was like trying to describe a living human being by describing his or her internal organs or cell-structures. It was nothing short of vivisection! In the most emphatic terms, Mahler forbade Hertzka to allow any such thing for the Eighth Symphony's world premiere. What mattered above all else was that the listener, having enjoyed the music directly, without any kind of intellectual or emotional supervision, should be able to intuit in some way the real 'inspiration or basis' behind its composition. So what then was the nature of the 'real meaning' Mahler felt he had drawn from the Eighth Symphony's original inspiration? When we have looked at that, at the Eighth Symphony itself, and at the effect it had at its sensational world premiere, we must consider what message, or messages, the world then heard in it – in Munich in 1910, and afterwards.

2

'Light of the Senses'

Mahler usually composed quickly, sometimes staggeringly so. But in the case of the Eighth Symphony the speed at which he got his ideas down on paper defies credibility. By all accounts (and there are several), the sketch score was completed in just eight weeks. Mahler's summer holidays – the only time in the year he was normally able to devote to uninterrupted composition – usually lasted around ten weeks. According to Alma, the first two weeks of their stay in the Alpine resort of Maiernigg, above the shore of the beautiful lake Wörthersee, actually saw almost no musical work. There was nothing unusual in this, Alma tells us: as often before, Mahler fretted about failing inspiration until, suddenly, the light went on. In this case, however, the sudden flood of ideas was like an Alpine deluge: 'superhuman energy' was how Alma described it. It seems from Alma's account that Mahler didn't even know in advance which text he was going to set in the symphony's first part, and hadn't brought a copy with him. But that was only a minor impediment. It happened one morning, just as Mahler had stepped over the threshold of his composing hut up in the wood above the house. The desire of his heart, for inspiration, suddenly found words, 'Veni, creator spiritus', and with them the music flooded into being. In no time at all the opening chorus was written down. But then came the problem: '. . . music and words did not fit – the music had overlapped the text. In a fever of excitement he telegraphed back to Vienna and had the whole of the ancient Latin hymn telegraphed back. The complete text fitted the music exactly.

Intuitively he had composed the music for the full strophes.'[1]

It sounds too good to be true – and what on earth would have been the cost of telegraphing the entire eight-verse text of the Latin hymn to Mahler at a time when post offices charged by the word? But the story is not simply the creation or elaboration of Alma's lively mind. The critic Ernst Decsey, writing just after Mahler's death in 1911, remembered the composer telling him the same story – more or less: Decsey gives the location as Altschluderbach, but it was only the later compositions, the Ninth and Tenth Symphonies and *Das Lied von der Erde*, that were written there. Decsey tells us that Mahler did have a text of the medieval Latin hymn *Veni, creator spiritus* to hand, but in this version some of the original words were missing. Decsey tells us vaguely that the music Mahler had envisaged was in some way too substantial for the text. Whether, like Alma, he means that 'words and music did not fit', or whether something structural in the larger sense is indicated, is impossible to tell. (Mahler did in fact cut some of the words of the medieval hymn in his setting.) Nevertheless Decsey too tells us that Mahler soon realised he had to see the original text, and that he contacted Karl Luze, director of the Vienna Court Orchestra, asking him to send him a copy of the complete text. When this arrived, says Decsey, Mahler was astonished and thrilled to discover that the music he had composed fitted the hymn's verse structure – or was it the individual words and phrases? – precisely.

One can argue about the details, but somewhere between those two accounts is, one strongly suspects, a real, extraordinary creative event – so extraordinary that to onlookers it appeared almost supernatural. It also gives the lie to any suggestion that Mahler set out on composing his Eighth Symphony with any specific 'meaning' in mind. For Mahler's younger friend, Arnold Schoenberg, there

was nothing at all remarkable in that. The creator, said Schoenberg, is merely the slave of higher providence. Composing is for
him not a blissful, fully conscious response to some kind of divine
inspiration, but more akin to a kind of trance state. According to
Schoenberg's recollection, the Eighth Symphony had spilled out
onto the paper rapidly and half-unconsciously – 'as though it had
been dictated to me', as Mahler once told him.[2] For all the apparent
extravagance of the language, it does make sense: surely Mahler
would have had to create the Eighth 'half-unconsciously'. Given the
speed at which the ideas were pouring out onto the paper he would
hardly have had time to assess them consciously, let alone pause to
consider what they might signify.

But by June 1910, as Mahler was looking forward eagerly to the
Eighth Symphony's premiere three months later, the question of
the music's 'real meaning' had crystallised in his mind. The notion
of setting the concluding scene of Part II of Goethe's verse drama
Faust had, it appears, been germinating for some time. Mahler was
an enthusiastic reader, and his knowledge of the classics of German literature was extensive. *Faust* – a work with similar iconic
status for German-speakers as Shakespeare's *Hamlet* holds for the
English – would have been essential reading in any case, but as
Ernst Decsey recalled, Mahler's passion for Goethe bordered on
identification – with the work, and even with the man himself.
Decsey remembered his impressions on first entering Mahler's living room: there were books everywhere, not only on the shelves
but piled high on tables, furniture, even on the floor. Apart from
the wide range of literary fiction there was a huge zoological encyclopaedia, and a copious supply of philosophical works. None
of this, Decsey felt, was there for display. Mahler was a vor-
acious reader, and in the evenings he liked nothing better than to

stretch out comfortably and have a friend read aloud to him from a favourite book. The author Decsey remembered Mahler asking for most often was Goethe, and in particular Part II of *Faust*. Even though it was clear Mahler knew huge chunks of the work by heart, he loved to savour special passages, to discover them anew by hearing them read by someone else. On one particularly memorable occasion, after Decsey had been reading to him for over an hour, he seemed to undergo a remarkable transformation, and for a moment at least Decsey was convinced that he was looking, not at Mahler, but at Goethe himself: 'his face was ennobled by contemplation, his nose became more pronounced. I gazed at him for a long time and the impression was confirmed: like Goethe.'[3]

It is precisely the kind of half-intoxicated, dream-like descriptive writing modern commentators delight in debunking; and yet, look at Rodin's famous bust of Mahler – the one dominating shop windows all over Munich in September 1910 – and it would appear that the French sculptor saw something similar. And one thing from Decsey's account remains essentially unchallengeable: Mahler knew his Goethe, and particularly *Faust* Part II, from the inside out. The words had been brewing away in his imagination long before that fantastically productive summer of 1906. By the time he picked up his pen, the music had more or less fallen into place in his unconscious mind. No wonder it was so ready to come flooding out onto the manuscript paper.

Mahler was by no means the first composer to tackle the final scene of Goethe's *Faust* Part II. It forms both the culmination and the focal point of Robert Schumann's strangely hybrid choral-orchestral *Scenes from Faust* (1844–53), and – some might say rather less successfully – it provides a relatively brief choral finale for Franz Liszt's programmatic *A Faust Symphony* (1854–7). Clearly Mahler loved the poetry, the sounds, rhythms and melodic contours of the words, and sometimes that's all a composer needs to set his or her imagination working. But by 1910 it was clear that Mahler felt that in some vitally significant way Goethe's message to the world was also his own – and that this chimed in beautifully with the meaning he found in the old Latin hymn, *Veni, creator spiritus* ('Come, creator spirit'), whose musical potential had revealed itself to him in a thunderbolt of inspiration. A hymn to the Holy Spirit, followed by a depiction of the arrival of a redeemed soul in Heaven and his presentation to the Mother of Christ – unsurprisingly some people coming to the Eighth Symphony for the first time presume that this is pure Roman Catholicism, or at the very least some form of Christianity, orthodox or otherwise. Even Michael Kennedy, one of Mahler's most insightful biographers, summarised the philosophical plan of Mahler's Eighth Symphony as at least partly an affirmation of Christian belief, fused with Goethe's 'symbolic' vision of the redemption of humankind through love, as represented by Goethe's *Ewig-Weibliche* – the 'Eternal Feminine'. Was he wrong to do so?

Before considering what Goethe meant, it might be more helpful to follow Mahler and begin with the Latin hymn *Veni, creator spiritus*. This is attributed to the Benedictine monk, and later Archbishop of Mainz, Rabanus (or Hrabanus) Maurus (?780–856), later celebrated as *Praeceptor Germaniae*, the 'teacher of Germany'. Colourful legends have grown up around the origins of some of the Roman Catholic Church's most famous texts, for instance the lovely but improbable story that the hymn *Te Deum laudamus* ('We praise thee, O God') was improvised antiphonally by the saints Ambrose and Augustine after the latter's baptism in AD 387. But in the case of *Veni, creator spiritus* the attribution to Maurus is still widely accepted. Today the hymn is regularly performed at liturgical celebrations of the feast of Pentecost, seven weeks after Easter Sunday, commemorating the descent of the Holy Spirit on Christ's twelve Apostles, Jesus's mother Mary, and a number of other female and male disciples, in fulfilment of Christ's own promise made before his ascent into Heaven. According to the narrative given in the second chapter of the Acts of the Apostles, the Holy Spirit descended on the disciples 'like a rushing mighty wind', accompanied by an apparition of 'tongues of fire', and those who received it were heard to speak ecstatically in many different languages. Some bystanders speculated that the disciples were merely drunk; others however instantly perceived something miraculous:

And there were dwelling at Jerusalem Jews, devout men, out of every nation under Heaven. Now when this was noised abroad, the multitude came together, and were confounded, because that every man heard them speak in their own language. And they were all amazed and marvelled, saying one to another, Behold, are not all these which speak Galileans? And how hear we every man in our own tongue, wherein we were born? . . . we do hear them speak in our tongues the wonderful works of God.[4]

An experience like the sudden descent of a mighty wind, tongues of flame, ecstatic utterances – how like Mahler's own experience of conceiving the music for his setting of *Veni, creator spiritus*, a setting that turned out, almost miraculously, to fit the words of the original text better than the imperfect version he remembered! Then there is that resounding endorsement in the biblical account of the universality of the Christian message – addressed to everyone, Jews like Mahler himself very much included. And what better language than music to declare 'the wonderful works of God', whatever their background and native tongue? In all like-lihood Mahler also knew that Goethe himself had valued *Veni, creator spiritus*, to the extent of making his own translation – so here was a direct link to the creator of *Faust*. One aspect of the hymn that would have appealed equally to Goethe and to Mahler is that – apart from the conventional Trinitarian doxology in the final verse – there is very little in the text that makes it exclusively Christian: other religions invoke divine spirits and acknowledge heavenly fathers. Perhaps on top of all this there was a personal memory: *Veni, creator spiritus* is usually sung at the service of con-firmation, and Mahler would almost certainly have heard it sung at his own reception into the Roman Catholic Church in Vienna on 23 February 1897 – perhaps to the beautiful medieval chant still sung in Catholic churches today.

Might there be an indication here that there was, after all, more to Mahler's conversion to Roman Catholicism than political prag-matism? To take up his post at the Vienna Court Opera, as he did later in 1897, Mahler had to be – as any significant Imperial Austrian court official had to be – a member of the Catholic Church. It is possible, but despite his respect for his friend and mentor Anton Bruckner's intense Catholic faith, and despite his well attested love for country churches and their often touchingly simple devotional images, for plainsong and the smell of incense, there is no evidence that Mahler ever seriously considered him-self an orthodox Catholic believer. Accounts of what he actually confessed to believing vary. The great soprano Anna von Milden-burg, who had an affair with Mahler in 1895, two years before his official 'conversion', recalled 'his love of nature, his humility in his own art, his religiosity, his faith and his love of God'.[5] But the composer's friend and biographer Richard Specht felt that for

Mahler, 'God' and 'nature' were more or less synonymous. Mahler was, Specht insisted, 'a complete pantheist and a wholehearted believer in the doctrine of eternal reincarnation'; though Specht also remembered Mahler saying, 'Only as a musician can I fully express my thoughts on this.'[6] Otto Klemperer went even further: Mahler, he recollected in *Meine Erinnerungen an Gustav Mahler* ('My Memories of Gustav Mahler'), was in essence a true child of the nineteenth century. For Klemperer, Mahler was first and foremost an adherent of the philosophy of Friedrich Nietzsche, ecstatic proclaimer of the Death of God, and like Nietzsche completely irreligious. If he was in any way 'pious', it was not the kind of piety to be found in prayer books. In placing Mahler in his time, culturally speaking, Klemperer almost certainly meant to indicate what the historian Eric Hobsbawm called 'the long nineteenth century', that is, the period between the dawning of the French Revolution in 1789 and the outbreak of the First World War in 1914. It was a period of huge change and upheaval in ideas about God and religion, as the power of both Catholic and Protestant states to impose belief on their apparently willing citizens began to fail, and new ideas rushed to fill the resultant vacuum. Thus we have Maximilien Robespierre's revolutionary 'cult of the Supreme Being', Immanuel Kant's decidedly moral but personally remote deity, followed by the still more abstract, historically evolving, self-actualising 'world spirit' of Hegel. Then, having found a chink in the door, serious doubt began to prise its way in. David Strauss's *Das Leben Jesu* ('The Life of Christ', 1836) sensationally applied new historical critical techniques to the Gospels and concluded that accounts of the miracles of Christ were later additions, and that Jesus himself could not have been divine. Five years later the philosopher Ludwig Feuerbach published *Das Wesen des Chris-*

tenthums ('The Essence of Christianity'), arguing, from an openly atheist standpoint, that the heavens were, in effect, a giant screen onto which human beings projected their deepest, and sometimes darkest, desires, urges and aspirations: God did not create mankind; mankind created God, in his (it was usually 'his') own image. Feuerbach and Strauss's works had a life-changing effect on their young English translator, Mary Anne Evans, later famous as the novelist George Eliot. Around the same time, Feuerbach and Hegel were formative influences on Karl Marx's philosophy of history – evolutionary, like Hegel's, but materialist, replacing spiritual agency with purely socio-economic forces.

It has been argued, quite plausibly in some cases, that Goethe understood and/or foresaw all of this, and that the two parts of *Faust*, read together, are a symbolic record of the evolution of such ideas, not only during Goethe's own long lifetime, but before and afterwards. For the scholar R. H. Stephenson, *Faust* is nothing less than a history of the life of the spirit as the West has understood it. But what would Goethe have made of the philosopher of whom, Otto Klemperer tells us, Mahler was effectively a disciple? It was Friedrich Nietzsche who famously proclaimed in his quasi-scriptural 'philosophical novel' *Also sprach Zarathustra* ('Thus Spake Zarathustra', 1883–5) that 'God is dead'. But despite his occasionally manic self-celebratory tone, there is nothing smug about Nietzsche's proclamation. God has died 'from his pity for mankind' – in other words the idea of a compassionate God is simply unsustainable in the face of the suffering human beings endure. And Nietzsche is painfully, agonisingly aware of the abysmal void created by the departure of God. At one point his prophet Zarathustra cries out, 'Come back / With all your anguish / Oh come back / To the last of all hermits . . . Oh come back / My unknown

God! My pain! My last – happiness!' One can imagine Mahler himself writing those words in one of his own darker moments: in fact they read rather like some of the desperate comments Mahler scrawled on the sketches of the Tenth Symphony he was struggling to complete during the crisis of summer 1910.

But while Nietzsche expressed brilliantly and powerfully the existential nightmare into which Godless mankind had fallen, his solutions to the problem – particularly his ecstatic proclamations of the imminent dawning of the 'superman' (*Übermensch*) and the attendant 'revaluation of all values' – have proved a great deal more controversial: 'fanfares of despair' was how the writer Erich Heller summed them up. Where was Mahler to turn for an answer? It came to him, he explained in a sequence of letters to Alma, from Goethe's *Faust* Part II, and then, via Goethe, from a much older source: the thoughts of the Ancient Greek philosopher Socrates, as expressed in Plato's dialogue *The Symposium*. Alma has been reading *Faust*, and her comments on its final lines, the enigmatic 'Chorus Mysticus', have excited him. The Eighth Symphony's full text will follow in due course, but for the moment it would be helpful to give the stanza in full:

Alles Vergängliche	All that is transient
Ist nur ein Gleichnis;	Is but a symbol;
Das Unzulängliche,	The unfulfillable,
Hier wird's Ereignis;	Here becomes real;
Das Unbeschreibliche,	The inexpressible,
Hier ist's getan;	Here it is done.
Das Ewig-Weibliche	The Ever-Womanly
Zieht uns hinan.	Draws us on.

After stressing that the interpretation of a work of art is 'something out of the ordinary', beyond the tools of rational analysis, Mahler observes that *Faust* is 'quite a jumble, since it was written over the course of a *long* lifespan'. It was indeed: nearly fifty years separate Goethe's first sketches for *Faust* from the completion of Part II in 1831. Naturally some of the content of the latter reflects the changes in Goethe's own attitudes in the course of that half-century (he was no rigid dogmatist), and the range and diversity of its thinking and subject-matter has perplexed many commentators (including, privately, Goethe himself). 'The essence', Mahler explains to Alma, 'lies in its artistic entity, which cannot be expressed in dry words.' Nevertheless he feels inspired by Alma's letter to try to make sense of his own conclusions. Everything in Goethe's text at this point is 'allegory', a symbol, and thus inexpressible in rational language: 'That which leads us forwards with mystical strength – which every creature, perhaps even every stone, knows with absolute certainty to be the centre of its existence, and which Goethe here calls *Eternal Femininity* . . . is the antithesis of eternal longing, striving, motion towards that goal – in a word, Eternal Masculinity . . .' It is this 'Eternal Femininity', says Mahler, that carries us forward, not masculine striving. It brings us at last to the point that the restless male urge on its own can never know. We are finally at peace, fully in possession of what we on this transient earth can only desire, strive for: 'Christians speak of "eternal bliss", and for the sake of my allegory I have made use of this beautiful, sufficiently mythological concept.'[7]

So like Goethe, Mahler too embraces Christian imagery, partly because it is 'beautiful' and 'sufficiently mythological', but also because it will be readily understood by the world to which he wishes to communicate his vision of the 'centre of its existence'. In this his thinking almost exactly parallels that of Goethe himself. This is all the more striking when one considers that even some of the finest scholars of German literature have misread what Goethe was trying to say here. Eliza Butler, for instance, in her much-acclaimed study of the Faust legend, *The Fortunes of Faust*, can barely conceal her disappointment at the way Goethe ultimately dispatches Faust's soul, cleansed and redeemed of everything that once made him distinctive, to a safely Roman Catholic heaven. In fact Goethe's attitude to Christianity fluctuated throughout his long life, but certainly as an adult he was no orthodox Christian believer. He explained his choice of Christian symbolism in a letter to a friend as follows: 'The concluding scene, where the redeemed soul goes aloft, was very difficult to bring about, and I could have easily lost my way amongst such metaphysical, hardly knowable things, if I had not been able to give my poetic ideas form and firmness through the sharply outlined figures and imagery of the Christian Church.'[8] One can imagine Mahler saying 'Amen' to all of that. Nonetheless, it should be stressed that from a Christian point of view, there are several highly unorthodox aspects to Goethe's view of Heaven: God the Father is hardly mentioned, and Jesus Christ is acknowledged as the Virgin Mary's 'divinely transfigured Son', which could be taken to imply that, before that divine transfiguration, he was not divine in essence. Mary herself, the 'Mater Gloriosa', may only have two lines to sing, but she is clearly central, the focus of every adoring gaze. Earlier in the final scene, the angel chorus delivers this judgement, more humanist than conventionally Christian:

Wer immer strebend sich bemüht,   Whoever strives constantly,
Den können wir erlösen!   Him we can redeem.

It is a thought that could have been addressed personally to Mahler.

A year later, in June 1910, Mahler writes to Alma again on this subject, now tracing the roots of his thinking beyond Goethe to the Ancient Greek philosopher Plato's dialogue *The Symposium*, which records a discussion between Plato's teacher Socrates and a group of friends on the theme of what is often called 'Platonic love' – mistakenly, it turns out: Socrates is not talking of a kind of love which has *no* erotic dimension. In essence what he says is the same as Goethe's assertion that all love has its roots in procreation, and in the higher creative urge. For Socrates and for Goethe procreation is an activity not only of the body but also of the soul, and both activities are fundamentally an expression of Eros, the 'creator of the world'. So Eros, not the third person of the Christian Holy Trinity, is the 'creator spirit' on whom Mahler calls so magnificently at the opening of the Eighth Symphony!

When the reader turns to *The Symposium*, says Mahler, he or she is initially captivated by the vitality and narrative drive. The characters are so remarkably alive, their exchanges so full of colour and feeling, that the element of philosophical contention can almost seem marginal: 'Only later does one appreciate the diversity of opinions proffered, and only at the very end does one realise what this carefully planned rise in intensity is actually leading to: that wonderful dialogue between Socrates and Diotima, in which Plato outlines and summarises his entire world.'[9] That comment about the 'carefully planned rise in intensity' will be crucial when we come to consider how the symphony's second part evolves towards its concluding Chorus Mysticus. It also ties in beautifully with Socrates' account of his discourse with Diotima, the speech that forms the climax of *The Symposium*. Love, says Plato's priestess in Percy Bysshe Shelley's majestic translation, is 'universally all that earnest desire for the possession of happiness and that which is good'; it is 'the desire in men that good should be for ever present to them'.

'Love, then, O Socrates, is not as you imagine the love of the beautiful.' – 'What, then?' – 'Of generation and production in the beautiful.' – 'Why then of generation?'– 'Generation is something eternal and immortal in mortality. It necessarily, from what has been confessed, follows, that we must desire immortality together with what is good, since Love is the desire that good be for ever present to us. Of necessity Love must also be the desire of immortality.'

Desire itself can, if sublimated to this great quest, draw us towards the infinite. It is the ladder on which we climb from the physical to the spiritual:

'He who has been disciplined to this point in Love, by contemplating beautiful objects gradually, and in their order, now arriving at the end of all that concerns Love, on a sudden beholds a beauty wonderful in its nature. This is it, O Socrates, for the sake of which all former labours were endured. It is eternal, unproduced, indestructible; neither subject to increase nor decay . . . All other things are beautiful through a participation of it, with this condition, that although they are subject to production and decay, it never becomes more or less, or endures any change. When any one, ascending from a correct system of Love, begins to contemplate this supreme beauty, he already touches the consummation of his labour.' [10]

The same desire condemned by Christianity as the sin of lust can, if its true object is understood, draw us towards the infinite, to perfection. For Plato, as for Goethe, lust is simply desire that fails to recognise its real, otherworldly goal, as Goethe emphasises, provocatively, in the penultimate scene of *Faust* Part II: one of the reasons that Faust's soul is able to elude the clutches of Mephistopheles at the last moment and slip into Heaven is that Mephistopheles is temporarily distracted by the angels' pert bottoms! In opposition to this stands 'Platonic love' in its true sense. It is for this that the massed choirs invoke the 'creator spiritus' in the Eighth Symphony's Part I:

Accende lumen sensibus,   Arise, light of the senses,
Infunde amorem cordibus.   Pour love into our hearts.

The composer Anton Webern recalled Mahler talking to him excitedly about this passage not long before the Eighth Symphony's premiere: this, he said, was the pivotal moment in Part I where, in response to the command 'Accende', the music rises up and anticipates the setting of the concluding scene from *Faust* in Part II. Here then is the true connection Mahler drew between *Veni, creator spiritus* and the concluding scene of *Faust* Part II. Written at a time when much Christian writing was fiercely ascetic, decrying the body as hopelessly corrupted by original sin, Rabanus Maurus's hymn offered hope for the physical being as well, acknowledging the 'light of the senses'. In the words of the ancient Latin hymn Mahler had read the message that had evidently struck Goethe too: fired by love, real erotic love rather than some disembodied ideal, we too can follow Socrates and scale the Heavens.

3

Why Symphony?

If this, then, was Mahler's message to the world, why did he decide
to convey it in a symphony? Why not choose opera, the medium
to which he had devoted most of his conducting career, and the
one in which Wagner had laid out his complex spiritual manifestos? Or if he preferred a more high-minded setting than the opera
house, why not some form of oratorio or semi-dramatic cantata?
There was a far more distinguished pedigree there when it came to
expressing ideas, particularly ideas of a religious or quasi-religious
nature. To understand Mahler's choice, we need to grasp what it
was that symphonic form – or rather symphonic thought and
expression – meant to him.

The most vivid, conveniently pithy explanation of Mahler's
position was provided by an eminent composer colleague. In
November 1907, after directing his final performance at the
Vienna Opera, Mahler went to Helsinki to conduct a concert of
music by Beethoven and Wagner. During his visit he struck up an
acquaintance with the man many regard as the other outstanding symphonist of Mahler's age, Jean Sibelius. Apparently Mahler
wasn't impressed by Sibelius's music, but he warmed to the man
himself: according to Sibelius the two men 'spent much time in
each other's company'. Sibelius was struck by Mahler's extreme
caution concerning his recently diagnosed heart condition: during
the summer of 1907 a doctor had identified a lesion of the heart,
causing Mahler some anxiety about his health, and resulting in
major, though possibly temporary revisions to his daily regime.

Walking, however, was still allowed, and Sibelius joined Mahler in some of his constitutionals, during which, Sibelius tells us, the two composers examined 'all the great questions of music thoroughly' – what a shame no one was on hand to take notes. As to what they might have concluded, Sibelius unfortunately tells us very little. There is however one precious, if brief account of an impassioned disagreement they had about the musical form that meant so much to both of them. At some point the conversation came round to the subject of the symphony. Sibelius said that what mattered for him was its 'severity and style' and 'the profound logic that created an inner connection between the motifs'. At this point Mahler disagreed passionately: 'Nein, die Symphonie muss sein wie die Welt. Sie muss alles umfassen.' (No, the symphony must be like the world. It must embrace everything.)[1]

Sibelius's and Mahler's remarks have both been quoted frequently, usually to support the notion of an extreme polarisation between these two composers' conceptions of symphonic thinking. It is however important to take into consideration the date of this conversation. Only the previous year Mahler had composed his Eighth Symphony, the work that throws its embrace wider than anything he had ever composed before, not just in its vast resources, but in its subject-matter: love, human creativity, the creation of the world, the redemption of the soul, the elemental reconciliation of 'masculine' and 'female' energies and, ultimately, a vision of the 'unfulfillable', the 'indescribable', made actual in music. Sibelius on the other hand had just finished his three-year struggle to complete his Third Symphony: a rigorously concentrated half-hour structure, for a classical-sized orchestra with just eight woodwind and nine brass, eschewing the kind of colouristic resources and effects Mahler had drawn so enthusiastically into his own musical embrace, and in its 'severity and style' echoing the austere ideals of the *junge Klassizität* ('youthful classicism') of Sibelius's friend, the virtuoso pianist and composer Ferruccio Busoni.

Yet it wasn't long before Sibelius's writings about 'the profound logic' of symphonic music began to take on a less forbiddingly abstract, more spiritual character that Mahler might well have found more sympathetic. In 1909 Sibelius informed his close friend and invaluable artistic confidant Axel Carpelan that he saw himself primarily as a vessel, a conduit for musical ideas whose source was mysterious. Mahler would have entirely agreed, as his comment to Schoenberg quoted above (see p. 33) confirms. 'What's essential', Sibelius continues, 'is this wonderful logic (let us call it God) that governs a work of art.'[2] In certain moods Mahler would call it 'God' too, and he would surely have warmed to Sibelius's increasingly pantheistic-sounding nature imagery, as recorded in the latter's diary entries of 1912. In one of these Sibelius memorably compares the symphony to a river, created by the coming together of various streams and gaining strength and momentum as it flows towards the sea. And the Mahler who had lovingly imitated the calls of birds again and again in his own scores would surely have felt the urge to embrace a fellow spirit if he had read Sibelius's account of how the famous horn motif in the finale of his Fifth Symphony had come to him, as a gift of nature. Standing by his house at Järvenpää he had been thrilled to watch sixteen swans take off from the lake and circle overhead before disappearing into the far-northern solar haze like a silver ribbon. The swans' cry became the woodwind melody soaring on high, their huge wing-beats the rising and falling horn figures. Nature's glory and its angst all in one visionary image! How dry talk of 'profound logic' and 'inner connection' between themes sounds

beside this; but they are present too – this also is nature. A couple
of pages further on in Sibelius's diary, Mahler would have found a
statement he could easily have made himself, though perhaps in
more emotive terms: Sibelius describes his symphonies as 'confessions of faith' from different stages of his life, and explains that the
reason that they are so different from one another is that the perspective, perhaps even the foundations of that faith kept shifting.[3]

It rings so true in both cases. Imagine if the two composers
had met a second time, say in the late summer or early autumn
of 1910: Mahler, his heart weakened, struggling to come to terms
with the devastating discovery of Alma's infidelity and the
spiritual crisis it precipitated; Sibelius rocked to his core by the
discovery of a tumour in his throat in 1908, by the ordeal of the
subsequent operation, the torture of waiting to know if the operation had been successful, and by terrible withdrawal symptoms
from the temporary renunciation of his twin life-supports, alco-
hol and tobacco. Imagine the two men showing each other the
symphonies they were writing at that time: Mahler his Tenth and
Sibelius his Fourth. Picture them meeting in Mahler's mountain
hideaway at Toblach, or at Sibelius's forest retreat at Järvenpää, the
sketch score of Mahler's Adagio finale lying open beside Sibelius's
Il tempo largo slow movement. The sparse, desolate textures, the
heavy, weary, wandering bass lines, the heart-rending cries from
a lonely solo flute, and above all the gaping, abysmal silences . . .
Neither of them would have needed to say very much: a grim nod
of acknowledgement would have been enough.

*

How then did a musical form that began life as a piece of
abstract, purely instrumental concert music, normally without texts,

programmes or any other form of verbal elucidation, evolve into a
vehicle for 'confessions of faith'? The title 'symphony' or 'sinfonia'
was well known in the music of the baroque era, when it usually
signified either an overture or an orchestral interlude in a vocal
work: the 'Pastoral Symphony' in Part I of Handel's *Messiah* is a
classic example. But the symphony as today's concert-goers know
it began to define itself in the middle to late eighteenth century,
in the midst of the period of radical intellectual ferment known
to historians as 'the Enlightenment'. In some ways the emergence
of the symphony parallels that of the modern realistic novel, also
on the rise in the eighteenth century, which many commentators
have linked to the increasing aspiration and influence of the afflu-
ent, educated middle classes in Western Europe.[4] One important
element embodied in both forms was the idea of development, of a
dynamic process of growth, of change. The relationship of artistic
forms to the prevailing social and political conditions of their age
– to the *Zeitgeist*, if you prefer a less materialistic slant – is often
complex and can elude even the most methodical unpicking. But
it isn't hard to see why the notion of development – of character in
a novel, even of a theme in a symphony – might have gone down
particularly well with aspiring middle-class audiences. In soci-
eties where aristocratic values prevail, character is not something
acquired through education, experience or personal struggle, it is
a given – it goes with one's social rank, and is fundamentally not
open to question. But in eighteenth-century Europe, these old-
established values were being challenged as never before, urged
on by such Enlightenment luminaries as Voltaire, Denis Diderot
and Jean-Jacques Rousseau. The aspect of Pierre Beaumarchais's
play *The Marriage of Figaro* (1778) that proved most scandalous
was its depiction of a lecherous count, corrupted by aristocratic

privilege, and his undoing by his clearly intellectually superior servants. The message was clear: ambitious members of the 'lower orders' no longer had to limit their horizons according to their status at birth. A door was opening, revealing to middle-class men – and, *mirabile dictu*, perhaps even to middle-class women – the prospect of becoming 'self-made', like the modestly born Corsican Napoleon Bonaparte who, by the end of the century, was leading the armies of Revolutionary France to victory across Europe and beyond. And in music, their spokesman was the generalissimo of symphonic form, Ludwig van Beethoven (1770–1827) – the very Beethoven who famously censured his royal patron, Prince Lichnowsky, in 1806, by informing him that princes were mere accidents of birth, whereas he, Beethoven, was unique, the true self-created man. The more old-worldly Goethe was horrified by Beethoven's refusal to show deference to his 'betters'; but for aspiring middle-class men – and women too – he was a trail-blazer in social as well as artistic terms.

Of course Beethoven did not create the symphony. He inherited its dramatic principles and broad formal outlines from Mozart, and above all from his teacher Joseph Haydn. Placed beside Mozart's 'Jupiter' Symphony (no. 41, 1788) or Haydn's 'London' (no. 104, 1795), Beethoven's own First Symphony (1800) seems relatively cautious, with only its explosive third-movement 'minuet' giving more than a hint of great things to come. But one of the many things Beethoven went on to achieve was to make the symphony far more novelistic: to heighten and extend its powers of musical narrative to the point where it could be said to communicate not only emotional processes and dramatic events, but even philosophical ideas. Talk of themes, developments and tonalities in music can be dry and forbidding for non-specialists, even for some musicians; but I urge the reader to stay with this, because what is at issue here isn't merely technical mechanics, but a musical life principle. To register the immensity of what Beethoven accomplished one has only to compare the First Symphony with two of its most iconic successors: the 'Eroica' (no. 3) and the Fifth. In Symphony no. 1, themes are developed – varied, fragmented and reconstituted – within the four individual movements, but at the end of each movement order and balance are restored and all tensions resolved. In the 'Eroica', however, something more fluid, less orderly – something psychologically 'realistic', one might say – is beginning to happen. After two hammer-blow opening chords from the full orchestra, cellos introduce a motif that rises and falls, then drops to a challenging dissonance. Throughout this long and dramatic first movement, that original motif goes on sounding its challenge, eliciting a variety of different responses. One of the biggest surprises comes at the beginning of the section conventionally labelled 'recapitulation': first a solo horn seems to come in with the leading motif too early, to be silenced, *fortissimo*, by the full orchestra; then the cellos bring back their motif in full, as at the start – only now it veers off in a totally unexpected new direction. Even at the end of the movement, where it seems that the main motif is at last to attain its long-delayed triumphant resolution, the trumpets appear to 'miss' the top note, the theme remains uncompleted: instead a massive dissonance from the full orchestra leads to a loudly emphatic, but arguably somewhat abrupt conclusion. For some listeners it is no surprise that such a qualified triumph should be followed by a uniquely dark-hued funeral march.

This sense that the first three movements of the 'Eroica' Symphony are not self-sufficient – that each contains 'issues' that are only fully resolved in the finale – is taken a stage further in Beethoven's Fifth. Now, for the first time in a symphonic work, there is a clearly identifiable motif that runs through all four movements. The famous opening outlines a rhythmic pattern, *da-da-da-DAH*, that dominates the first movement, re-emerges in the second in the *fortissimo* brass and timpani fanfares (and later in the cellos' nervous echoes), then returns to haunt the following Scherzo as an ominous horn tattoo. From that last form it then morphs into the throbbing repeated timpani notes that rise in an elemental crescendo to sweep the music without a break into the finale, where *da-da-da-DAH* is transformed into a hortatory *da-Dah-Dah-DAH* figure, later thrillingly sounded by trombones through surging orchestral textures. For the conductor Sir John Eliot Gardiner there is a distinct echo here of the French Revolutionary ode, *Hymne dithyrambique*, by Rouget de l'Isle (author of both text and and music of *La Marseillaise*), and particularly of its leading motif 'la liberté'.[5] In this, and in its many other developmental adventures, the fate of *da-da-da-DAH* (or is that *la li-ber-TÉ*?) is closely involved with the Fifth Symphony's overall tonal journey, from dark, fraught C minor to blazingly optimistic C major. It is a narrative of hope, of the overcoming of the forces of darkness by determined, heroic effort – on one level much less definite than words, on another far more visceral. Remember Mahler's words to Richard Specht: 'Only as a musician can I fully express my thoughts on this.' Beethoven could have used those very words for himself.

Many composers after Beethoven imitated his narrative symphonic techniques, though few had very much to add to them, at least not in the first half of the nineteenth century. There is one towering exception, however: the Frenchman Hector Berlioz (1803–69). The young Berlioz was enthralled by Beethoven's symphonies – or at least by the first eight of them. At this stage the

choral Ninth was widely regarded as unperformable, and quite possibly insane. A performance of the Ninth Symphony's three purely
orchestral movements in Paris in 1839, directed by the conductor
François Habeneck, was a revelation for many, but at this stage the
hugely complex choral finale was clearly still considered a no-go
area. In any case, by then Berlioz had already composed his most
influential symphonic score, the *Symphonie fantastique* (1830), a
work much admired (and frequently conducted) by Mahler. Berlioz intended his *Symphonie fantastique* to tell a story, an intensely
personal story; and he provided several literary programmes to
ensure audiences got the message. But it is the way the music itself
evokes moods, landscapes, terrifying crowd scenes and witches'
sabbaths that has made it so enduringly popular – that, and its
vivid, compelling depiction of a process of psychological transformation: the mental disintegration of its febrile, love-tormented
artist-hero, and the gradual debasement in his mind of his love
object, symbolised by a theme Berlioz called the *idée fixe*. At first
beautiful, elegant, winsome on violins and flute, it turns eerily distant, then mocking at the end of the fourth movement, only to
undergo a shocking transformation in the finale, where it becomes
a grotesque dance on piccolo (E flat) clarinet, pungent oboes and
obscenely gurgling bassoons. The ideal beloved is finally revealed
as a hideous witch, cackling triumphantly over the hero's apparently still conscious corpse. This passage clearly left a deep imprint
on Mahler: think of the mocking high clarinets in the funeral
march from Mahler's First Symphony, or the way the E flat clarinet
sneers at the previously aspiring trumpet theme towards the end
of the Ninth Symphony's *Rondo-Burleske*. In everything, from the
instrumental colours to the almost cartoon-like storytelling, Berlioz is unmistakably the father figure.

But Mahler's Eighth Symphony would have been unthinkable without the epoch-making example of Beethoven's Ninth – and without the efforts on its behalf of one iron-willed man: Richard Wagner. In 1829, the sixteen-year-old Wagner got hold of a score of the Ninth Symphony (an achievement in itself in those days) and was enormously impressed by what he saw, so much so that he immediately set about making a piano transcription of the whole work – over an hour's worth of music. Around this time Wagner seems to have conceived the notion that he might one day unearth for the world the treasure still hidden in this work, but although he conducted the other symphonies on various occasions, he clearly decided that the Ninth should wait. Hearing Habeneck's 1839 Paris performance of the first three movements was a major spur to his ambitions, but it wasn't until Palm Sunday 1846 that Wagner was at last able to conduct the entire Ninth Symphony, including the choral finale, in Dresden. It was a colossal success: Wagner's insistence on extra rehearsal time, which had caused such consternation amongst musicians, singers and court officials, was now judged to have been entirely justified. The Ninth Symphony was not an aberration, a symptom of megalomaniac ambition or of mental decline exacerbated by increasing deafness; it was one of the highest achievements of German musical genius, comparable with Bach's *St Matthew Passion*, which had itself been triumphantly resurrected by Felix Mendelssohn just seventeen years earlier after years of neglect.

For that historic 1846 Dresden performance, Wagner provided a programme note which argues not only that Beethoven's Ninth Symphony is a coherent, triumphantly achieved artistic statement, but that it represents something revolutionary in European art. Wagner charts, in glowing prose, the emergence of 'the great chief theme' from a 'spectral shroud' – by 'theme' he means not only the first movement's mighty unison theme at the height of the first crescendo, but also what he sees as the music's philosophical theme, 'a titanic struggle of the soul, athirst for joy, against the veto of that hostile power that rears itself 'twixt us and earthly happiness'. He follows the symphony's 'flight from despair . . . in breathless haste to snatch a new and unknown happiness' in the scherzo, then sighs in relief as the slow movement's tones 'turn its turbulence to gentle melancholy! It is as if a memory were awakened, the memory of purest happiness from early days.' But it is with the transition from the third to the fourth movement, opening with a wildly dissonant fanfare-like 'shriek of horror', that Wagner's reading reaches its climax, in prose that – paradoxically from Wagner's point of view – seems to be straining for musical utterance:

With this opening of the last movement Beethoven's music takes on a more definitely speaking *character: it quits the mould of purely instrumental music, observed in all three preceding movements, the mode of infinite, indefinite expression; the musical poem's urging forward toward a crisis, a crisis only to be voiced in human speech. It is wonderful how the master makes the arrival of Man's voice and tongue a positive necessity, by this awe-inspiring recitative of the bass-strings; almost breaking the bounds of absolute music already, it stems the tumult of the other instruments with its virile eloquence, insisting on decision, and passes at last into a song-like theme whose simple stately flow bears with it, one by one, the other instruments, until it swells into a mighty flood.*

In this remarkable, revolutionary passage, says Wagner, we hear purely instrumental music's most heroic attempt to date to express the fullness of joy. But ultimately it must fail: the 'Ode to Joy' theme, presented by cellos and basses and elaborated by the full orchestra, sinks back, and suddenly the terrifying fanfare from the very beginning of the movement piles in again, *fortissimo*. If instruments cannot provide the way from this to joy, what can? For Wagner there is only one possible answer:

The human voice, with the clear sure utterance of articulate words, confronts the din of instruments; and we know not at which to wonder most, the boldness of the inspiration, or the naivety of the master who lets that voice address the instruments as follows:

Ihr Freunde, nicht diese Töne!*	No, friends, not tones like these!
Sondern lasst uns angenehmere anstimmen	But let us sing a strain more cheerful
und freudenvollere!	and agreeable!'[6]

Up to this point, one can imagine Mahler reading with approval – especially the younger Mahler, creator of the so-called 'Resurrection' Symphony (no. 2), in whose ultimately choral finale an impassioned, purely instrumental quasi-recitative is eventually taken up by a solo contralto voice, spelling out in now fully articulate terms the symphony's message of hope and consolation:

O glaube, mein Herz, o glaube,	O believe, my heart, o believe,
es geht dir nichts verloren!	Nothing is lost to you!
Dein ist, was du gesehnt!	Yours is what you longed for,
dein was du geliebt,	yours what you loved,
was du gestritten!	what you fought for!

* Wagner is in error: Beethoven wrote 'O Freunde . . .'

But for Wagner, the reconciliation of music and sung words in Beethoven's Ninth Symphony wasn't an end in itself, it was only the beginning. Like many of the German romantics before him, Wagner turned to Ancient Greece for inspiration, and for confirmation of his own intuitions. His ideal was the playwright Aeschylus's great trilogy, the *Oresteia*. The age of Aeschylus, Wagner argued, was the only time in history when art had lived up to its full potential. Not only did dramas like the *Oresteia* embody universal truths about human beings through the skilful use of myths, the dramatisation of these widely shared myths in an artful public spectacle would also help draw individuals together to form a community, a nation. This drawing together was also reflected in the very nature of the art-work, in which song, dance, instrumental music, poetry and mime were fused in a grand, vibrant synthesis. 'Before what phenomenon do we stand with more humiliating sense of the impotence of our own frivolous culture than before the art of the *Hellenes*?', Wagner wrote in an essay, *The Art-work of the Future*, three years after that triumphant Dresden performance of Beethoven's Ninth.[7] The separation of the arts since the Greek Golden Age – their splitting off into seemingly self-sufficient independent entities – had been a process of grievous decline. In allowing themselves to become separated, these art forms had also become emasculated, emptied of their true spiritual content and finally, pitifully, they had fallen victim to commercialism. Beethoven had sounded the first blast of the trumpet against this monstrous process of degradation. Now it was up to Wagner to complete the task: the Drama of the Future would rise up spontaneously when Comedy, Opera, Pantomime and all the other old theatrical forms had exhausted themselves, along with the social conditions that sustained them and which they in turn reflected. No, the term drama was insufficient: revolutionary change in social conditions and values would breed of itself an even bolder conception, the Art-work of the Future. But for that, an even more profound change – a spiritual change – was necessary. The Art-work of the Future could not arise of its own volition, but only in harmony with the conditions of life as a whole: 'Only when the ruling religion of Egoism, which has split the entire domain of Art into crippled, self-seeking art-tendencies and art-varieties, shall have been mercilessly dislodged and torn up root and branch from every moment of the life of man, can the *new religion* step forth of itself to life; the religion which includes within itself the conditions of the Artwork of the Future.'[8] Political upheaval was not enough. The revolution must bring about a change in the whole of human life, a change whose expression demanded the tools of religion – but not the old religion. That was itself corrupted by the colossal 'egoism' of the old power- and wealth-fixated world.

It is tempting to say that this is the point at which Mahler and Wagner go their separate ways. But perhaps it would be more accurate to say that, if we look at Mahler's symphonies in chronological sequence, we can see him moving further and further away from Wagner's position. For Wagner, the symphony as 'absolute music' had effectively been dealt a death blow by Beethoven's Ninth. Composers such as Wagner's contemporary Johannes Brahms, whose four symphonies continued to explore musical form for its own sake, rejecting programmes, titles, or any kind of reconciliation with the spoken or sung word, were the embodiment of 'crippled, self-seeking' art. In orchestral music, Wagner's champion – and later father-in-law – Franz Liszt had pointed another way forward with his 'symphonic poems', in which the music was held to illustrate subjects from classical mythology, romantic literature, history, even the visual arts. That was acceptable – 'progressive'; writing symphonies with numbers, keys, opus numbers and nothing more was emphatically not.

When Mahler's Symphony no. 1 first appeared in 1888, it was furnished with a title, *Titan*, taken from the novel of that name by the then widely read German writer 'Jean-Paul' (Johann Paul Richter, 1763–1825); in fact for its first two performances the symphony was actually billed as a 'symphonic poem'. In addition to the detailed descriptive programme note that accompanied the performances, listeners were provided with other clues as to possible larger meanings. There were the extensive quotations from Mahler's song cycle *Lieder eines fahrenden Gesellen* ('Songs of a Wayfarer'), composed in 1884, the year he began work on the symphony, and the connection to the novel's hero and his eventual spiritual triumph is underlined in the symphony's loudly affirmative coda by a striking echo of the figure 'And he shall reign' from the 'Hallelujah' chorus of Handel's *Messiah*.

An even more lengthy and elaborate programme accompanied some of the early performances of the Second Symphony. In addition there were sung texts: the poem 'Urlicht' (Primal Light) from the folk collection *Des Knaben Wunderhorn* ('Youth's Magic Horn'), sung by the contralto in the brief fourth movement, and a choral setting of the first two verses of Friedrich Klopstock's so-called 'Resurrection Ode' (from which the symphony gets its nickname), much expanded by Mahler himself. And who could miss the clear message of the black funeral march in the first movement, with its desolate 'Out, out brief candle!' ending? The trouble was that, even when provided with such clear aids to comprehension, people would go off in alarming imaginative directions of their own or, worse still, take it all much too literally. Alma remembered Mahler describing how, during a trip to St Petersburg, one member of his audience had stunned him by doing precisely that. Apparently a beautiful and intensely voluble old Russian lady had approached Mahler with an urgent question. Sensing that her own death was near, she pressed him to tell her what she might expect in the afterlife – after all, hadn't he depicted it all so vividly in his Second Symphony? When Mahler attempted to disabuse her, she sent him on his way frostily. It seems this wasn't the message Mahler's programme note had led her to expect.

It is easy to understand Mahler's frustration. Even today, as with the Eighth Symphony, commentators and (in the experience of this writer) listeners still presume that the Second Symphony's message of 'resurrection' is fundamentally Christian – an expression of faith in an afterlife that Mahler either felt or wanted to convince himself that he felt. But Mahler was an immensely complicated being, talking in Christian terms one moment, of reincarnation the next, then professing himself an 'adherent' of the militantly atheist Nietzsche. There are times in interpreting his work when it is well to remember the challenging words Beethoven wrote on the manuscript of the original version of his song 'Klage' (Lament): 'Manchmal is das Gegenteil auch wahr' (Sometimes the opposite is also true). In the programme note Mahler provided for a performance of the Second Symphony in Dresden in 1901, he wrote, 'Behold, this is no judgement . . . There is no punishment and no reward. An overwhelming love illuminates our being. We know and *are*.'[9] Those last two sentences are particularly revealing. Mahler may have had his doubts about a benign, omnipotent personal 'God', but it seems he never really doubted the transcendent power of love itself. As for 'We know and *are*' – that may be the true significance of 'resurrection' for Mahler: a rising from the dead into the fullness of life not in a world to come but here and now. As in Henrik Ibsen's almost exactly contemporary play *When We Dead Awaken*, or Tolstoy's novel *Resurrection* (both published in 1899, four years after the Second Symphony's premiere), the challenge is to rise above mortal fears, to experience spiritual rebirth in this life – or in the words Mahler added to Klopstock's 'Resurrection Ode', 'Cease from trembling! Prepare yourself to live!'

In any case there was always something tugging at Mahler from within, telling him that music was music, and spoke on its own terms: 'Only as a musician can I fully express my thoughts on this.' As early as 1896, when he drew up his first programme note, at the request of a young journalist admirer named Max Marschalk, Mahler felt the need to begin with a caveat. He would, he said, regard his work as having failed completely if he found it necessary to give anyone even an indication of its mood-sequence. What mattered to him above all was not the detailed account of an 'event', but much more that of a 'feeling'. The transition from purely orchestral music to music with sung text in the fourth movement, and particularly in the final chorus, throws 'an illuminating light' on the earlier movements, but it should not be regarded as explaining or in any way defining them.[10]

This is a core reason why, for Mahler, the ideal vehicle for his kind of message had to be the symphony rather than Wagnerian 'total work of art' (*Gesamtkunstwerk*). Music, with its unique ability to communicate a 'mood-sequence', had to be first and foremost. It was not about setting forth 'events', still less rational concepts, but about 'feeling'. However much Mahler admired and was stirred by Wagner, and despite the masterful performances he gave of Wagner's operas – especially *Tristan und Isolde* and

Die Meistersinger – it seems he was most persuaded by Wagner the musician, and least by Wagner the preacher. If Mahler had been a thoroughgoing Wagnerian then the latter's final great achievement, *Parsifal* – described by its composer as a 'Festival Play for the Consecration of the Stage' (*Bühnenweihfestspiel*) – could have offered a model to Mahler of how to convey his ideas of Eros, creation and the *Ewig-Weibliche* in dramatic form. But for Mahler, it seems, *Parsifal* was too much about ideas and not enough about music: Ernst Decsey remembered Mahler describing it as a work that gave the impression of being composed by one of Wagner's slavish intellectual disciples rather than by the master himself.* As for opera beyond Wagner, by 1906, the year of the Eighth Symphony's composition, Mahler had had too much gruelling practical experience of the operatic world to nurture any particularly fond hopes there. During that same year Mahler was involved in the Salzburg Music Festival, which was then marking the 150th anniversary of Mozart's birth. The Mozart biographer Bernhard Paumgartner remembered Mahler after the rehearsal, laying bare his bitter frustration with opera houses and what he now felt were the idiotic attitudes of opera practitioners and their followers. A revolution was needed, he insisted, a fundamental change of approach, especially in the repertoire system, which he loathed. One could try for, and occasionally even meet with, a kind of success, but as soon as an opera became a repertoire production people stopped thinking about it – a legion of practical problems quickly swept centre stage. In a concert performance of a symphony there was at least the possibility that, for a precious

---

* Though Mahler's reaction on hearing *Parsifal* for the first time in Bayreuth in 1883 had been intensely enthusiastic.

hour or so, everyone's mind might be focused on higher things.

Mahler considered various titles, and began devising pro-gramme notes for his next Symphony, the Third, but by the time of the premiere, in Krefeld in 1902, all had been dropped. Two years earlier, in 1900, Mahler met a young musicologist named Ludwig Schiedermair, who was writing a book about him. Schiedermair joined Mahler and a group of admirers for celebratory drinks after the Munich performance of the Second Symphony in Octo-ber that year. At one stage in the proceedings some unfortunate person brought up the subject of programme notes. According to Schiedermair Mahler jumped up from the table and threw himself into a tirade. Programme notes gave an utterly misleading pic-ture. Far better to let the public form its own opinions, explore its own emotional reactions to the music they were hearing. If the composer manages to make his audience feel the emotions he felt when writing it, so much the better; if not, words were no help. Music may come close to words, but of itself it expresses so much more than words can. At this point, Mahler seized his glass, drained it to the dregs, and cried, 'Perish all programmes!'[11]

*

Even so, while a composer should never *tell* his audience what it is they are hearing – force them to read his or anyone else's 'pre-judgements' while they are listening – he can at least provide *hints*, particularly in the form of suggestive sound symbols. The birdsong in the first movement of the First Symphony, and in the finale of the Second, is a good example: if nothing else, this seems to say 'nature' in some form or other. The symphony Mahler began the year after that meeting with Ludwig Schiedermair, his Fifth, begins and ends with two arresting sound symbols. The first movement is actually entitled *Trauermarsch*, 'funeral march' – not that we really need telling. After the stark opening trumpet fanfare, the slow, heavy martial tread, the shuddering string trills and deep, rasping horn notes clearly evoke Death in full grotesque pomp. Then, at the end of the symphony, the brass chorale that so nearly brings the stormy second movement to a triumphant conclusion returns in radiant affirmation, sounding through upward-surging, downward-cascading strings. It's clearly a hymn of praise, and what's more – as Mahler's German-speaking audience would readily have recognised – it sounds a lot like the kind of hymn of praise with which his older friend Anton Bruckner had closed several of his symphonies. And there, in the climactic phrase, is an unmistakable echo of the old German hymn 'Wie schön leuchtet der Morgenstern', (How brightly shines the morning star). Affirmation, praise, possibly of the love that, according to the biblical Song of Solomon, is 'strong as death' – all that can be divined by the listener, if he or she wishes. But anything more categorical than that is beyond the language of feeling, in which, Mahler always insisted, music could express infinitely more than words.

The Fifth Symphony, however, shows Mahler hinting at possible interpretations via another means: one revealed to him by another master of symphonic form, Franz Schubert. Mahler loved Schubert's music, championing his 'Great' C major Symphony in the concert hall at a time when many still had doubts about Schubert's mastery of long-term formal processes, and captivating his student friends with his performances of Schubert's solo piano works. Less rigorously purposeful in his creation of large-scale structures than his hero Beethoven, Schubert nevertheless makes compelling use of the huge time-spaces he inhabits: 'heavenly length' was how Robert Schumann famously summed up the 'Great' C major in a review of the work's posthumous 1839 premiere in his magazine, *Neue Zeitschrift für Musik* ('New Music Journal'). He does this partly through the mesmerising repetitions of dance and song-accompaniment rhythms, and above all through the glorious long-breathed melodies that float above and through them. Mahler owes a great deal to this, as the French novelist and critic Romain Rolland was quick to recognise. No one, said Rolland, better expressed the grace and charm of the *Ländler* and waltz tunes that so fascinated Schubert, and perhaps no other composer came so close to the essence of Schubert's 'moving and voluptuous melancholy'.[12]

It is worth noting that by the time Mahler conducted Schubert's 'Great' C major Symphony in New York on the opening night of the Philharmonic Society's 1910–11 season he seemed to have undergone a further shift in his attitude to Schubert's long-term musical thinking. As a reviewer from the *New York Times* noted, Mahler had dropped his previous practice of cutting substantial chunks of Schubert's symphony, allowing it to speak for itself in all its 'heavenly length'. Not every critic was convinced, but several admitted that the symphony's drama and musical logic were actually improved when it was heard in full. Long exposure to Schubert's music had evidently convinced Mahler that – despite the claims of influential critics like George Bernard Shaw – Schubert really did know what he was doing.

One other big thing Mahler and Schubert had in common is that they were both equally masters of symphony and of song. Mahler's ear for the musical and emotional nuances of the German language can, at its best, be as finely tuned as Schubert's; and, as with Schubert, the overlap between lieder and symphonic works can be highly suggestive, especially for those who like hunting out autobiographical meanings in music. The presence of a

set of variations on the song 'Der Tod und das Mädchen' (Death
and the Maiden) at the heart of Schubert's String Quartet in D
minor, D810, isn't just an arresting structural feature: it's a key to
interpreting the character of the other three movements (all, like
the song, implacably minor-key), and a possible clue to Schubert's
state of mind at the time he wrote it. So too is the suddenly chilling
reference to the agonisingly nostalgic song, 'Schöne Welt, wo bist
du?' (Beautiful world, where are you?), in the seemingly idyllic,
prevailingly out-of-doors Octet, D803, composed the same year
as the quartet (1824). And what are we to make of the eerie similarity between the main first movement theme of the 'Unfinished'
B minor Symphony, D759, and the song 'Der Zwerg' (The Dwarf),
a shadowy study in perverse sexuality? Both were composed at a
time when members of Schubert's intimate circle were seriously
concerned about the influence of his friend, the restless and faintly
Mephistophelean Franz von Schober.

The point about these citations, references or allusions, however, is that they fall some way short of being definitive. They still
leave the imagination plenty of room to play creatively, to 'form
its own thoughts' as Mahler put it. So too do the echoes of Mahler's own songs in his purely orchestral Fifth Symphony. After the
menacing funereal opening comes a more intriguing emotional
signpost: the softer march theme that follows on strings is clearly
related to a song Mahler wrote around the same time, 'Der Tam-
bourg'sell' (The Drummer Lad), which tells of a very young army
deserter facing execution – no more grandeur, just pity and desolation. So here we have two starkly contrasted images of death.
This could be intuited from the music alone, but for those who
know the song this poignant echo puts flesh on the musical idea.
The famous Adagietto fourth movement, for strings and harp, was

clearly intended as a kind of love-song without words to his future wife, Alma. Here he quotes from one of his greatest songs, 'Ich bin der Welt abhanden gekommen' (I am lost to the world) from his *Rückert Lieder*. This is the song mentioned above that ends with the phrase 'I live alone in my heaven, in my love, in my song', and at this point in the Fifth Symphony Mahler actually quotes the violin phrase that accompanies 'in my love, in my song'. Alma herself would have recognised that, and read its meaning – or at least Mahler would have hoped she would.

This invocation of human love and song proves to be the true turning point in the Fifth Symphony. But before we get to the final hymn-like invocation of the 'morning star' (alias the planet Venus, named after the Roman goddess of love), there comes another reference to one of Mahler's songs – the most explicit yet, and the most purely joyful. This is another song from the classic folk collection *Des Knaben Wunderhorn*: 'Lob des hohen Verstandes' (In praise of lofty intellect). The song tells of a singing contest between the birds of the field and forest, judged by a donkey, who awards the prize to the cuckoo as his is the only 'song' he can understand. This unmistakable jibe at Mahler's critics is followed by his most impressive display yet of contrapuntal skill (some of those critics had accused Mahler of being weak in contrapuntal technique), culminating in the now fully triumphant return of the chorale from the second movement. One doesn't need to 'get' any of these references to be stirred by Mahler's Fifth Symphony, or to be able to make some kind of sense of it; and discovering these song connections probably wouldn't be revelatory for most sympathetic listeners. Yet they add to our pleasure, and they strengthen our appreciation of the music's 'mood-sequence', without at the same time being entirely prescriptive.

These then were the symphonic techniques Mahler had evolved by the time he came to write his Eighth Symphony: Beethoven's dramatisation of the processes of thematic development and harmonic change, heightened by Berlioz; his use of sung texts to elucidate but never fully explain the play of feelings, which is music's true territory; and Schubert's evocation of song, either as sweeping or lilting quasi-vocal melody or as a tantalising clue to more complex, possibly multi-layered meanings. Armed with these, Mahler could now set out to create a symphony that would 'embrace the world'.

INTERLUDE

Behind the Scenes: Alma and Walter, August–September 1910

There is one advantage to being a work widow: it gives one plenty of opportunity to pursue one's own private concerns without too much fear of discovery. With Mahler safely occupied in his composing hut, or away conducting, Alma sends off letter after letter to Walter Gropius from the mountain resort of Toblach. She will try to be calm, she tells him more than once, but soon the intensity of her longing betrays itself. In one undated letter, probably early in August, she sends Gropius news that must have chilled his heart. She has decided that she will 'probably' go with Mahler to New York at the end of the year, when he leaves to take up his new appointment at the Metropolitan Opera. Why? Because Mahler insists he cannot live a single day without her. The responsibility is too great: she *must* go with him. How is she getting along, she asks on her lover's behalf? *Remarkably well* – the words are underlined, the added emphasis more than hinting at doubts. But she wants him to write to her every day, *poste restante* – in other words, the local post office will hold the letters until she calls to claim them – but at least once a week he must write to her *directly* (underlined), and especially on her birthday, 31 August. Business matters over, things soon turn much more intimate: she wants him to send her his jacket, since he has worn it, and *his dear* hands (more emphasis) have held it. Before he posts it, he must kiss it on the neck band, and she will do the same on receiving it. Mahler is leaving for Munich on 3 September, so if he sends it on Friday 2nd, she will be able to perform her act of devotion in complete safety, before she leaves three days later.

Then more about Mahler. It's painful, she says. He fires off tele-grams almost hourly from Innsbruck: 'All good and evil powers accompany me – Over all reigns the victress – Good Night my Lyre – I feel nothing but longing.' She fears for his sanity, she tells Gro-pius, and so does her mother. This 'idolatrous' obsession that he now carries for her, this deluge of desperate confession and clamour for reassurance 'can hardly be considered normal any more'. A break, then Alma evidently resumes the letter later. Now, she reveals, she is lying in bed, writing by the light of her splendid three-branched Empire candelabra. 'I am *with you so intensely* that you must feel me. You *always* give me such great pleasure!' His noble nature, his freedom from all forms of pettiness and mean-mindedness, means that he too understands and respects Mahler and his artistic voca-tion – in other words he *must* understand why she has to go to America with him. Yet she insists that time will come when they will lie together, when nothing can separate them but sleep. Quite how and when she thinks this will occur Alma does not reveal, but of one thing she is quite sure: 'Someone who has once loved you, and found your love, can *never* again lead a life with another man.' She signs herself simply, 'Your wife.'[1]

A few days later Alma writes again. She has to, she tells Gro-pius. She misses him as a friend with whom she can talk about everything – especially of things not of this world. What a glorious life it would be if they could do this all the time. How she loves the highest features of his nature: his intellect, his artistry – which she'd known must be sublime even before she had seen a pencil stroke of one of his drawings – his talent for living, his charm, and last but not least his sheer physical beauty – to say nothing of his nobility and kindness. Indeed, Walter's physical attractions are far from 'least' in her estimation. Then comes something startling: 'At that time I still believed that I was still carrying your sweet, beloved essence in me towards a new development – and was so rich – I didn't know myself – *whereas* today, now I am completely destitute, I do know it!!' Of course she is 'dreadfully sorry' for Mahler. He must know that she has absolutely no physical desire for him. On the contrary, she fends him off, and has been completely successful in this – is that completely true, or is it meant to reassure her lover? She feels she belongs to Gropius so intensely that contact with another man, even her husband of eight years, would be an act of infidelity to him: 'My husband – write, do write! – That is all we have now.'[2]

It is 3 September, and Mahler has set off for Munich. He is 'still crazy', Alma tells Gropius, and she is afraid he will remain so. She describes how she drove him down to the railway station – an emotionally gruelling experience. Mahler was close to tears, and possessed by the fear that once he'd left she would go off with 'someone else' – was Mahler unable or unwilling to say with whom? Perhaps – he's clutching at straws now – time will make her lover's image fade. 'What length of time could do that?! – *he knows* that without me he cannot live. *I know* that I will respect and protect him – but love only you. *How* can we get out of that!?'

Then, soon after the premiere of the Eighth Symphony, Gropius drafts a letter to Alma Mahler. Now it is Walter who feels the need to be calm. He has thought this through carefully during the night, and has interrogated himself on every single thought. It is imperative that he faces up to everything with complete honesty and openness, especially in the light of what happened the last time he and Alma met, the day before. But he has one pressing request: she must not be 'hard-faced and composed' as she was yesterday. She must not try to hide her suffering from him – he knows the truth. There must be no more illusions, hiding from reality can only make things worse. And there is one question above all which she must answer – please! 'When was the first time you became intimate with G[ustav] again?'

So that was the bombshell. Not only has Mahler triumphed musically, spiritually, he has won the battle for Alma's heart too. Not that Walter entirely blames her. An experience like that, such an overwhelming artistic victory – how could it be otherwise? It was the same for him, he confesses resignedly. 'G's music moved my heart so much that I left the concert with this feeling that we could not hurt him, we must bow down to this man. As I read the biography the feeling grew stronger in me, and I met you yesterday with the intention of telling you that we must remain pure.' He sees it clearly now. In comparison with Mahler's outstanding qualities, both as man and as artist, he himself has been unable to win over Alma so completely that she was prepared to sacrifice everything for him. For someone like her – a momentary glint of steel here – the sheer physical presence of such a strong-willed person as Mahler would inevitably win out against the 'bungled scribbling' of a lesser mortal, trying to contend for her from a long way off. 'His will was simply stronger and more mature, and compelled you to surrender.'[3]

But it seems the letter was never sent.

4

God or Demon?

Emil Gutmann's message had been received and duly assimilated: this was to be a climactic event in Munich's artistic history. The city, the *Neues Münchner Tagblatt* ('New Munich Daily') proudly reported, was once again leading the world in the field of music – a more-than-implied dig at its main musical rivals, Paris and Vienna. The buzz in and around the city was that any self-respecting cultured individual just had to be there. The concert was billed to start at 7.30, though the audience began to arrive at least an hour in advance. By seven o'clock, around a thousand people had already taken their seats. Inside the Musik Festhalle, the *Neues Münchner Tagblatt* reporter sized it all up with a mixture of breathless awe and studied irony. Despite the intimidatingly high price of admission, the huge hall was sold out to the last seat. The quality of dress, he said, proclaimed a prevailingly wealthy, in some cases clearly aristocratic audience, while the eccentricity of some of the other costumes indicated membership of a different kind of 'aristocracy': the intellectual and artistic elite. The reporter was also struck by something else: something that, like Gutmann's saturation publicity tactics, places the Eighth Symphony's Munich premiere on the cusp of the modern age. Many of those attending the premiere arrived in cars – there were hundreds of them, the writer tells us excitedly, rattling and roaring from the city and its environs, leaving a huge cloud of petrol fumes that took a while to subside. Today, German car manufacturers dominate the prestige end of the global automobile market, while the German engineer Karl Benz is widely credited as the inventor of the modern car – the patent for his first engine was granted in 1879, the year after Mahler completed his studies at the Vienna Conservatory. But despite the tremendous push towards industrialisation in the newly unified Germany, interest in the automobile was slow to take off on its home ground. France was quicker to catch on, in fact until almost the end of the nineteenth century Benz sold more cars in France than he did in Germany. In America Henry Ford's famous mass-produced Model T had been introduced in 1908, the year of Mahler's debut at New York's Metropolitan Opera; in 1909 Count Zeppelin had founded the world's first airline, and the first commercial Zeppelin flights followed in 1910. But when it came to private automobiles Germany still lagged behind. A mass outing of cars was something worth noting in Munich in 1910, as was the effect it had on the atmosphere.

Still, in contrast to the United States of America, in Germany in 1910, the car was still largely the plaything of the wealthy upper classes. When the cars drew up outside the Musik Festhalle, it was representatives of the old order that stepped down from them: the *Neues Münchner Tagblatt* reporter dwells on the impressive turnout by the aristocracy and the *haute bourgeoisie*. A legend has grown up that there were also crowned heads of state in that first audience. This turns out to be untrue, but Prince Ludwig Ferdinand of Bavaria (who would have been King if the German states had failed to unify in 1871) was there, as was the heir to the throne of Spain and, more significantly, the Archduchess Gisela, daughter and eldest surviving child of the Austrian emperor Franz Joseph. So too were the Princess Thurn und Taxis, Princess Marietta zu Hohenlohe and Paul Clemenceau, brother of the French prime minister. Germany's great musical royal house was represented by Siegfried Wagner, son and heir of the composer. Naturally the

Lord Mayor of Munich was in prominent attendance. There was a strong representation from Mahler's old fiefdom, the Vienna Court Opera, including the star sopranos Anna von Mildenburg and Selma Kurz, Mahler's conductor protégé Bruno Walter and his stage and graphic designer Alfred Roller. The eminent Viennese critic and Mahler champion Julius Korngold was there with his thirteen-year-old son, Erich Wolfgang Korngold, whose ballet *Der Schneemann* ('The Snowman') had been a sensational success at its Viennese premiere just five months earlier. Also there were three authors of important Mahler studies: Guido Adler, Richard Specht and Paul Stefan. There were at least four literary lions from the German-speaking world – Hugo von Hofmannsthal, Thomas Mann, with his wife Katia, Arthur Schnitzler and Stefan Zweig – along with Nietzsche's friend and secretary, Peter Gast. Composers present included Max Reger, Richard Strauss, Anton Webern (reporting back to his 'Second Viennese School' colleagues Arnold Schoenberg and Alban Berg) and Alexander Zemlinsky, Alma's lover until he was supplanted by Mahler in 1901. There was also an impressive array of critics, from Germany and Austria naturally, from America, and from France, amongst the latter the composers Paul Dukas and Camille Saint-Saëns. Saint-Saëns later confessed to finding Mahler's music 'unbearable', but given his extreme prejudice against almost all forms of modern music that is no great surprise. There is also a rumour, as yet unsubstantiated, that the maverick English composer John Foulds was there for at least one of the performances, which may then have sowed creative seeds for the world-embracing *Symphony of East and West* Foulds was working on at the time of his death in 1939. The young conductor Leopold Stokowski was definitely present, however, and the experience gave him the courage and determination to defy opposition and bring about the Eighth Symphony's American premiere in Philadelphia on 2 March 1916. Stokowski's performance was so successful that the symphony was performed again in Philadelphia, and then at New York's Metropolitan Opera House.

As we've already seen, the concert was billed to start at 7.30, but Mahler didn't make his entrance onto the stage until exactly 7.45 – a spontaneous decision, or a carefully planned one? Either way it had the desired effect, stoking up the tension to exactly the right level. The French magazine *Le Monde musical* reported how the nervous, excited chatter built steadily during the quarter of an hour that followed the expected start time; and when the tiny figure of Gustav Mahler made his way effortfully through the close-compacted mass of performers, a thunderous cheer suddenly erupted throughout the hall. Mahler climbed the steps to the rostrum, then turned and bowed as the applause broke over him in waves. The critic Maurice Baumfeld, writing for a New York German-language newspaper, described the audience rising to its feet spontaneously, *en masse*, at Mahler's appearance on the platform, as though they were greeting the arrival of a king. At a signal from Mahler the massed forces rose as one with military precision – which the clearly patriotic French reporter for *Le Monde musical* couldn't help diagnosing as typically Teutonic. But neither could he prevent himself from being blown away by the symphony's opening: the thunderous chord of E flat major from the hall's powerful organ, then the sound of massed voices piling in together with a great cry of 'Veni, creator spiritus' – the *Le Monde musical* reporter puts the number of choral singers at four hundred, but judging from some other accounts this was probably a conservative estimate.

Even more extraordinary, however, was the performance that followed, during which, with a few well-calculated gestures, and carefully directed glances from his famously piercing eyes, Mahler urged on his musical troops to feats that perhaps even they themselves would not have thought possible. Alma describes the experience in ecstatic terms, and although she omits any account of its effects on the balance of power in her relationships with her husband and her lover, something of that can perhaps be intuited. Not only Munich itself, but others from many lands, she notes with swelling pride, had come to pay tribute to *her* husband. The reception at the symphony's first public performance eclipsed even the 'rapturous' enthusiasm at the final rehearsal. As the audience rose to its feet to acknowledge Mahler's arrival on the stage, then fell back into breathless silence in anticipation of the much-hyped musical experience, Alma sat in her box, 'almost insensible from excitement'. As for the music itself, that raised the experience to yet another exalted level: 'And then Mahler, god or demon, turned those tremendous volumes of sound into fountains of light. The experience was indescribable. Indescribable too the demonstration which followed. The whole audience surged towards the platform.'

Alma tells how she waited behind the scenes, deeply stirred by the whole experience, until the clamour had died down. Then she joined her husband for a triumphal drive to the hotel where a victory reception had been arranged. Even there the adulation pressed on them like flood waters. A rich, notoriously eccentric American from New York stood in their way and stammered out that there had been nothing to compare with it since Brahms – evidently an unworthy comparison in Alma's eyes. 'We pushed past him', she tells us gleefully, 'by main force.'[1] One can't help noticing her repetition of the triumphal 'we'. There are few aphrodisiacs more powerful than public success – especially success on this scale. It was, as most of Mahler's commentators agree, the greatest single triumph of the composer's life, and one of the most remarkable public successes in the whole history of Western classical music, certainly in Munich's history – and this was the city that had seen premieres of masterpieces by Wagner and Strauss. Did the 'whole audience' really surge towards the platform to honour Alma's 'god or demon' at the end? Other accounts differ; but even if not, her hyperbole is surely symptomatic of her feelings.

Unsurprisingly, PR mastermind Emil Gutmann was inspired to flights of lyricism – no doubt partly fuelled by proprietorial pride. When Mahler stepped onto the platform, he tells us, 'everyone felt that a primeval, well-organised being, capable of life, was about to acquire a heart, which would now begin to beat . . .' And then 'the lips of all humanity thronging on the sacred mountain opened for the first time in the fervent cry: "Veni, creator spiritus".'[2] For the German writer Emil Ludwig, Mahler stood revealed simply as a 'magus', a kind of black magician. How different it all was from the dubious, cultish mass devotion manifested at Wagner's Bayreuth Festival – this was truly visionary. Ludwig also noted how, at the end, as the thunderous waves of applause swept from the hall to the platform, Mahler was particularly keen to acknowledge the heroic efforts of the children's choir. So too did Bruno Walter, even though his role had been to coach the vocal soloists. Walter remembered how, when the performance was over and the audience's ecstatic applause swept through the hall like a great tidal wave, Mahler made a point of hurrying up the steps on the platform to the children's chorus, delightedly grasping the hands of each tiny performer in turn. It was crucial for Mahler, Walter felt, to acknowledge the contribution of youth to his hymn to Eros and the heavenly spheres. This was the composer who had portrayed the emotions of childhood with such tenderness (and, at the same time, unsettling honesty) in his Fourth Symphony, and who had already lost his adored elder daughter; one can well understand why the children's contribution meant so much to Mahler. But for Walter there was a dreadful pathos in all this too. Walter knew how concerned Mahler was after the diagnosis of his heart condition, and recalling the Munich premiere some forty-five years later he knew how little time Mahler had left to live. But there has to be more to this than just hindsight. The soprano Lilli Lehmann, who had sung for Mahler at the Vienna Opera, knew far less than Walter about Mahler's health, and his anxieties about it, but she seems to have realised from the start what few others in the hall had recognised. This was to be the last time Lehmann saw the composer, and from his arrival on the stage she was shocked by his appearance. He seemed to have aged so much since they'd last worked together. The performance of the symphony moved Lehmann deeply, but it wasn't all pleasure: 'The second part of the Symphony . . . touched me painfully. Was it he, his music, his appearance, a premonition of death, Goethe's words, reminiscences of Schumann, my youth? I don't know; I only know that for the whole of the second part I gave way to emotion which I could not control.'[3]

After all the excited accounts of the Eighth's Symphony's overwhelming, oceanic effect, and of Mahler's 'demonic' direction, it is something of a relief to come across Lehmann's more nuanced reaction, her insight into this music's half-hidden complexities. Just as intriguing from this point of view is the description provided by Anton Webern, reporting back to his friend and former teacher Arnold Schoenberg, apparently trapped in Vienna by work commitments and financial hardship. Given the extreme delicacy of many of Webern's mature compositions – to the point where the silences can often be as eloquent as the handful of notes they punctuate – his reaction is telling:

I can't tell you how beautiful Mahler's symphony is. A wealth of ideas, and intensity of emotion, the most supernatural emotion. In the second part there is a stillness and tenderness: 5 harps, Celeste, Mandolines, Pianoforte, harmoniums with soft woodwinds and muted brasses and pp singing by three women's voices canon diminuendo right down to pppp – entry of the 'Chorus Mysticus'! It is indescribable.[4]

The two works Webern wrote following this transcendent experience, the *Five Pieces for Orchestra* op. 10 (1911–13) and the *Six Bagatelles for String Quartet* op. 9 (1913), could each be seen partly as a distillation of what he had learned in such moments. In the mere fourteen pages of score that comprise the *Five Pieces* the overwhelmingly dominant dynamic markings are *p*, *pp* and *ppp*; just as telling is the use of harp, celeste, mandolin, organ (presumably harmonium), and the muting of the tiny brass section (just three instruments) throughout. The even more radically concise *Six Bagatelles* barely rise above a whisper. This was one of those astonishingly concentrated compositions in which, according to Schoenberg, Webern had been able to condense the richness, complexity and intensity of a novel into a single musical gesture, and express 'a wealth of ideas, and intensity of emotion' in the merest breath. Webern had been heading in this direction before 1910, but the experience of Mahler's 'stillness and tenderness' in the Eighth Symphony was clearly a major signpost.

What of the reactions of some of the other major creative figures present at the Eighth Symphony's premiere? The critic Julius

Korngold remembered his thirteen-year-old son Erich Wolfgang being intensely excited by the whole process, but when Korngold junior described the impression made on him by Mahler during the rehearsals and the first performance years later, it was Mahler the magician-conductor he recalled. Listening to the slow movement of Korngold's Violin Concerto (1945), however, it is possible to hear a connection between its exquisite, hushed, voluptuous textures, and especially its delicate use of harp, celeste and vibraphone, and those still, tender sounds in Part II of Mahler's symphony that so entranced Webern. Mahler's half-friend, half-rival Richard Strauss had confessed to being sceptical about the Eighth before the performance, and the experience of hearing it seems to have hardened his heart still further. But how much of this was an honest reaction to the musical experience itself, and how much was jealousy at seeing Mahler achieve such an overwhelming success in Strauss's own home city, a city where Strauss himself had never quite managed to score such a colossal hit? Strauss's next major work, *Eine Alpensinfonie* ('An Alpine Symphony', begun in 1911), uses a huge orchestra – the largest Strauss ever employed in a symphonic work – and in its colouristic effects and use of offstage brass it could be read as an attempt to outdo Mahler: this from the composer who earlier in 1910 had apparently told Mahler that from now on he would write only operas, and that he was done with symphonic works. The subject of Strauss's symphony is one that one would have thought was guaranteed to appeal to every true Münchner: a portrayal of an exciting day's adventure climbing and descending from a peak in the Bavarian Alps. But by the time *An Alpine Symphony* was complete, in 1915, the catastrophe of the First World War had begun to unfold, and the cultural climate in Germany had changed almost out of recognition.

What then of the literary figures who witnessed Mahler's triumph? 'I could have written about great premieres', Stefan Zweig
begins in *The World of Yesterday*, heading the list that follows with
Mahler's Munich triumph, but that, frustratingly, is as far as he
goes – and the fact that he gets the symphony's number wrong (he
refers to it as 'Mahler's Tenth') is not encouraging.[5] The novelist
and dramatist Arthur Schnitzler tells us still less, which is an even
greater shame: it would have been fascinating to read the reactions
of a writer so fixated with eroticism, and with female eroticism
in particular, to Mahler's hymn to Eros and the *Ewig-Weibliche*.
But the reaction of one writer to the 1910 premiere has become
famous – legendary even. Thomas Mann had met Mahler in
the hotel after the performance, and had presumably offered his
congratulations. Even so, he still felt the need to write to Mahler
about his experience. He had been incapable, he told Mahler, of
expressing how deeply indebted he felt to the composer for the
impressions created by that momentous event. It was a message
for his age, expressed in the most profound and sacred terms. All
Mann could do in return, he confessed, was to offer him a copy
of his most recently published novel – a trifling gift, but one the
great man might find tolerably entertaining. The book in question was *Königliche Hoheit* ('Royal Highness', 1909), not generally
counted amongst Mann's finest achievements. But the book Mann
began the following year, the novella *Der Tod in Venedig* ('Death
in Venice') would be another matter entirely, and this time there
was a direct connection to Mahler, one that Mann acknowledged
in a letter written ten years later, to the book's illustrator, Wolfgang
Born. To Mann's astonishment, Born (without any prompting
from the author) had portrayed the novel's protagonist, Gustav von
Aschenbach, in a manner that strongly recalled Mahler. Could this

have been pure coincidence? The novel's very conception, Mann reveals, was influenced by the shocking news of Mahler's death in 1911, so soon after that overwhelming triumph in Munich. The after-effects of that shock fused with other impressions and ideas germinating in his mind at the time, and from which *Der Tod in Venedig* was soon to spring, with the result that 'when I conceived my hero who succumbs to lascivious dissolution, I not only gave him the great musician's Christian name, but also in describing his appearance conferred Mahler's mask upon him'.[6]

Had Born intuited what until then Mann had kept a close secret? There is a link in the final sentence of *Death in Venice* that apparently ties in Mann's story, and its hero, with Mahler's own triumph and tragedy. Aschenbach's body has been discovered, 'and that same day a respectfully shocked world received the report of his death' – just as Mann himself, about to set off for Venice from the island of Bioni (now Brijuni), on the opposite coast of the Adriatic Sea, received the reports of Mahler's woefully premature death from the Viennese newspapers. The link was clearly conclusive enough for the director Luchino Visconti, whose film *Death in Venice* (1971) emphasises the connection between Gustav von Aschenbach and Gustav Mahler by changing the former's profession from writer (in Mann's novella) to composer, by having the hero, played by Dirk Bogarde, made up to look remarkably like Mahler, and by using the Adagietto from Mahler's Fifth Symphony, along with the Nietzsche setting 'O Mensch! Gib Acht!' (Oh Man! Take heed!) from the Third, to represent Aschenbach's own thoughts and feelings during the working out of the story.

But remember that Mann himself described the connection between Aschenbach's appearance and personality as 'loose and hidden'. And how many Mahler-lovers, reading Mann's letter, have stumbled over Mann's comment about how his hero 'succumbs to lascivious dissolution'? It could be argued, tenuously perhaps, that Mahler did eventually succumb to a form of 'dissolution' in 1911, though he fought against it with all his usual strength and tenacity until almost the end. But 'lascivious'? It's time to take a closer look at the Aschenbach–Mahler connection, and to find out if there is any verifiable spiritual kinship between the real flesh-and-blood composer, his music, and Mann's fictional writer.

Birth in Munich, Death in Venice

The first thing to be said is that the composer whose music and character obsessed Thomas Mann throughout his creative life was not Mahler, but Richard Wagner. The case of Wagner outlined a paradox that troubled Mann, and which he wrote about again and again, developing the issues he identified in several of his novels and short stories. One of Mann's last acts, before leaving Germany in 1933, was to deliver a lecture entitled 'The Sorrows and Grandeur of Richard Wagner', containing amongst other things a note of coded protest against the Nazi regime. Alongside this was yet another attempt to make sense of the issue that had troubled Mann about Wagner since early adulthood: how was it that Mann could be drawn so irresistibly to Wagner as an artist, when as a thinker, and above all as a personality, he appeared to him so thoroughly suspect?

But the connections between Wagner and *Death in Venice* are profound and multi-layered. It was Wagner, after all, who had died in Venice, in 1883. And it was to Wagner that Mann turned, in July 1911, while staying at the Grand Hotel des Bains, on the city's sea coast, in a short essay called 'Coming to Terms with

Richard Wagner', written – like some of the sketches for *Death in Venice* – on the hotel's headed notepaper. At one point in the novel Aschenbach is depicted composing a short but intensely focused essay as he watches the exquisitely beautiful boy Tadzio playing on the beach in front of the hotel. The inference that the subject and content of the essay is more or less the same as that of 'Coming to Terms with Richard Wagner' is hard to resist. In his own essay, Mann questions himself as to the true nature of his youthful response to Wagner's music. It was, he admits, the experience of hearing and seeing Wagner that provided a more important stimulating influence on his own youthful artistic ambitions than anything else he encountered at the time. It was Wagner, the 'Master' he both adored and envied, who had challenged him to produce something comparable himself, if only on a more modest scale. But however intoxicated the young Thomas Mann may have been, did he ever really believe in the artistic message Wagner seemed to be trying to convey? That is what he now asks himself. Perhaps, in all honesty, there was a terrible truth in all this. Could it even be that all art contained an element of deception, of demagoguery, a compound of theatrical manipulation and impish trickery? Yet even if this were entirely correct, Mann confessed that whenever some evocative melodic phrase or harmonic twist from one of Wagner's works found its way to his heart, he still found himself startled by the joy he felt again, as his defences yielded yet again to Wagner's 'clever and ingenious wizardry, full of yearning and cunning'.[7]

For all his conscious, rational scruples, developed and reflected on at length in later life, whenever Mann heard Wagner's music his instinctive response remained the same, flooding him with memories of his youthful passion, and the intense feeling of creative promise associated with it. Perhaps the impression that the music also offered profound truths, glimpses into things of deep significance, was a delusion; but if so, was this the kind of delusion without which, as Nietzsche had admitted, human beings might not be able to live? *Death in Venice* can be seen in part as an attempt to work through this paradox creatively, rather than rationally – analysing the problem only ever seemed to tie Mann in mental knots. Two books by Nietzsche appear to have been particularly influential: the early *The Birth of Tragedy*, written in 1872 when Nietzsche was still a disciple of Wagner; and *The Case of Wagner*, from 1888, well after Nietzsche's final falling out with Wagner, in which the composer's work is presented as a dangerously enchanting form of sickness. With this in mind, Venice, in Mann's novella, looks increasingly like an embodiment of Nietzsche's later position: the supremely artistic city that floats, dreamlike and seductive, above the mud and waters of a stagnant lagoon, provides the nourishment and breeding space for the plague that kills Aschenbach, along with many others in the city. At the same time *Death in Venice* can be understood, like many great ghost stories, as a parable of what Freud called 'the return of the repressed' – the 'repressed' in this case being the Greek god Dionysos, and all the dark, powerful, unconscious energies he represents. In *The Birth of Tragedy*, Nietzsche argued that the polarity between the gods Apollo (order, rationality, categorical thought, sunlight) and Dionysos (ecstasy, emotionalism, sexual abandonment, night) was fundamental to the human experience. Gustav von Aschenbach, we are told in Mann's novella, is a devotee of Apollo, a preacher of moral resolution, whose novel *The Abject* is conceived as a challenge and a rebuke to an age obsessed with psychology, an age that by seeking unconscious motivations for so many of our actions blurs the moral dimension. There must be no shilly-shallying: the abyss within must be confronted with clear-eyed fortitude, not excused with soft-hearted humanitarianism. To understand is not necessarily to forgive: far from it. The devil must be called out. In short, Aschenbach has repressed his own Dionysos, and on one level, *Death in Venice* is the story of Dionysos's revenge.

If those final words don't sound a lot like Mahler, that's because they aren't. Mahler was, as Otto Klemperer has told us, a devotee of Nietzsche. Mahler knew and understood Nietzsche's conception, set forth in *The Birth of Tragedy*, of an Apollo–Dionysos polarity in the human mind, resolvable (if only temporarily) through the experience of beholding classical tragic drama, resulting in what Aristotle had called a 'catharsis' (purging) of the emotions. *The Birth of Tragedy* was almost certainly a crucial influence on Mahler's Sixth Symphony – the symphony he at one early stage actually called 'Tragic' – which just about manages to contain its volcanic emotional outpourings in what is in fact Mahler's most 'classically' proportioned symphonic structure. Here then is an image of reconciliation, such as Nietzsche described in *The Birth of Tragedy*, not of repression of one side of the spiritual–mental equation. As for Mann's account of how Aschenbach magisterially rejects all forms of compassion for the abyss – what could be less Mahlerian than this? This is the composer who in the Third Symphony's finale begged his God for forgiveness for every living creature: 'Father, see these wounds of mine! Let not be lost one creature of thine.'[8] This is the Mahler who worshipped Dostoyevsky, unmatched chronicler of the abysses in the human soul and for Mahler the greatest of all psychologists; it is the Mahler who argued that the symphony 'must be like the world. It must embrace everything', and who scandalised his critics by placing banality, *grotesquerie*, sentimentality and acrid sarcasm alongside his most sublime and poignantly beautiful utterances.

The question would now appear to be, not how far Gustav von Aschenbach resembles Gustav Mahler, but whether there is any resemblance at all beyond that of superficial appearance? I believe that there is. First of all there is the tribute Mann paid, in his letter to Wolfgang Born, to how Mahler's 'intense personality' had 'left the strongest impression' on him. The Mahler described again and again in magical imagery – 'magus', 'god or demon', 'wizard' – at the Eighth Symphony's premiere, who imposed his will with such ruthless energy on the vast forces he urged on to such overwhelming effect, could be seen as a kindred spirit to Mann's ruthlessly disciplined, driven writer-hero. Yet all the demonic imagery might suggest something else too: something far darker and more anarchic. Here, for the novelist, at the age of thirty-five, was a return to that blissful spirit of youthful intoxication comparable, he tells us in 'Coming to Terms with Richard Wagner', to an intense and illicit love affair. Like Wagner for the young Thomas Mann, Mahler's Eighth Symphony, and its composer's spirit-conquering direction, had filled the older writer once more with a longing, perhaps again coloured with envy, to produce something similar, if only on a more modest scale. That 'something similar' – far more modest in scale but devastating in effect – was *Death in Venice*, I would argue, which contains, in its Dionysian dream sequences, perhaps the most oceanic, voluptuously beautiful prose Mann ever created. Mahler's Eros had become Mann's *creator spiritus*: the novella's references to Plato's writings, including *The Symposium*, show how close the two men had come in their understanding of that concept. And there is, I believe, a particular tribute to Mahler's Eighth and to its effect on Mann – unconscious, perhaps, but no less genuine for that – at the end of the novella. In his letter to Wolfgang Born, Mann talks about 'hidden' connections to Mahler, beyond the recognition of readers; and by a bizarre, inexplicable twist of fate, one of the most striking of those connections has remained hidden to most Anglophone readers for decades. In the old Penguin translation of *Death in Venice* by H. T. Lowe-Porter, for a long time the only translation commercially available in English, the moment of Aschenbach's death is rendered as follows. Aschenbach is, as so often in the story, watching the beautiful boy Tadzio intently, now from his deckchair beside the sea. As he follows the boy's graceful movements, his head resting against the chair-back, he recalls the moment when Tadzio's 'twilit grey eyes' first met his own. Eventually Aschenbach falls into a kind of trance, outwardly appearing unconscious, yet with his gaze still fixed upon the boy:

It seemed to him the pale and lovely Summoner out there smiled at him and beckoned; as though with the hand he lifted from his hip, he pointed outward as he hovered on before into an immensity of richest expectation.

Some minutes passed before anyone hastened to the aid of the elderly man sitting there collapsed in his chair . . .

It is a heartbreakingly beautiful moment, a kind of Wagnerian *Liebestod* ('love-death') expressed in luminous prose, and Lowe-Porter's translation gets closer than most to the beauty of Mann's original German. But for reasons that have never been explained, Lowe-Porter leaves out key sentences at various stages in *Death in Venice*, and at this point comes perhaps the strangest omission of all. After the sentence that ends, 'he pointed outward

as he hovered on before into an immensity of richest expectation',
Mann's text contains another sentence: 'Und wie so oft, machte er
sich auf, ihn zu folgen' (And as so often before, he got up to follow
him). Without that final sentence, Tadzio is simply the Freudian
Thanatos, the death-wish; with it, he is also Eros – as Mahler said,
the true 'creator spirit' – beckoning the novella's hero to his death,
but inspiring its author to 'follow him', to experience the urge that,
as Goethe put it, 'draws us onward', and thus to produce what
some would say was Thomas Mann's greatest achievement. *Zieht
uns hinan* – these are the closing words of Mahler's Eighth Symphony, rising in one of the greatest climactic waves in all music.
With that shattering, orgasmic culmination in mind, it is surely
not stretching credibility too far to see *Death in Venice* as the Platonic love child of Mahler's Eighth Symphony.

5

Approaching the Inexpressible: Words and Music in Mahler's Eighth Symphony

Part I: *Veni, creator spiritus*

Veni, creator spiritus	Come, Creator Spirit,
Mentes tuorum visita.	Visit the minds of your people.
Imple superna gratia,	Fill with heavenly grace,
Quae tu creasti pectora.	Those whose hearts you have created.

The enthralled reaction of the reporter from *Le Monde musical* to the opening of Mahler's Eighth has been shared by countless listeners in the twentieth and twenty-first centuries. It is an awe-inspiring way to begin a symphony: the thrilling chord of E flat from the full organ, then the great choral shout of 'Veni, veni creator spiritus'; yet at the same time it is a striking reminder of Mahler's practicality as a musician. His first experiences of working with orchestras and singers in spa towns and provincial opera houses had taught him that sometimes even good musicians need help. It might have been possible to find around five hundred singers with perfect pitch, but to rely on them to come straight in with a massively assertive chord of E flat major, exactly in tune, could have led to disaster in the concert hall. The *fortissimo* organ chord – or rather, bass pedal note quickly followed by full chord on the keyboards – is not only a tremendous call to attention, it provides the initial notes for all the singers in the two massed choruses, ensuring that each one can enter with full confidence.

And confidence is needed. This is not the first of Mahler's symphonies to begin *fortissimo*, but in character it is quite unlike any opening he had ever contrived before. On this subject Mahler revealingly remarked to Richard Specht that 'All my previous symphonies are merely the preludes to this one. In the other works everything still was subjective tragedy, but this one is a source of great joy.'[1]

The transformation from 'subjective tragedy' to objective, collective 'joy' is reflected in the very character of the first theme. Four of Mahler's earlier symphonies (nos. 2, 3, 5 and 6) begin with marches, and the first movement of the Seventh quickly develops into one, but the character of all of these is prevailingly dark, grim, and unequivocally minor-key. The marches in the first movements of the Sixth and Seventh Symphonies bear a strong family likeness, and strong echoes of both themes can be heard in the Eighth Symphony's march-like opening, 'Veni, veni creator spiritus!' But now the rhythmic pattern is augmented, the upward leap thrusts itself even higher, and the mode is pure bright major: 'I'm still the same Mahler,' it seems to say, 'but now I'm not the self-focused tragedian, but the bringer of joy!'

Symphony No 6, First Movement

Symphony No 7, First Movement

Symphony No 8, Part One

Ve - ni,   ve - ni, cre - a - tor   spi - ri tus!

Symphony No 8, Part One (Fig 3)

Spi - ri-tus;   o   cre-a - tor - ve - - - - - - ni,

Soon afterwards a second motif emerges, as Mahler characteristically plays around with the word ordering of the hymn: 'spiritus, o
creator veni' (Ex 5.1). This is soon swept aside by the original 'Veni,
veni creator' theme, but it will turn out to be important later on.

As for the collective element in this hymn of 'joy', Mahler was
a huge admirer of J. S. Bach, and according to the Mahler scholar
Donald Mitchell, one work of Bach's in particular was an important influence on Part I of the Eighth Symphony: the motet *Singet
dem Herrn ein neues Lied* ('O Sing unto the Lord a New Song').
This setting of the Biblical Psalm 96 is an ecstatic communal outpouring of praise to God – 'O ye kindreds of the people, give unto
the Lord glory and strength' – and Bach's setting is a magnificent,
intricately contrapuntal paean of joy which, like the first part
of Mahler's Eighth, makes use of thrilling antiphonal contrasts
between its two mixed four-part choruses. One of the glories of
contrapuntal writing in Western classical music is the impression
it gives of many distinct voices combining in a single purpose. For
this reason Wagner made much use of Bachian counterpoint in
his hymn to his ideal civic community, *Die Meistersinger* – and
since the Eighth Symphony's premiere several commentators have
noted resemblances in its Part I to Wagner's most joyous masterpiece, and particularly to its intricately polyphonic Prelude.

This mood of confident, forward-striding exultation, with voices
calling to each other, urging each other on, continues for about
three minutes, then it quickly subsides into a new theme ('Imple
superna gratia') and a new emotional character. In the conversation

with Specht quoted above, Mahler claimed that this first movement was in strict symphonic form, despite being sung throughout.
That would mean that Part I was cast in a fundamentally classical
'sonata form'. Sonata-form movements fall into three parts: 'exposition', in which the main themes are introduced; 'development', in
which these themes are dramatically broken down and recombined
in sometimes striking new forms; and 'recapitulation', in which the
main themes return in more or less their original form, only now all
anchored in the home key. Analyses of putative sonata-form movements can easily come across as pedantic nitpicking. Perhaps the
best way to approach it is to follow the example of Charles Rosen in
his magnificent study *The Classical Style* and view this 'form' more
as a kind of dynamic principle: a mode of thinking rather than a set
of rules to contain that thought. The essence of that principle could
be conveyed in a phrase from the poet William Blake: 'Without contraries there is no progression.'

Mahler certainly springs a 'contrary' on us now. The tonality
eases downwards into D flat major for what textbooks call the
'second subject'. This is very much on the 'flat' side of the tonic
E flat, and movements in this direction have often been held to
express passivity in tonal music. In a classical sonata-form movement, however, the composer would normally make a move to the
'sharp' side to heighten the intensity, by which standards Mahler's move could be viewed as unorthodox. Mahler has his reasons,
however. After the loud opening invocation to the Creator Spirit,
the supplicants now place themselves in an attitude of receptiv-
ity, waiting for the divine gift to be bestowed. The writing is still
contrapuntal, but it is liquid, melodious, flowing, the orchestration softer, warmer, more mellifluous. Intimate solo voices replace
the massed utterances of huge choirs. The use of an ensemble of

solo voices, rapturously intertwined, after the bold assertions of choruses and orchestra, directly recalls the final solo quartet in the 'Ode to Joy' finale of Beethoven's Ninth Symphony; only by placing it so early in his own choral symphony, Mahler subtly draws attention to the fact that he has gone one better than Beethoven, creating a musical argument that is both symphonic and sung throughout. There are echoes too of the ravishing solo quintet from Act III of Wagner's *Meistersinger*. At the same time the second theme itself, introduced by the solo soprano ('Imple superna gratia'), may contain a half-memory of the Gregorian chant 'Veni, creator spiritus' which, as we have noted, Mahler probably heard at his service of reception into the Roman Catholic Church in 1897. There is a similarity in the opening melodic turn, and the twofold rise that follows, conflated into one phrase by Mahler.

Veni creator spiritus

Symphony No 8, Part One (Fig 7)

Qui diceris Paraclitus,	You who are called the Paraclete,
Altissimi donum Dei,	Gift of the most high God,
Fons vivus, ignis, caritas	Fount of life, fire, divine love
Et spiritalis unctio.	And the balm of the spirit.

As choral voices, sometimes reduced in number, join in discreetly with the solo voices, the prayer turns to dwell on the nature of the Holy Spirit, now addressed as the 'Paraclete', alternatively rendered in Christian writings as 'advocate' or 'comforter' (from the Greek *para*, 'beside', and *kalein*, 'to call'). A word about gender may be in order here. The Latin 'spiritus' is masculine, in keeping with prevailingly masculine conceptions of God in Christian traditions; but as Mahler almost certainly knew from his youthful Jewish religious studies, the Hebrew word for spirit, *ru'ach*, is feminine, as it is in the Aramaic language Jesus himself would have spoken. If so, this would strengthen the link between the Christian concept of 'spirit' and the creative *Ewig-Weibliche*, hymned in the closing stages of Part II. As we shall see, it is a link that Mahler carefully underlines in his musical setting.

Gradually, however, the serenity begins to cloud over, and a highly chromatic violin line troubles the harmonies, gradually building to a more urgent version of the opening 'Veni, veni' from full chorus. Just as this seems to be building to a solid climactic confirmation on 'superna gratia', the tempo lurches forward and the mood darkens still further, with shrill high woodwind and ominous deep bell strokes as the key shifts downwards a semitone into a sombre D minor. The chromatic violin line is taken up by a solo violin, marked *accel. ohne Rücksicht auf das Tempo* ('accelerating without regard for the main tempo'), heightening the sense of unease. The earlier mood of collective joy appears to be shifting back into the sound-world of 'subjective tragedy' that dominated the purely orchestral Fifth, Sixth and Seventh Symphonies. It is orchestral forces that have engineered this transition, but the voices now provide the explanation.

Infirma nostri corporis	Strengthen our frail bodies
Virtute firmans perpeti,	With enduring moral strength,
Accende lumen sensibus,	Blaze out, light of the senses,
Infunde amorem cordibus.	Pour love into our hearts.

As the orchestra's harsh tumult subsides, the choral voices enter with a subdued, shadowy, dissonant version of the once radiant 'Veni, veni', to the words 'Infirma nostri corporis'. 'Infirm-ity', human weakness, is brought into the spotlight. The prayer for strength, 'Virtute firmans perpeti', appears to bring new hope, with a very Bachian inversion (i.e. turning a theme upside-down, inter-val by interval) of the original 'Veni, veni creator' motif in imitation, growing in resolution; but this too is suddenly cut off, to be replaced by eerie low tremolando strings, muted brass, nerve-tingling high pizzicato violins and more deep bell strokes. Eventually the tempo drops, and the tonality sinks by another semitone into a funereal C sharp minor, as dark-toned choral basses introduce a prolonged polyphonic meditation on the word 'Infirma'. Although the mood does lighten, with a slightly more hopeful shift back to D (major this time), the movement's original driving energy seems to have flagged. But it is at this very point that Mahler rouses himself stupendously. A startling *fortissimo* orchestral outburst, marked *Plötzlich sehr breit und leidenschaftlichen Ausdruck* ('With sudden very broad and passionate expression'), lifts the music into a radi-ant E major – significantly also the key for some of the most ecstatic outpourings in the Symphony's second part. And now begins the passage Mahler identified to Anton Webern as the turning point of Part I, where the music follows the text's command to 'arise' and anticipates the transfiguration of Part II.

This ferociously impassioned *fortissimo*, with the first violins shooting upwards *fff*, would be arresting enough in itself: it's clear that the music has entered a new emotional phase. But Mahler heightens the tension with a thrilling theatrical device. Soloists and both choruses quickly sound out the first syllable of 'Accende' (arise); then comes a brief pause, before the '-cende' is delivered by all the voices with pile-driver support from the full organ, now marked *Mit plötzlichem Aufschwung* ('With sudden impetus'). The falling fourth originally associated with 'Veni' now sets in motion a sweeping, aspiring theme which will play a much more important part in the symphony's second part: the structural and spiritual bridge that Mahler pointed out to Webern is both tonal and thematic. After an oceanic high point on the word 'amorem' (love), the boys' choir enters for the first time,* the distinctive bright sound of the young voices cutting through the rich, active choral and orchestral texture like a beam of light through storm clouds. The notes they sing are highly significant, for they outline exactly the same melody as that intoned by the boys' voices at their first entry in the opening chorus of Bach's *St Matthew Passion*. In the Bach, the boys enter in the key of G; but transpose their notes to the chorus's home key of E and the connection becomes obvious.

J.S. Bach: St Matthew Passion, Opening Chorus
(transposed to E major)

Symphony No 8, Part One (Fig 40)

Bach's chorus is an expression of lamentation mixed with anticipated triumph, foretelling both Christ's Passion and his Resurrection;

---

*Actually this isn't quite the first entry: the ever-practical Mahler has the boys double the choral altos at the words 'Accende lumen sensibus' and 'Infunde', giving them a few precious moments to find their voices before this exposed entry.

Mahler at this point is intent more on the final spiritual victory. But the Bach is also a distinctly communal outpouring, again with intricate counterpoint and antiphonally placed choirs suggesting a multitude of minds concentrated upon a single thought. There must have been many in those first Munich performances who would have caught the reference, if only subliminally.

Hostem repellas longius	Drive the enemy far from us
Pacemque dones protinus.	And grant us lasting peace.
Ductore sic te praevio	With you going before us as leader,
Vitemus omne pessimum.	May we avoid all evil.

Now the tone turns combative. Trombones thunder out rapid groups of seven notes, clashing with the 4/4 beat to create an effect of extreme rhythmic turbulence; meanwhile the first chorus delivers dissonant shouts of 'Hostem' ('the enemy'), underlined by high-straining woodwind, whoops from the eight horns and sharp, percussive chords from the organ. This splendid, masterfully organised melee eventually manages to arrive back at the home key for the second two lines of the stanza ('Ductore sic te praevio . . .'). At this point Mahler exhibits his Bachian credentials to the full by launching a stirring double fugue (a fugue based upon two leading themes), utilising both the original 'Veni, veni creator' motif and the slightly later 'spiritus, o creator veni' figure. It is, in textbook terms, a remarkably orthodox fugue, with the leading vocal entries always on either the tonic (E flat) or the dominant (B flat), and yet the vitality and power of the writing make it all feel stunningly fresh and original. There is nothing neo-baroque or otherwise picturesquely archaic about this writing. The lessons Mahler had learned during his summer holidays, when he pored over the keyboard works of Bach, had obviously gone in deep. Bachian counterpoint has become his own language – and how he glories in it here.

Tu septiformis munere	With your sevenfold gifts
*Digitus paternae dexterae . . .**	You are the finger of God's right hand . . .
Per te sciamus da Patrem	Through you we know the Father,
Noscamus . . . Filium.	Recognise . . . the Son,
**. . . spiritum*	. . . the Spirit,
Credamus omni tempore.	In whom we believe at all times.

As the fugue unfolds, the words of the hymn's next two verses are drawn in and intermingled with those of the previous verse. Typical of the way Mahler plays with the word ordering is the boys' repeated-note shout of 'credamus' (we believe), just before the seven soloists[†] proclaim 'Per te credamus omni', mixing words from the first and last lines of verse 6. Intentionally or not, Mahler's use of seven vocal soloists beautifully parallels the hymn's mention of the 'sevenfold gifts' of the spirit – this is the kind of musical number symbolism Bach loved and incorporated again and again, not only in his religious works. Then, as the key twists back up again to a radiant E major, the words and music of 'Accende lumen sensibus' return (this time without the dramatic pause), enriched by closely worked motivic imitations throughout voices and orchestra. Just when it seems the excitement is on the point of becoming uncontainable,

---

* Here Mahler cut the words, '*Tu rite promissum Patris, / Sermone ditans guttura*' (Justly promised by the Father, / You transform our utterances into speech).
** Here Mahler cut the words '*atque*' (also) and '*Te utriusque*' (You also).
† The third solo soprano is silent in Part I.

all seven soloists sweep upwards to the notes of the 'second subject', now to the words 'Veni, creator', and the full orchestra, chorus and organ, enhanced by three clashed pairs of cymbals, thunder into the recapitulation: 'Veni, veni creator spiritus', as heard at the very beginning of the symphony. There have, in fact, been several points in this movement where the return of the opening motif in the home key may have appeared to signal a recapitulation (despite what he said to Specht, Mahler's attitude to classical sonata form is somewhat looser than his double fugue technique). But the return of the opening words along with the original motif, in the home key, along with a substantial amount of the music that originally followed, gives this return added emotional and intellectual force. It is directly comparable to one of those thrilling moments in Beethoven's symphonic first movements where, after long, compli-cated strife, the heroic main theme storms back in, trailing clouds of glory. Infirmity is a thing of the past; frail humanity has been transfigured by the creator spirit.

Da gaudiorum praemia.	Grant us the rewards of joy.
Da gratiarum munera.	Grant us the gifts of grace.
Dissolve litis vincula,	Dissolve the bonds of strife,
Adstringe pacis foedera.	Make fast the treaties of peace.

It is when we come to the expected return of the 'second subject' that Mahler's unorthodox – or perhaps it would be better in this context to say 'creative' – attitude to sonata form is evident again. As the choral voices quietly intone the words 'Pacem' (peace) and 'protinus' (lasting), adapted from the fourth verse of the hymn, low woodwind and string basses begin the theme originally associated with the phrase 'Imple superna gratia', now securely in the home key of E flat. But what follows is not a conventional return of the second theme but an extended contrapuntal meditation on the themes of both the first and second thematic groups. This integration of musical motifs from various stages in the symphonic argument matches the way Mahler mixes texts from different verses. There is nothing arbitrary about this: the emphasis is clearly on peace as a consequence of 'the gifts of grace'. The prayer 'Adstringe pacis foedera' (make fast the treaties of peace) is followed by more calls of 'pacem, pacem', a hushed imprecation to drive away the enemy ('Hostem repellas'), and a resolute crescendo on 'vitemus omne pessimum' (May we avoid all evil). The way Mahler extracts and remixes words and phrases from different verses indicates that his grasp of Latin grammar was sound enough. It is unlikely that he learned much Latin at school, in which case his imaginative handling of the *Veni, creator spiritus* text is another tribute to his diligence and determination as a self-educator in adult life.

The original 'Veni creator' motif now strides forth from the orchestra in muscular imitative counterpoint, then comes a wonderful opening out in E major: the key of 'Accende lumen sensibus' and the 'bridge' to Part II. The horns call out the first three notes of the 'Veni creator' motif, echoing like horn calls across Alpine valleys – a rare glimpse in this movement of the mountain pastoral mode that featured prominently in the first movements of the Sixth and Seventh Symphonies, and which is to move centre stage at the beginning of Part II of the Eighth.

Gloria Patri Domino,	Glory to the Lord our Father,
Natoque, qui a mortuis	To him you bore, who from death
Surrexit, ac Paraclito	Rose again, and to the Paraclete,
In saeculorum saecula.	Throughout all ages.

As in many Christian hymns, the final verse of *Veni, creator spiritus* is a reworking of the traditional Trinitarian 'Gloria', praising in turn Father, Son and Holy Spirit. Strikingly, however, Christ is not mentioned by name, any more than he is in the closing scene of Goethe's *Faust* Part II. This may well be one of the features that attracted Goethe to this text. 'To him you bore, who from death rose again' could, with a little imaginative recalibration, be taken to refer to the mortal human supplicant, transfigured by the spirit – and thus to Faust himself, reborn to new life in the Eighth Symphony's second part. As in Mahler's 'Resurrection' Symphony, the notion of death and rebirth also allows for a humanist interpretation: 'Cease from trembling! Prepare yourself to live!'

If so, that would account for the extraordinary burst of new energy that marks the beginning of the coda, and indeed for its tempo marking, *Wieder frisch*: 'Again vigorously'. This final section draws together all Part I's leading motifs in a thrilling race to the finish, returning from the 'bridge' key of E major to a magnificently grounded E flat major at the close. Boys lead off with the 'Gloria', to the three-note 'Veni, ve–' motif (Ex 5.1) from the very beginning of the Symphony. The two soprano soloists take up this motif at half speed, twisting the harmony thrillingly onto the dominant of E flat, then both choruses enter *fortissimo* with the words 'Gloria sit, gloria sit domino' to the full theme associated with 'Veni, veni creator spiritus'. The 'sit' ('let it be') is Mahler's own addition to the hymn text, allowing him to fit the words exactly to the rhythm of the original motif. Also caught up in this great tidal wave of elation are the 'Imple nostra gratia' second theme, the 'Infirma' motif and later (delivered by boys and reinforced by the extra offstage brass), the 'Accende lumen sensibus' theme from the movement's central climax. The introduction of offstage trumpets and trombones for the first time in the symphony emphasises the role of the latter theme as a 'bridge' to the music of Part II. Finally Mahler takes us back into E flat via a traditional 'plagal' cadence: in other words the two-chord harmonic movement traditionally associated with a liturgical 'Amen' – as Mahler would have been perfectly well aware. As it does so, the offstage trumpets and trombones sound out the theme associated with 'spiritus, o creator veni' (spirit, o creator, come), and the Eighth Symphony's first part comes to a thunderously affirmative close.

Just before the end, however, there is one more detail that is worth dwelling on, as it shows how Mahler could creatively transform the musical models he sometimes drew upon in his own music. In the past, Mahler's detractors would frequently enjoy pointing out ways in which his ideas were indebted to those of other composers. It is a highly disingenuous argument, as just about every great composer has taken and transformed motifs, sometimes even whole structures, from forebears who were important to him or her. Stravinsky is said to have remarked that good composers don't imitate, but rather steal from works they admire, and it could be argued that, whereas the imitator only borrows, the thief makes someone else's property entirely his own. In Mahler's case there has from time to time been an added antisemitic dimension to this: one of Wagner's most poisonously influential claims in his essay *Jewishness in Music* was that the Jew was not an original creator, only a synthesiser of the ideas of others. But here, in his hymn to the 'creator spirit', Mahler shows what a truly original artist can do with an idea he 'steals' from another. The 'Sanctus' from Beethoven's monumental *Missa solemnis* ends, like Part I of Mahler's Eighth Symphony, with a plagal cadence, though unlike the Mahler it is delivered as an awestruck *pianissimo*. As Beethoven's final hushed 'Amen' begins, scales rise upwards quickly on the strings, like a breath of incense, before the movement comes to its serene close. What Mahler does with this idea, however, transforms it almost beyond recognition. As the boys and the trumpets sound out the 'Accende' theme, with its association with 'arising', Mahler sets in motion a thrilling sequence of rising scales, beginning in the bass and ascending to the sopranos, over and over again. As a musical image it is like flames mounting upon flames, ever higher, and the effect on the listener – not to mention the performers – can be overwhelming. The release of the final turn to the tonic chord comes not a moment too soon. Beethoven's hushed benediction is extended and elevated into a colossal wave of cosmic abandonment. Theft, if that is what it is, has resulted in transfiguration. And with this gesture Mahler's community itself is also transfigured, or as Mahler himself put it in a letter to Willem Mengelberg: 'It is no longer human voices, but circling planets and suns.'

*

Both the tone and the manner of address now shift completely. Polyphony, 'many voices', now yields to song-like lyricism as Mahler turns to speak, not for the community, but for the striving individual, archetypally embodied in Goethe's Faust. A Christian hymn is followed by a strange kind of dramatic action. This is not the first time a composer had incorporated elements of theatrical drama into a work called a 'symphony': Berlioz had done the same with scenes from Shakespeare's most famous love story in his 'dramatic symphony' *Romeo and Juliet*, though unlike Mahler he rewrote them extensively in the process. Berlioz's wordless instrumental 'setting' of lines from the play in his symphony's 'love scene' may well have influenced Mahler's orchestral writing in the

Eighth Symphony's second part, some of which does seem to strive towards vocal, even verbal expression. The orchestral palette has also changed. Apart from during the orchestral interludes introducing and following Part I's 'Infirma' episode, instrumental colour has not played an important expressive role, tending instead to support and amplify the sounds of the human voices. Now it steps into the foreground: we are presented with a whole new range of instrumental timbres including, for the first time in the symphony, glockenspiel, celeste, piano, harmonium and harps – though those only make their presence felt later in the movement.

The scene too has moved to another plane. This is no longer humanity imploring Heaven for the gift of the Holy Spirit; we are now in Heaven itself. It is however one of the most thought-provoking features of Mahler's Eighth Symphony that the move towards the heavenly spheres is initially accompanied by the darkest music in the whole work. The shadows temporarily cast in the first part's 'Infirma' section now lengthen and deepen. Explaining why that should be is no easier than rationalising Goethe's quasi-Christian symbolism. Is the role of the darkness here – as T. S. Eliot famously put it – to heighten our sense of the glory of light? Or does it have another, less ancillary role in the story? According to Richard Specht, Mahler had wanted to set this scene from *Faust*, and particularly its hymn to the Mater Gloriosa/*Ewig-Weibliche*, for many years – almost certainly long before he met Alma. What matters here of course is not so much what Goethe intended, but what Mahler made of it. The answer, as we shall see, is a complicated one, but that surely only makes it all the more absorbing and, one might add, more authentically Mahlerian.

Part Two: Final Scene from Goethe's *Faust*, Part II

(*Mountain gorges, forest, cliffs, wilderness. Holy anchorites
amongst the rocky clefts, up and down the mountain sides.*)

Here is a definite first: no other symphony before Mahler's Eighth
includes a scenic stage direction. Granted, Berlioz does specify a
location for the Love Scene in his *Romeo and Juliet*, but there is no
detailed description, as here. To be exact, Mahler places Goethe's
description of the landscape at the point where the voices enter for
the first time, after the purely orchestral introduction. Opening
the score at random, without knowing that what one was looking
at was a symphony, one might easily conclude that this was an
opera, and that this was the point at which the composer expected
the theatre curtain to rise. In fact the orchestra has already set the
scene, in ten minutes of powerfully atmospheric music.

The orchestral prelude begins with an ethereal high tremolando
E flat on first violins, *sforzando pianissimo*, reinforced by a quietly
clashed pair of cymbals. Deep down in the bass, pizzicato cellos
and basses make it clear that this is now E flat minor, with a sombre transformation of the once-aspiring 'Accende lumen sensibus'
theme from Part I. Above this, flutes, clarinets and oboes extend
the bass theme plaintively while the E flat tremolando persists in
the violins. The fact that we are still in E flat – and so strongly
committed to E flat – is in itself very striking. If one includes Symphony no. 10, only half of Mahler's symphonies begin and end in
the same tonality. None of Mahler's great symphonic precursors –
not even the extravagantly experimental Berlioz – had abandoned
the notion of commitment to a home key. But right from the start,
Mahler had taken a more progressive attitude to tonality, making
it an essential feature of the narrative drama of his symphonies.

Symphony no. 1 may begin and end in D, but the finale begins in a harsh F minor, and the long climb back to the bright splendour of D major is an integral part of the psychological process Mahler described as 'from inferno to paradise'. In Symphonies nos. 2, 4, 5, 7 and 9 this kind of tonal-emotional progressive thinking is extended over the whole structure. It isn't simply that these symphonies begin in one key and end in another. Symphony no. 5, for instance, sets out in C sharp minor, but soon forsakes it for new tonal territory, aspiring towards D major in the second movement, touching it for a moment, then losing it; it is only in the finale, however, that D major is at last confirmed as the symphony's true goal, and the hope glimpsed in the second movement becomes reality. None of Mahler's other symphonies remains as consistently tonally anchored to one key as the Eighth. In fact, it is one of the most arresting features of the orchestral introduction to Part II that, while the other orchestral sections may stray from E flat minor, the violin tremolando repeatedly brings us back, either to the original E flat, or to its dominant, B flat. Is Mahler working hard to stress the continuity of this desolate, sparse music with the thunderous, swarming, affirmative sounds that ended Part I? Whatever his intention, this long-sustained tremolando E flat in the introduction to Part II does create a mounting sense of expectation, even for modern listeners familiar with this device from its recurring use in film and TV drama scores.

At the same time, the melodic writing, so wintry and spare at first, grows increasingly intense, with cellos rising at one point to an astonishingly anguished outburst. The three-note stepwise rising–falling figure first intoned by flutes and clarinet to a simple dotted rhythm is clearly an important motivic 'seed', and much of the subsequent melodic writing derives from it in some way or another. After the woodwinds' long threnody, occasionally echoed by horns, the tempo increases and the violins press forward to a climax of desperate, almost expressionist intensity. The eerie violin solo in the first part's 'Infirma' section, so quickly forgotten in the music's tidal sweep to collective exultation, contained a latent hint of potential violence; now that potential is fully released. As the prelude subsides back into its original *Poco adagio* tempo, imploring or protest turns into lamentation, again based on the 'Accende lumen sensibus' theme. We are about to begin the process of ascent towards the 'light of the senses', and yet the music seems to be mourning its loss, or even its unattainability. So far this is some of the most anguished music Mahler had yet composed: in character, if not in thematic material, it wouldn't sound out of place in *Das Lied von der Erde* or the Ninth Symphony, both of which represent a very different phase in Mahler's spiritual development.

As the prelude falls back again into E flat minor, this time to a deep bass note on bass clarinet, contrabassoon, cellos and basses, there comes the first flicker of light. Three flutes, *ppp*, begin what could be a faint foretaste of a jaunty march. It doesn't last long, and its little dotted opening figure (taken from the flute and clarinet melody at the very start of the movement) soon falls heavily, via oboes and trumpet, into the inky depths on tuba and low woodwind. The tremolando E flat sounds again, with the sombre pizzicato version of 'Accende lumen sensibus' reassembling itself in cellos and basses. The orchestral prelude has now run its course.

CHOR UND ECHO	CHORUS AND ECHO
Waldung, sie schwankt heran,	Woodland sways about us,
Felsen, sie lasten dran,	Rocks lie heavily beside,

Wurzeln, sie klammern an,	Roots grasp tightly,
Stamm dicht an Stamm hinan.	Trunks close to trunks.
Woge nach Woge spritzt,	Wave upon wave sprays,
Höhle, die tiefste, schüzt.	The deepest cave protects.
Löwen, sie schleichen stumm –	Lions stalk silently,
Freundlich um uns herum.	Friendly, around us,
Ehren geweihten Ort,	Honouring this sacred place,
Heiligen Liebeshort.	Sanctuary of Sacred Love.

Take a look at Goethe's words here, and if Mahler's setting is familiar, try to forget it. What kind of atmosphere and scenery do Goethe's lines convey? This is certainly a mountain 'wilderness', of the kind outlined in the scenic stage direction; but the cave 'protects', the lions are 'friendly' – as one would expect in a 'sacred place'. Mahler's setting however is skeletal, bleak, forbidding. The sombre pizzicato version of 'Accende lumen sensibus' stalks, like Goethe's lions, in the bass, but there is nothing particularly friendly about it. The male choral singers' chant-like adaptation of the movement's opening dotted figure ('schwankt heran') has a primitive funeral quality. The profusion of rests, breaking up the choral lines, gives the impression that the singers are half holding their breath, though whether in excitement or dread is left to the listener to decide. Only at the final mention of the sacred place ('Ehren geweihten Ort . . .') is there a slight hymn-like warming of the tone, with an accompanying softening to E flat major, but it is only for a moment. The violin tremolando persists, and the pizzicato version of 'Accende lumen sensibus' continues its forlorn tread in the bass, now with little hushed cries of pain from flutes, clarinets and solo oboe, then solo horn. It seems nothing has changed. In fact the process of ascent is just about to begin.

PATER ECSTATICUS	PATER ECSTATICUS
(auf- und abschwebend)	*(hovering up and down)*
Ewiger Wonnebrand,	Eternal flame of joy,
Glühendes Liebeband,	Radiant bond of love,
Siedender Schmerz der Brust,	The breast's seething pain,
Schäumende Gotteslust!	Foaming Divine bliss!
Pfeile, durchdringet mich,	Arrows, pierce though me,
Lanzen, bezwinget mich,	Lances, subdue me,
Keulen, zerschmettert mich,	Cudgels, smash me,
Blitze, durchwettert mich!	Lightning, shoot through me!
Dass ja das Nichtige	That everything worthless
Alles verflüchtige,	Might pass away,
Glänze der Dauerstern,	That the everlasting star may shine,
Ewiger Liebe Kern!	Seed of Eternal Love!

The final hushed cry from woodwind and horn suddenly grows, *molto crescendo*, and the baritone soloist, identified as Pater Ecstaticus, enters in a confident E flat major, warmly supported by massed strings. Pater Ecstaticus is the first of the three male priestly figures introduced by Goethe in the closing scene of *Faust* Part II, their presence paralleling that of the three saintly women who appear later in the drama as the Mater Gloriosa, or *Ewig-Weibliche*, draws near. His name derives from the Ancient Greek *ekstasis*, literally 'standing outside oneself', or even 'beside oneself' – transcending the limitations of one's own body in mystical communion with the divine, as reflected in Goethe's direction (retained by Mahler), 'hovering up and down'. His words, 'Ewiger Wonnebrand' (Eternal flame of joy) – Mahler's nickname during the Munich rehearsals – take the hints of a theme presented in the orchestral prelude and transform them into something definite and strongly memorable. Not only so but the rhythm, *Dah – da-da Dah – de-Dah*, fits well with many subsequent key phrases in Goethe's text. Mahler's use of these leading motifs has been compared to Wagner's *Leitmotif* technique, but attempts to give them symbolic name-tags has proved markedly less successful than for Wagner's music dramas. The words 'Ewiger Wonnebrand' are sung to a melodic and rhythmic pattern very similar to that intoned by the male voices to the words 'Waldung, sie schwankt heran' (Woodland sways about us) in the previous chorus; but the character, and with it the apparent meaning, has changed radically. One can imagine Pater Ecstaticus wearing the half-blissful, half-exquisitely pained expressions of one of El Greco's adoring saints or angels. His words border on the sado-masochistic: are the sufferings he begs to be permitted welcomed for their power to cleanse the soul, or as pleasures in their own right? Mahler's music seems to entertain both possibilities. As this solo powers forwards and upwards, driven partly by the musical energy in the 'Ewiger Wonnebrand' motif, it becomes clear that Mahler's use of this leading idea here is essentially symphonic: it drives the musical argument rather than adding nuances of meaning to Goethe's words. And yet as the ecstasy subsides, in a downward cascading sequence of string figures ('wave upon wave sprays', as the previous chorus put it), the return of the 'Accende lumen sensibus' theme, now strong and hopeful on trumpets, does convey a more than musical significance: the notion of 'ascent', previously sombre and dispirited, has acquired new force through Pater Ecstaticus's intercession. This is a telling example of how Mahler 's use of his thematic material in his Eighth Symphony – and particularly in this second part – is poised brilliantly between abstract symphonic argument and dramatic, conceptual development. On

one level it is a musical argument, more or less self-sufficient; on
another it not only tells a story but unfolds a philosophy.

Like many a good story however, this one also includes sudden
reversals, and one of those is about to take place right now.

PATER PROFUNDUS

(tiefe Region)

Wie Felsenabgrund mir zu Füssen
Auf tieferm Abgrund lastend ruht,
Wie tausend Bäche strahlend fliessen
Zum graussen Sturtz des Schaums der Flut,
Wie strack, mit einigem kräftigen Triebe,
Der Stamm sich in die Lüfte trägt:
So ist es die allmächtige Liebe,
Die alles bildet, alles hegt.
Ist um mich her ein wildes Brausen,
Als wogte Wald und Felsengrund!
Und doch strürzt, liebevoll im Sausen,
Die Wasserfülle sich zum Schlund.
Berufen, gleich das Tal zu wässern;
Der Blitz, der flammend niederschlug,
Die Atmosphäre zu verbessern,
Die Gift und Dunst im Busen trug:
Sind Liebesboten! sie verkünden,
Was ewig schaffend uns umwallt.
Mein Innres mög es auch entzünden,
Wo sich der Geist, verworren-kalt,
Verquält in stumpfer Sinne Schranken,
Scharfangeschlossnem Kettenschmerz!

O Gott! beschwichtige die Gedanken,
Erleuchte mein bedürftig Herz!

PATER PROFUNDUS

(from the depths)

As the rocky abyss at my feet
Rests upon a still deeper abyss,
As the thousand brooks flow brightly
Towards the awesome plunge of foaming flood,
As straight the tree, driven by its own force,
Raises itself into the air:
So it is with Almighty Love
That shapes and watches over all things.
Everything around me thunders,
Like waves of forest and rock!
The lightning that crashes down in flames,
To purify the atmosphere
That carried poison and foul fog in its breast:
All are Love's messengers, proclaiming
The creative force that flows about us.
May it also quicken me within,
Where my spirit, confused and cold,
Torments itself in the confines of my dull senses,
In the pain of my tight fetters!
O God! soothe my thoughts,
Pour light into my needy heart!

Abruptly the key changes back to E flat minor, and the bass voice
of Pater Profundus sounds, following the exact meaning of his

name, 'from the depths'. This is the point in the Eighth Symphony where the expression of spiritual agony reaches its most extreme. The terrifying rocky abysses conjured up scenically by Goethe are transformed into something more existential by the music. Mahler, the lover of high mountain landscapes, certainly relishes the awe-inspiring scenery: as Pater Profundus describes the vertiginous drop at his own feet – an abyss resting upon an abyss – three clarinets and four bassoons deliver a wonderful tremolando shudder. But the *Sturm und Drang* conveyed by the soloist's wide upward leaps and the turbulent, fragmented writing for the orchestra has its roots in more than landscape. Goethe's Pater Profundus is confident in his assertion that these alarming phenomena are portents of divine healing, but Mahler's soloist seems to be flailing around desperately seeking confirmation. His utterances are closer to those of the prisoner Florestan in Beethoven's *Fidelio*, conjuring a fleeting image of his wife Leonore out of his own darkness and abandonment, or of the sick Tristan, in Act III of Wagner's *Tristan und Isolde*, endlessly scanning the horizon for a sign of the ship he half-hopes, half-doubts will bring his lost Isolde back to him.

Mahler knew both those operas extremely well: *Fidelio* was one of the operas he conducted most often, and his *Tristan* was legendary. But Florestan and Tristan are both tenors; there is an operatic baritone role closer in character to that of Mahler's Pater Profundus, and the music that accompanies his tortured ravings is strikingly close to that of the Eighth Symphony at this point, especially the violins' downward plunging figures, and the cellos' and basses' upward-thrusting responses. This is Amfortas, King of the Grail Knights in Wagner's *Parsifal*, who for his betrayal of his sacred cause has been punished with a wound that will not heal. Amfortas's description of his physical, and still more his spiritual torture is the dark heart of the opera's first act. Despite what he may have said to Ernst Decsay, *Parsifal* evidently made a much deeper impression on Mahler than he was prepared to admit. Could it be that Wagner's disturbingly powerful depiction of a wounded soul in *Parsifal* evoked a sympathetic response from Mahler? There are reasons to think so, reasons that may become clearer when we come to consider Mahler's meeting with Sigmund Freud, late in the summer of 1910.

Unlike Amfortas however, Pater Profundus is granted his moments of hope. As he delivers his final prayer, 'Pour light into my needy heart!' (*mit Inbrunst*; 'with ardour' or 'inner burning'), previous hints of 'Accende lumen sensibus' solidify into a nearly perfect restatement on trumpet and trombone, poised on the edge of a new, brighter tonality: C flat, or as it is soon to be spelled out, B major – anticipated, significantly, at the point where Pater Profundus tells us that earthquake, lightning and flood 'are all Love's messengers'. The 'Ewiger Wonnebrand' motif now returns warmly on cellos and horns, initiating a magnificent long accelerating crescendo.

(*The next two choruses are sung simultaneously*)

ENGEL	ANGELS
(*schwebend in der höheren Atmosphäre, Faustens Unsterbliches tragend*)	(*Soaring in the higher atmosphere, bearing Faust's immortal essence*)
Gerettet ist das edle Glied	Saved is the noble limb,
Der Geisterwelt vom Bösen:	Restored from evil to the spirit world
Wer immer strebend sich bemüht,	Whoever strives constantly,
Den können wir erlösen!	Him we can redeem.

Und hat an ihm die Liebe gar   And indeed, Love from on high

Von oben teilgenommen,   Has taken part in his destiny.

Begegnet ihm die selige Schar   The blessed throng comes to meet him

Mit herzlichem Wilkommen.   With heartfelt welcome.

CHOR DER SELIGER KNABEN   CHORUS OF BLESSED BOYS

(*um die höchsten Gipfel kreisend*)   (*circling the loftiest peaks*)

Hände verschlinget   With hands entwined

Freudig zum Ringverein!   In a joyous round-dance,

Regt euch und singet   Rouse yourselves and sing

Heilige Gefühle drein!   Of sacred emotions!

Göttlich belehret,   Taught by God,

Dürft ihr vertrauen;   You may be sure;

Den ihr verehret,   Him whom you honour

Werdet ihr schauen.   You shall behold.

Wagner is said to have defined composition as 'the art of transition'. If so, he would surely have been impressed by the way Mahler engineers his transitions in Part II of the Eighth Symphony. How striking that at this point he should have chosen to leave out the dialogue between Pater Seraphicus and the Chorus of Blessed Boys by which Goethe effects his transition. Instead, Mahler chooses to let the music lead us into the Boys' angelic round dance. Generally speaking, the structure of the closing scene of *Faust* Part II lends itself very easily to setting by 'numbers' in the operatic sense – i.e. as a sequence of arias, ensembles, choruses etc. As we have already seen in the solo for Pater Profundus, Mahler's experience in the opera house has left its mark on the music. But the overall effect of Part II of Mahler's Eighth is not really operatic: the steadily evolving flow of the ideas, partly originated, partly steered by Mahler's masterly development of his leading themes, is more symphonic than theatrical, while the 'numbers' themselves (and not just the solo numbers) have more of the character of orchestral songs – not surprisingly, given Mahler's experience as a song composer of genius, and given his increasing doubts about the opera house as a platform for conveying the loftiest ideas. There is a case for regarding the Eighth Symphony's second part as a symphonic song cycle, the songs themselves linked by orchestral transitions which emerge from and flow into the sung sections so seamlessly that continuity is always maintained. Sibelius's comparison of symphonic development to the current of a river would thus apply as aptly to the second part of Mahler's Eighth as it does to the opening movement of his own Fifth Symphony, in which a moderately paced first section gradually transforms itself into a steadily accelerating scherzo. Thirteen years after the premiere of the Eighth Symphony, Alexander Zemlinsky completed his *Lyric Symphony*, for soprano and baritone soloists and orchestra, in which seven settings of poems by the Indian poet Rabindranath Tagore are similarly interlinked by orchestral interludes. On one level, Zemlinsky's symphony was unmistakably inspired by Mahler's 'song symphony', *Das Lied von der Erde*, for contralto and tenor soloists with orchestra. But in *Das Lied von der Erde* the songs are presented as separate movements. When it came to the art of transition, Zemlinsky's model was surely Mahler's Eighth, which made such a powerful impression on him at the first Munich performance.

What Mahler has engineered here, however, is not just a transition into a new song, but into a new stage of the symphonic argument which in itself embodies the 'carefully planned rise in intensity' Mahler so admired in Plato's *Symposium*. Several commentators have noted that Part II can be divided into three distinct sections, or perhaps movements, resembling a symphonic slow movement, scherzo and finale, although there has been some disagreement about where the 'scherzo' ends and the 'finale' begins – in itself a tribute to Mahler's skill in creating river-like changes of character. (Attempts to locate the exact point at which Sibelius's *Molto moderato* first movement becomes a scherzo founder for the same reason.) There does seem to be some correspondence, however, between the movement type in Part II and broad tonal areas. The opening slow movement is centred on E flat minor; but during Pater Profundus's solo there has been an increasing feeling of aspiration towards C flat/B major. It is in this key that the women's voices now enter, for the first time in Part II, *Allegro deciso*, to words that every educated German-speaker in Mahler's day would have known. This is one of the most famous utterances in the whole of Goethe's *Faust*: 'Saved is the noble limb, / Restored from evil to the spirit world: / Whoever strives constantly, / Him we can redeem.' Unsurprisingly Mahler sets these words to the 'Accende lumen sensibus' theme. The message is clear: it is by striving that we can ascend. The boys follow, to the same notes as in their first entry in Part I, now transposed down into B major. All this makes perfect sense in terms of Mahler's overall philosophical scheme; what is surprising is the style of the setting. One would expect a German-speaking composer to treat these words with special respect – as Robert Schumann does in his *Scenes from Faust* (1844–53). Schumann builds a stirring choral-orchestral crescendo at 'Gerettet is das edle Glied', with the vocal entries imitating triumphal trumpet fanfares. Mahler's setting, however, borders on the irreverent. One can imagine the boys, hands linked, laughing and high-kicking in delight at the prospect of welcoming Faust's redeemed soul to Paradise. The orchestral colours and textures, previously sombre or turbulent, now flash and dance athletically. The avoidance of a solid orchestral bass for most of this double chorus adds to the impression of weightlessness. We are no longer amongst the rocks and gnarled tree roots, straining upwards, but amongst the clouds, peering down.

The breeziness of Mahler's setting – his apparent refusal to take it too seriously – does mean that the weighty import of these words can easily be missed by the listener. This may initially seem odd: striving and redemption were central preoccupations in Mahler's earlier symphonies, indeed they are the very heart of the message of the Second, the 'Resurrection'. But as Mahler told Richard Specht, his intention here was to move away from 'subjective tragedy' and offer instead 'great joy'. The Angels and the Blessed Boys welcome the tragic, striving Faust joyously, but they do so in the character of a scherzo – a word that, before it was adopted by Haydn and Beethoven for their rapid dancing symphonic movements, originally meant a 'joke'. Redemption may honour strenuous aspiration, but ultimately it is the work of divine grace.

DIE JÜNGERN ENGEL

Jene Rosen, aus den Händen
Liebend-heiliger Büsserinen,
Halfen uns den Sieg gewinnen,
Und das hohe Werk vollenden,
Diesen Seelenschatz erbeuten.
Böse wichen, als wir streuten,
Teufel flohen, als wir trafen.
Statt gewohnter Höllenstrafen
Fühlten Liebesqual die Geister;

Selbst der alte Satansmeister
War von spitzer Pein durchdrungen,
Jacuhzet auf! es ist gelungen.

THE YOUNGER ANGELS

These roses, from the hands
Of Love-consecrated penitent women,
Helped us to achieve the victory
And complete the sublime plan
By capturing this priceless soul.
Evil yielded when we strewed them,
Devils fled when we struck them.
Instead of the allotted tortures of Hell
The spirits felt the torment of Love;
The master of the devils himself
Was pierced by searing pain.
Rejoice! It is achieved.

For the chorus of the Younger Angels, Mahler stipulates a 'selection of lighter voices from the women of the first choir'. The music calms down now, with gently rustling strings and chattering woodwind and the light, spangly touch of a triangle; but the marking *scherzando* indicates that Mahler doesn't want the mood of divine playfulness to be forgotten. In the women's lilting lines there is just a hint of the deliciously seductive Flower Maidens' song from Act II of *Parsifal*: the 'love-consecrated penitent women' of whom the Younger Angels speak have not lost their winning sensuality – nor should they in a work celebrating 'Eros as creator of the world'. The image of the rose underlines this distinctly non-Christian double meaning. In Roman Catholic writing the rose has, at least since medieval times, been a symbol of the Virgin Mary, and of her 'immaculate conception', unstained by sexual contact; but it has also long been an erotic token in Western European culture – the gift the male suitor traditionally gives to the object of his affections on St Valentine's Day.

The final cries of 'Rejoice!' lead to a robust, cheerful orchestral climax, like the previous chorus in the symphony's home key of E flat major, but suddenly the bass slips to D, as it did at the beginning of the 'Infirma' section in Part I, and with that the uneasy music associated with that shift returns too, though less harshly scored on woodwind and strings. Was it the talk of devils and hell that precipitated this change? The words of the next chorus provide an explanation.

DIE VOLLENDETEREN ENGEL

THE MORE PERFECT ANGELS

(*Chor mit Altsolo*)

(*chorus with alto solo*)

Uns bleibt ein Erdenrest	There still remains on Earth
Zu tragen peinlich,	A remnant, painful to bear,
Und wär er von Asbest,	And even if it were asbestos,
Er ist nicht reinlich.	It could not be pure.
Wenn starke Geistekraft	When a strong spiritual power
Die Elemente	The elements
An sich herangerafft,	Has seized upon,
Kein Engel trennte	No angel can divide
Geeinte Zweinatur	The combined dual nature
Der innigen beiden:	That remains within;
Die ewige Liebe nur	Only Eternal Love
Vermag's zu scheiden	Is able to separate them.

The Chorus of the More Perfect Angels enters to the subdued, shadowy, dissonant harmonies heard in Part I at the words 'Infirma nostri corporis' – itself a distortion of the symphony's opening 'Veni'. Human 'infirmity', weakness, is once again centre-stage. The 'flashback' effect is underlined by the return of the uneasy violin solo that originally accompanied those words. This connection is essential to Mahler's overall scheme. The *Veni, creator spiritus* hymn spoke of the need to strengthen human frailty with divine moral power; Goethe's verses now talk of humanity's 'combined dual nature', which only 'eternal love' can remedy. This is a reference to a passage in Part I of *Faust* which, again, many in Mahler's audience would have known. Faust cries out in frustration at the 'two souls' that dwell within him, constantly fighting against each other. One aspires upwards to 'rarefied ancestral spheres'; the other clings to the 'gross' delights of the material world. The duality hinted at in the image of the rose is now spelled out. But as in the 'Infirma' section of Part I, a way out is indicated musically as the alto solo rises hopefully: once again the inversion of the symphony's opening 'Veni creator' motif sounds out in imitation, with the male voices joining in for the first time since the first chorus of Part II, and the tempo quickens again. Considerations of human frailty are important, but they must not impede the process of ascent.

(*The following choruses, along with Doctor Marianus's first eight lines, are sung simultaneously*)

DIE JUNGEREN ENGEL	THE YOUNGER ANGELS
Nebend um Felsenhöh	Beside the rocky heights,
Spür' ich soeben,	I have just beheld,
Regend sich in der Näh	Stirring nearby,

Ein Geisterleben.	A movement of spirits.
Die Wölkchen werden klar:	The little clouds become clear:
Ich seh bewegte Schar	I see a lively crowd
Seliger Knaben,	Of blessed boys,
Los von der Erde Druck,	Free from Earth's constraints,
Im Kreis gesellt,	Gathered in a circle,
Die sich erlaben	Delighting themselves
Am neuen Lenz und Schmuck	In the fresh spring and the glory
Der obern Welt.	Of the higher world.
Sei er zum Anbeginn,	Let it be to him a beginning,
Stegendem Vollgewinn	For his growing perfection,
Diesen gesellt!	To be joined to their company!

CHOR SELIGER KNABEN   CHORUS OF THE BLESSED BOYS

Freudig empfangen wir	Joyfully we receive
Diesen im Puupenstand;	This soul in pupal form;
Also erlangen wir	Secure in the assurance
Englisches Unterpfand.	That we will become an angel.
Löset die Flocken los,	Free him from the flecks
Die ihn umgeben!	That cover him!
Schon ist er schön und gross	Already he is beautiful and great
Von heiligem Leben.	With sacred life.

DOCTOR MARIANUS   DOCTOR MARIANUS

*(in der höchsten, reinlichsten
   Zelle)*

(in the highest, purest cell)

Hier is die Aussicht frei,	Here the view is unrestricted,

Der Geist erhoben.	The spirit lifted up.
Dort ziehen Fraun vorbei,	There women are drawing near,
Schwebend nach oben.	Hovering upwards.
Die Herrliche, mitteninn,	The Glorious One amongst them,
Im Sternenkranze,	In a crown of stars,
Die Himmelskönigin,	The Queen of Heaven,
Ich seh's am Glanze.	I see it from her radiance.

The third, climactic phase of the scherzo section takes as its starting point that faint hint of a jaunty march, sounded by the three flutes in the orchestral prelude to Part II, now growing in strength as the Younger Angels tell of a 'stirring . . . a movement of spirits' indicating that Faust's redeemed soul is ready to join the heavenly company. The soul however only exists in 'pupal form'; it is yet to become an angel, freed from the 'flecks' of human imperfection. But as the Younger Angels proclaim a 'fresh spring' for Faust, the glockenspiel sparkles for the first time in the symphony. As ever, Mahler carefully times his use of orchestral colour according to his philosophical programme. Also for the first time in Part II we hear the voice of the tenor, Doctor Marianus. 'Doctor' here is meant in the original Latin sense of 'teacher', so this third priestly figure from the closing scene of *Faust* Part II is one who instructs in the knowledge of Mary. His appearance is timely, for the Mater Gloriosa herself is now drawing near, and the prevailingly male utterance we have heard so far in this scene is about to yield to the female: 'There women are drawing near, / Hovering upwards.' This is one of the most arresting features of the ending of *Faust* Part II. Part I of the drama had begun with a Prologue in Heaven, in which the participants were exclusively male. Goethe's depiction of his female heavenly beings as eternal-feminine redeemers and eroticised penitents has understandably drawn stern criticism from some modern feminist writers, but for an age in which depictions of Heavenly beings – not only the Holy Trinity but also the angelic hosts – were predominantly male, this feminisation of the 'company of Heaven' would have been extremely challenging.

Doctor Marianus's entry takes Mahler's interlinking technique to new heights. The choral voices are marked *fortissimo*, but Doctor Marianus is instructed to sing his first notes *piano*, as though at a great distance, though growing in strength, so that he gradually emerges, just as the Queen of Heaven, whose coming he proclaims, draws ever nearer to receive the soul of Faust. We have returned to the key of B major, so this music could also be seen as rounding off the scherzo section, but Doctor Marianus's slow fade-up (Mahler anticipating the use of microphones in modern concert performances and recordings) is so elegantly dovetailed with the scherzo's climax that it makes dividing up Part II anatomically into separate movements all the harder. What follows is perhaps the most beautiful transition in the whole symphony.

[DOCTOR MARIANUS]

Höchste Herrscherin der Welt,
Lass mich im blauen,
Ausgespannten Himmelszelt
Dein Geheimnis schauen!
Billige, was des Mannes Brust
Ernst und zart bewegt
Und mit heiliger Liebeslust
Dir entgegenträget!
Unbezwinglich unser Mut,

[DOCTOR MARIANUS]

Highest Mistress of the World,
Let me, in the blue expanse
Of Heaven's outstretched canopy,
Behold your mystery!
Allow that which moves the heart of m
Earnestly and tenderly,
And with the holy bliss of Love,
That draws us towards you!
Invincible is our courage,

Wenn du hehr gebietest;	When you nobly command us;
Plötzlich mildert sich die Glut,	At once the heat lessens,
Wie du uns befriedest.	As you grant us peace.

DOCTOR MARIANUS UND CHOR	DOCTOR MARIANUS AND CHORUS
Jungfrau, rein im schönsten Sinn,	Virgin, pure in the loveliest sense,
Mutter, Ehren wurdig,	Mother, worthy of all honours,
Uns erwählte Königin,	Queen, chosen by us,
Göttern ebenbürtig.	Equal to the gods.

Now the *Ewig-Weibliche* is addressed directly. The tempo remains the same as at the end of the scherzo section, but as Doctor Marianus delivers his solo, it begins to relax. The tonality is E major, associated with 'Accende lumen sensibus' in Part I, the 'bridge' between the Eighth Symphony's two parts – and the key again performs a bridging function here. The music remains in E major while the tenor pours out his most voluptuous words of praise and entreaty to the Mater Gloriosa. But at the words 'Plötzlich mildert sich die Glut' (Suddenly the heat lessens) the harmony falls back to the symphony's home key, E flat major, and 'peace' does indeed begin to spread through the orchestral textures. Then Doctor Marianus leads the choral voices, beginning with the basses and rising in mounting rapture to the altos, in his hymn to the Virgin, Mother and Queen. His own line rises too into its brightest, clearest register, peaking on a high B flat on 'Königin' (Queen) – the 'Kö' being exactly the right vowel sound to focus the tenor voice thrillingly at this point. (Mahler's experience in the opera house tells yet again.) His final line, 'Göttern ebenbürtig', is left open, its tritone dissonance unresolved. Consciously or not, Mahler has drawn attention to one the most strikingly heterodox elements – from a Christian point of view – in Goethe's text. This Mary is 'equal to the gods': are there pagan deities in Goethe's Heaven? It would certainly fit with his thinking – Mahler's too, it would seem. He removes Goethe's next seven lines, so that the chorus immediately responds to the potentially blasphemous 'equal to the gods' with the direct hymn to the Virgin as the 'incorruptible', who allows souls 'led astray' to approach her 'intimately'.

Throughout Doctor Marianus's solo it is unclear whether the Eighth Symphony is still in its 'scherzo' phase, or whether in fact the 'finale' has already begun. Rather than trying to come down dogmatically on one side or other, is it not better simply to enjoy the ambiguity? The Queen of Heaven is very near – so near we can almost touch her. Yet she has not quite arrived yet. When she does, we know that we have truly entered Paradise, and the final stage of Mahler's 'great joy-bringer'.

(*Mater Gloriosa hovers into view*)

CHOR

CHORUS

Dir, der Unberührbaren,   You, the incorruptible,
Ist es nicht benommen,   It is not beneath you,
Dass die leicht Verführbaren   To allow those easily led astray
Traulich zu dir kommen.   To approach you intimately.
In die Schwachheit hingerafft,   Falling into weakness,
Sind sie schwer zu rettn.   They are hard to rescue.
Wer zerreisst aus eigner Kraft   Who, trusting in his own strength,
Der Gelüste Ketten?   Can tear off the chains of desire?
Wie entgleitet schnell der Fuss How easily the foot slips
Schweifem, glattem Boden!   On that slippery ground!

CHOR DER BUSSERINEN	CHORUS OF PENITENT WOMEN
(und Una Poenitentium)	(and Una Poenitentium)
Du schwebst zu Höhen	You soar into the heights
Der ewigen Reiche,	Of the eternal realms,
Vernimm das Flehen,	Accept their supplication,
Du Ohnegleiche,	You, beyond compare,
Du Gnadenreiche!	You, rich in mercy!

As Doctor Marianus concludes his solo, high strings sound a strong chord of E flat major, *fortissimo–pianissimo*, and the horn confidently intones the 'Accende lumen sensibus' theme. But almost immediately the harmonies twist back up onto the dominant of *E* major, and a great liquid wash of rising and falling arpeggios is heard on piano and harps – who have up to this point been silently awaiting their cue. Then, to a soft-toned accompaniment of harmonium and solo harp, violins intone a long, hushed but highly expressive theme marked *schwebend* ('hovering') and *vibrando* ('vibrating'). This kind of ardent, sweet melodic writing is a reminder that Mahler was also a great Verdi interpreter; at the same time it recalls Alma's account of how moved Mahler was by the naive but patently sincere devotional imagery of Austrian rural Catholic churches. This is the part of the Eighth Symphony that has most divided musicians and critics: sweet simplicity or, as one eminent composer-writer suggested to me, 'shameless kitsch'? A lot depends on the listener's point of view – and, possibly, prejudices. The British sociologist and literary commentator Richard Hoggart had some challenging things to say on this subject. Hoggart was responding to critics who had accused George Orwell of sentimentality in his depictions of ordinary working-class life in

The Road to Wigan Pier. In his thought-provoking introduction
to the Penguin edition of Orwell's book, Hoggart described how,
when it first appeared, even some of the critics who were most
sympathetically disposed to Orwell's challenging socio-political
message drew up short at his depictions of the homelier aspects
of English working-class life. Grim, harsh reality was fine; what
bothered them, it seems, was the expression of tender human
emotions – of warmth, or love. Hoggart noted how often the word
'sentimental' cropped up in such comments. Was this right – was
there something dubious in Orwell's account of the ordinary day-
to-day lives of the people he encountered? Or was it a kind of
defence, an escape mechanism – a way of avoiding dealing with
acutely sensitive emotional issues? Hoggart felt sure it was the latter, in most cases at least. And perhaps it is the same for others
with Mahler's sweetly poignant depiction of childlike longing for
a heavenly 'happy ever after'. After all, how many of us have never
felt a similar pang of yearning, however strenuously we may try
to suppress it? When a piece of music provokes a strong adverse
reaction, it is always worth asking if the real reason might be that
it touches something sensitive in the listener that he or she would
rather not acknowledge.

The male choral voices now intone a hymn that seems to reach
out quietly towards the Mother Goddess – though at the mention of human weakness ('Schwachheit') the piano and all the
harps suddenly deliver three sharp *fff* chords, *rauschend* – 'noisily
rustling'. The celeste joins the piano, tremolando, as the women's
voices augment those of the men. The hymn rises in a great
ecstatic wave, then at its high point comes the entry of Una Poenitentium, 'A Penitent', who turns out to be Faust's former lover
Gretchen – seduced, lured into mortal sin, but finally redeemed.

The Chorus of Penitent Women partly echoes, partly supports her vocal line. The image of fallen women, prostrate in repentance, is an image that is commonly erotically charged in nineteenth- and early twentieth-century literature and opera (by men), and Mahler revels in it here – this is after all a song of praise to Eros from a very male perspective. But as the three part-historical, part-legendary women join the heavenly throng, the tone changes completely, and the tempo increases to *fliessend* ('flowing').

MAGNA PECCATRIX

(St. Lucae VII, 36)

Bei der Liebe, die den Füssen
Deines gottverklärten Sohnes
Tränen liess zum Balsam fliessen
Trotz des Pharisäerhohnes,
Beim Gefässe, das so reinlich
Tropfte Wohlgeruch hernieder,
Bei den Locken, die so weichlich
Trockneten die Heilgen Glieder –

MULIER SAMARITANA

(St. Joh. IV)

Bei dem Bronn, zu dem schon weiland
Abram liess die Herde führen,
Bei dem Eimer, der dem Heiland
Kühl die Lippe durft berühren,

MAGNA PECCATRIX

(Luke VII, 36)

By the love that anointed the feet
Of your divinely transfigured Son
With tears as well as balm,
Despite the mockery of the Pharisees,
By the vessel that so richly
Poured down sweet fragrances,
By the hair, that so gently
Dried those holy limbs –

MULIER SAMARITANA

(John IV)

By the well, to which once

Abraham led his flocks,
By the pail, which cooled
The lips of the Saviour,

Bie der reinen, reichen Quelle,   By the pure, rich spring,
Die von dorther sich ergiesset,   Which issues from that place,
Überflüssig, ewig helle   Overflowing, ever bright,
Rings durch all Welten fliesset –   Streams through all worlds –

MARIA AEGYPTICA   MARIA AEGYPTICA

(Acta Sanctorum)   (Acts of the Saints)

Bei dem hochgeweihten Orte,   By that most holy place,
Wo den Hernn man niederliess,   Where the Lord was laid to rest,
Bei dem Arm, der von der Pforte   By the arm, that before the entrance
Warnend mich zurückestiess,   Thrust me back warningly,
Bei der vierzigjährigen Busse,   By the forty years' penance
Der ich treu in Wüsten blieb,   To which in the desert I remained
                                           faithful,

Bei dem seligen Scheidegrusse,   By the blessed words of parting
Den im Sand ich niederschrieb –   Which I wrote in the sand –

ZU DREI   ALL THREE

Die du grossen Sünderinnen   You, who from great sinners
Deine Nähe nicht verweigerst   Do not withold your presence,
Und ein büssendes Gewinnen   And reward penitence
In die Ewigkeiten steigerst,   With entry to the infinite,
Gönn auch dieser guten Seele,   Grant also to this good soul,
Die sich einmal nur vergessen,   Which forgot itself but once,
Die nicht ahnte, dass sie fehle,   Which never realised that it sinned,
Dein Verzeihen angemessen!   Your due forgiveness!

Of the three women introduced here, two are from the Bible, and the third, Mary of Egypt, comes from the *Acta Sanctorum*, a huge encyclopaedia of the lives of the great Roman Catholic saints, compiled by Jesuit scholars, first published in the seventeenth century, but greatly extended and adapted over a period of nearly three hundred years. Magna Peccatrix, 'a great sinner', is the 'sinful woman' (presumably a prostitute) who in the Gospel of Luke anointed Jesus's feet. A tradition grew up in the middle ages that this unnamed woman was actually Mary Magdalene, who became close to Jesus and was the first person to discover the empty tomb after his crucifixion, and therefore the first to testify to his resurrection. Whether Goethe or Mahler made that equation is hard to say, but the message of this identification – that a great sinner can become a great saint – is one that would have appealed to both. Mulier Samaritana, 'The Samaritan Woman', meets Jesus at the well in St John's Gospel. The fact that this simple, apparently uneducated woman understands Jesus's message, when the learned religious man in the previous chapter did not, is of enormous significance.

As for Mary of Egypt, she is the patron saint of penitents. According to legend, this Mary lived a highly dissolute life, driven, the *Acta Sanctorum* tells us, 'by an insatiable and irrepressible passion', until, seeing an icon of the Blessed Virgin, she was struck with profound remorse and committed herself to the life of an ascetic hermit in the desert. Goethe's scenic stage direction, faithfully reproduced by Mahler near the beginning of Part II, tells us that the mountain landscape is the territory of 'holy anchorites', male hermits, but this female hermit is allowed to approach closer to the heavenly throne. The music is, as Mahler marks it, 'flowing'; it is also remarkably fresh, spring-like, after the humid eroticism of the previous hymn – a response, no doubt, to the image of the 'pure, clear spring' flowing from the well where the Samaritan woman encountered Jesus. It is closer in mood to the cheerful childlike procession at the heart of the first movement of Mahler's Fourth Symphony, the symphony that ends with what Mahler called 'a child's view of paradise') – the strings' trills accompanying Maria Aegyptica are particularly redolent. Eventually all three women unite in a remarkably light-hearted trio, singing the violins' formerly ardent *schwebend, vibrando* theme at first in imitation – an effect closer to a classroom canon than to Bachian counterpoint – and finally all together as the women unite in prayer for the newly arrived soul of Faust. The string trills and rippling harp writing are now enhanced by a solo mandolin. (Mahler asks for the mandolin part to be strengthened later.) After the dark, Wagnerian near-expressionism at the beginning of Part II this all feels remarkably light, airy – expressive not of Northern European angst but of what Thomas Mann's Tonio Kröger described as the 'velvet-blue skies, heady wine and sweet sensuality' of the Mediterranean south, whose liberating scent can sometimes be detected in the air of Mahler's adopted home city, Vienna.

UNA POENITENTIUM

(*sonst Gretchen genannt, sich anschmiegend*)

Neige, neige,
Du Ohnegleiche,
Du Strahlenreiche,
Dein Antlitz gnädig meinem
  Glück!

UNA POENITENTIUM

(*otherwise known as Gretchen, approaching closely*)

Turn, turn,
You beyond compare,
You rich in radiance,
Deign to look upon my
  happiness!

Der früh Geliebte,
Nicht mher Getrübte,
Er kommt zurück.

The once beloved,
No longer stained,
Is coming back.

SELIGE KNABEN

(in Kreisbewegung sich nähernd)

Er überwächst uns schon
An mächtigen Gliedern,
Wird treuer Pflege Lohn
Reichlich erwidern.
Wir wurden früh entfernt
Von Lebechören;
Doch dieser hat gelernt:
    Er wird uns lehren.

THE BLESSED BOYS

(approaching with circular movement)

Already he outgrows us,
With mighty limbs,
Our true care he will reward
With ample recompense.
We were taken early
From the chorus of the living,
But this man has learned much:
    He will teach us.

UNA POENITENTIUM

Vom edlen Geisterchor umgeben,
Wird sich der Neue kaum gewahr,
Er ahnet kaum das frische Leben,
So gleicht er schon der heiligen
    Schar.
Sieh, wie er jedem Erdenbande
Der alten Hülle sich entrafft,
Und aus ätherischem Gewande
Hervortritt erste Jugendkraft!
Vergonne mir, ihn zu belehren:
Noch blendet ihn der neue Tag!

UNA POENITENTIUM

Surrounded by the noble spirit
    choir,
The new arrival is hardly yet aware,
He hardly senses the newborn life,
See how he breaks his earthly bands
And shakes off the old husk,
And from the ethereal garment
The strength of earliest youth comes
    forth!
Allow me to enlighten him:
The new day dazzles him!

This is the point in the closing scene of *Faust* Part II at which Goethe identifies 'Una Poenitentium' as Gretchen. It is her turn now to intercede for Faust, and to describe the emergence of his new redeemed self, 'in pupal form', from the 'old husk' of his former sinful self. A reader of the complete *Faust* drama might well ask her- or himself at this point exactly where it was that Faust went through the necessary process of repentance. His final words in the scene previous to this brim over with self-satisfaction and pride in his 'indelible' achievement. As a lover of *Faust*, Mahler would have known that well enough, but his concern here is not with the old Faust, but with the 'newborn life', dazzled with the new day: the child awakening with joy to the loving glance of its all-powerful, all-forgiving mother. His music cheerily sweeps aside any such reservations. Una Poenitentium sings her supplication, 'Neige, neige, du Ohnegleiche' to the rapt melody sung at the beginning of the finale by the violins, but it is now almost folk-like in its sparkling simplicity. As the Blessed Boys enter however, we can perhaps for a moment put ourselves in Mahler's place, directing his musical troops at the Eighth Symphony's triumphant Munich premiere. Witnesses tell us of his particular delight in the keen participation of the boys' – or, rather, children's – choirs. Perhaps he allowed himself a moment of self-indulgent delight as they sang the words, 'But this man has learned much: / He will teach us'.

Gretchen's solo reaches its final climax with a confident crescendo on the same music that marked the apotheosis of the phrase 'Imple superna gratia' (Fill with heavenly grace), early in Part I. There it reached its peak, not with the anticipated massively affirmative cadence in E flat major, but with a surprising lurch forward into the shadowy 'Infirma' section. This time, however, it comes to rest gratefully in a clear, serene B flat major: much slower, with twinkling high celeste, as horns and trumpets present the 'Accende lumen sensibus' theme in hushed imitation. B flat falls naturally to the tonic E flat, *morendo* (dying away). Something momentous is about to happen.

MATER GLORIOSA

Komm! Hebe dich zu höheren Sphären!
Wenn er dich ahnet, folgt er nach.

MATER GLORIOSA

Come! Raise yourself to higher spheres!
When he senses you, he will follow.

Up till now we have heard only seven vocal soloists, but for a brief moment an eighth, another soprano, joins the Heavenly Company. Mahler does not ask this singer to reach any higher than the other two sopranos, but she must do so *pianissimo*. Realising the challenge involved – especially as this singer has had no chance to warm up during the performance (if she remains onstage throughout, that is) – Mahler gives her an alternative at the high point of her solo, allowing her to soar up to her top B flat rather than hit it square on. The latter is however much more effective: given a first-class singer and an understanding conductor it can be the true emotional high point of the work. A tradition has sprung up of placing the Mater Gloriosa offstage, like the extra brass. This is not only thrillingly theatrical: it also means that the singer can prepare herself vocally for this moment backstage, then steal into place just before this crucial solo.

As Mater Gloriosa enters, *dolcissimo* ('very sweetly'), she intones Goethe's 'Komm!' twice. By repeating the word, Mahler ties it to the opening shout of 'Veni, veni' in Part I. In terms of sound, however it is at the other extreme from that great organ-enhanced exclamation: the celeste continues its softly tinkling tremolandos; flute and harp harmonics delicately pick out the notes of the theme now associated with Gretchen's 'Neige, neige, du Ohnegleiche'; strings stir rapturously for a moment then fall back in awed silence. The men of the second chorus quietly repeat the word 'Komm!', then Doctor Marianus takes centre stage again to deliver his final exhortation.

DOCTOR MARIANUS	DOCTOR MARIANUS
(*auf dem Angesicht anbetend*)	(*in prostrate worship*)
Blicket auf zum Retterblick,	Look upwards into the eyes of salvation,
Alle reuig Zarten,	You frail repentant ones,
Euch zu seligem Geschick	Thus to blessed destiny
Dankend umzuarten!	You may gratefully transform yourselves!
Werde jeder bessre Sinn	May all your better thoughts
Dir zum Dienst erbötig!	Be ready to serve you!
Jungfrau, Mutter, Königin,	Virgin, Mother, Queen,
Göttin, bleibe gnädig!	Goddess, be ever merciful!

Mahler reproduces Goethe's stage direction *auf dem Angesicht anbetend* – prostrate, or more exactly 'praying on his face' – on the tenor part above Doctor Marianus's first words, but for a singer to take this literally would be fairly catastrophic. It is an indication of emotional stance: Doctor Marianus is the last solo male voice permitted to speak in the presence of the *Ewig-Weibliche*, and he must do so in an attitude of utter, self-abnegating reverence. His opening phrases match his instruction to the faithful company: 'Look upwards'. In the background the second chorus repeats its invocation: 'Komm! Komm!' As the first great wave subsides, the motif associated with Pater Ecstaticus's 'Ewiger Wonnebrand' returns, its restless, forward-striving quality enhanced by its association now with the word 'auf' (upwards). As Doctor Marianus's urgent repeated cries of 'bleibe gnädig!' (be ever merciful!) reach their peak, on another thrilling high B flat, the chorus takes up the strain: 'Look upwards'. The harmonies grow more ardent and luscious, the tonality raises itself for one last time in the key of E major, then the tempo presses forward and the orchestra alone leads the way to an overwhelming climax, with a screaming high trumpet and the seminal three-note 'Veni, ve–' motif blasted out by four trombones, *fff*. This is the moment of maximal joy–pain intensity in the Eighth Symphony: the image of Christ on the cross, the supreme expression of the agony and ecstasy of self-sacrificing love, may well come to mind. It is possible to read it as pure masochism; but whatever one decides, it is a reminder that the emotional landscape of Mahler's Heaven is highly complicated, and susceptible to many different readings.

The trombones' motif is repeated, then replayed at half speed, *diminuendo*, with sprays of colour from celeste, piano and harps, gradually dissolving into a great pool of calm. We now come to the passage that so moved Anton Webern with its 'stillness and tenderness'. Celeste, piano, harps, harmonium and high string harmonics conjure a sound picture like the barely agitated surface of water, with jewel-like reflections of sunlight in its tiny wave-lets. Against this a solo piccolo sings an exquisite high song, like a child's pipe. For a moment it is the image of serenity – but then a cloud passes over the sun. The rippling stops, a hushed but pained dissonance sounds on muted horns and trombones, and the happily piping piccolo line is taken over by a much more strained-sounding high clarinet. It is one of those moments where, in the midst of apparent bliss, the music seems to ask, 'Is this for real?' These moments of self-questioning are achieved with great subtlety – and a great deal depends, of course, on how the per-formers interpret them – but the poignancy can be real enough. It comes unsettlingly close to a haunting remark of Nietzsche's Zarathustra, supposedly uttered at a moment of supreme spiritual achievement: 'O zerbrich, zerbrich, Herz, nach solchem Glücke, nach solchem Stiche!' (Oh break, break, my heart, after so much happiness, after so much pain!)

CHORUS MYSTICUS	MYSTIC CHORUS
Alles Vergängliche	All that is transient
Ist nur ein Gleichnis;	Is but a symbol;
Das Unzulängliche,	The unfulfillable,
Hier wird's Ereignis;	Here becomes real;
Das Unbeschreibliche,	The inexpressible,
Hier ist's getan;	Here it is done.
Das Ewig-Weibliche	The Ever-Womanly
Zieht uns hinan.	Draws us on.

Whatever one makes of the previous orchestral passage, emotionally speaking, it is another superb example of Mahler's mastery of
the art of transition, leading expertly into the opening of the final
Chorus Mysticus. Both choirs enter *ppp*, marked 'wie ein Hauch'
(like a breath), an instruction Schoenberg reproduced in the last
of his *Sechs kleine Stücke* ('Six Little Pieces') for piano, composed
in 1911 in memory of Mahler. The motif to which the choruses
sing the opening words is the one that launched Pater Ecstaticus's
'Ewiger Wonnebrand' monologue, and to which Doctor Marianus
urged his fellows to look 'upwards into the eyes of salvation'. The
chorus rises in a beautifully measured slow tread – or, rather, the
top line rises. The bass falls, and in keeping with the haunting
ambiguity of the previous orchestral episode, there is something
double-edged about the languishing harmonies, especially the
twist on the word 'Gleichnis' (symbol): it could be joyous abandonment, but it could just as easily be a lament. The astonishing
vocal hand-over between the stratospherically high first and second sopranos could be Faust swooning ecstatically into the arms
of the Heavenly Mother, but it can also have an eerie, keening quality. The mood brightens appreciably as harps once again add their
swirling arpeggios and the celeste glitters above, and still more
when the male voices take up the figure previously associated with
Gretchen's 'Neige, neige' and triumphantly declare 'Ewig! Ewig!'
(Eternally! Eternally!). Gradually the full orchestra (minus the
offstage brass) enters, drawing us, like the *Ewig-Weibliche*, ever
onwards, until the full organ thunders in, supporting all the voices
in a massive restatement of the first two and last two lines of the
Chorus Mysticus. And on the final shout of 'Hinan!' (Onwards!),
the offstage brass enter for only the second time in the symphony.
The E flat major chord on which they coincide is in fact the only

moment in the whole of Part II where almost the entire forces are heard together. The extra trumpets and trombones call out an augmented, hymn-like version of the symphony's opening 'Veni, veni creator spiritus', echoed in the main orchestral brass sections. Finally comes another colossal plagal 'Amen' cadence, with the orchestral trumpets shooting up to a spine-chilling high C, then the harmony falls back to the tonic E flat. The three-note 'Veni, ve–' motif sounds on the offstage trumpets and trombones, its final leap straining even higher. With one final, emphatic E flat major chord, Mahler, 'god or demon', ends his hymn of praise to Eros as 'creator of the world'.

6

Questions of Identity

'I am thrice homeless,' he used often to say. 'As a
native of Bohemia in Austria, as an Austrian among
Germans, and as a Jew throughout the world.
Everywhere an intruder, never welcomed.'[1]

This is one of the most famous of the many remarks attributed to
Gustav Mahler. It has to be remembered that it is presented to us
by Alma – and with Alma it is always worth asking if there is any
hidden agenda behind what she says. But then surely the same
could be said, to a greater or lesser extent, of any of the remarks
or opinions attributed to Mahler by his friends, however close.
Nevertheless, one of the reasons why this quotation has become
widely popular is that for many Mahler-lovers it evidently rings
true. There is plenty of evidence that Mahler did consider himself
an outsider wherever he made his home – except possibly when he
was amongst his beloved Alps, where he chose to compose, whenever possible. But the image of the alienated 'intruder' is surely
far closer to what Mahler himself called the 'subjective tragedy'
of the first seven symphonies than it is to the declared character
of the Eighth, his 'source of great joy'. It all depends, of course,
on whether one takes what Mahler said about the Eighth at face
value. Perhaps the opposite is also true here, too – in which case,
how do these differing senses of home and homelessness make
themselves felt in the Eighth Symphony?

Mahler's aphorism lists four possible identities: Bohemian,

Austrian, German and Jewish. The first of these should be treated with caution. In my research I have never been able to find another instance of Mahler referring to himself as a Bohemian, and efforts to find specifically Bohemian (as opposed to generally Czech) elements in his music tend to come across as either vague or tendentious, though it is clear that Mahler knew some Czech folk melodies, and as an adult he retained at least a basic knowledge of the Czech language. Mahler was born on 7 July 1860, in a poor village then called Kalischt (now Kaliště), in what was then Bohemia, but he was only a few months old when the family moved to the more sizeable and prosperous town of Iglau (now Jihlava), in the neighbouring province of Moravia. Iglau itself was predominantly German-speaking, thanks to a large influx of migrant Austrian and German workers, and to the presence of a sizeable Austrian barracks, which gave the town the feeling of an Austrian imperial outpost amid lands with a vaguer, more conflicted ethnic identity – a sense enhanced by the double fortifications that surrounded it. Mahler's friend, and later chronicler, Guido Adler, remembered Iglau as a 'German-speaking island in a foaming sea of nationalism'.[2] Perhaps it might be better to render 'a native of Bohemia in Austria' as 'a provincial in Vienna'. Mahler's friend Anton Bruckner, a native of rural Upper Austria, also suffered greatly from Viennese metropolitan snobbery.

But the other three identifications – Austrian, German and Jewish – do carry weight, for reasons which will be expanded upon in the following sections; and more importantly, each can be said to have a bearing on the character of Mahler's Eighth Symphony. Perhaps we should add a fourth identity, this time defined not in terms of ethnicity: 'Everywhere an intruder'. For this reason we can now consider the Eighth Symphony from four different perspectives:

the Austrian, the German, that of the intruder – the 'homeless'
outsider – and, running through each of these three identities, 'a
Jew throughout the world'. It is crucial to stress the latter, as – for
a variety of reasons – some of his biographers have tended to play
down this important facet of Mahler's sense of self. Even in the
recollections of some of his closest associates the picture wavers
somewhat. Otto Klemperer, a Jew who converted to Catholicism then returned to Judaism in later life, observed that Mahler
found himself attacked by both antisemites and philosemites,
and viewed both camps coldly from his 'homeless' perspective.
But in Alma Mahler's *Memories and Letters* there appears what
looks like an unexpectedly candid account – unexpected, because
in other places Alma makes little attempt to conceal her (probably) casual antisemitic attitudes. Introducing Mahler's close, and
intellectually highly influential friend Siegfried Lipiner, she finally
dismissed him as a 'bogus Goethe in his writing and a haggling
Jew in his talk'.[3] But talking later of Mahler himself, Alma provides
a memorable account. The 'Jewish question', she tells us, bothered
Mahler considerably. He had often been on the receiving end of
antisemitic attacks – especially in the Viennese press – and one
particular incident had left a bitter imprint. When Mahler had
been chosen as director of the Vienna Court Opera in 1897, Wagner's widow Cosima, whom Mahler had greatly admired, had tried
to block his appointment solely because he was a Jew. (Cosima
Wagner's antisemitism could be every bit as virulent as her husband's, and she was even less inclined to make exceptions on the
grounds of talent.) Alma mentions again Mahler's attraction to
some forms of Roman Catholic mysticism; in contrast she insists
that Jewish religious rites 'never meant anything to him'.

But he was not a man who ever deceived himself, and he knew
that people would not forget he was a Jew because he was sceptical
of the Jewish religion and baptised a Christian. Nor did he wish it
forgotten, even though he frequently asked me to warn him when
he gesticulated too much, because he hated to see others do so and
thought it ill-bred. No one dared tell him funny stories about Jews;
they made him seriously angry. And how right he was in this.[4]

The thought of Mahler repeatedly asking Alma to police his
gestures, in case anyone thought he was being too Jewish, is desperately sad. But there is at least one questionable assertion here.
What are we to make of Alma's claim that the Jewish ritual 'never
meant anything to him'? As Norman Lebrecht points out in his
book *Mahler Remembered*, there is plenty of evidence that the
young Mahler had strong links with the newly formed synagogue
in Iglau. His father, Bernhard, was a member of the Committee of
the Iglau Community, and his mother, Maria, was evidently highly
devout, and no doubt took care to encourage similar devotion in
her eldest surviving son. Mahler's school reports show outstanding achievement in Mosaic religious studies, and there is a report
of him playing the piano, at the age of twelve, at a service at the
Iglau synagogue in celebration of the wedding of the Archduchess
Gisela – who thirty-seven years later would attend the premiere
of the Eighth Symphony. The records of the Iglau synagogue have
not survived – probably they were destroyed after the Nazi annex-
ation of Austria (the *Anschluss*) in March 1938 – but it is highly
likely that Mahler had his bar mitzvah there, at the conventional
age of twelve, i.e. around the time of the synagogue concert mentioned above. There he would have heard plenty of Jewish music,
and it isn't hard to make out the exuberant dance melodies and

rhythms of the Eastern European klezmer band in the third move-ment of Mahler's First Symphony, or of Jewish folk lamentation in the strings' hushed threnody in the funeral-march first movement of the Fifth. Hearing these two passages side by side might suggest a painfully divided attitude to his heritage on Mahler's part. One can hardly help noting the sudden switches from tenderness to lacerating sarcasm – or is it both at the same time? Klemperer wasn't quite right: Mahler was indeed an 'outsider', but whatever else he may have felt himself to be, he was a Jewish outsider.

So then we have four different possible identity 'takes' on Mahler: the Austrian, the German, the Outsider ('Homeless') and the Jew. How might these manifest themselves in the Eighth Sym-phony? For reasons which will hopefully soon become clear, we will start with the German.

A Gift to the Nation

One comment Mahler made about his Eighth Symphony has baffled several of his commentators: he refers to it as his 'gift to the entire nation' (*Geschenk der ganzen Nation*).[5] Mahler goes on to call it 'a great joy-bringer', thereby aligning the work directly with Beethoven's Ninth Symphony, and particularly with its conclud-ing *Ode an die Freude*, 'Ode to Joy'. But where the Schiller text set by Beethoven offers its 'kiss to the whole world' (*Diesen Kuß der ganzen Welt!*), Mahler offers his to 'the entire nation' (*der ganzen Nation*), by which, it seems clear enough, he specifically means the German nation. Mahler a German nationalist? It seems unlikely, and yet it is possible to argue that there were aspects of the Eighth Symphony that Mahler considered specifically German. For a start, there is the setting, in the symphony's significantly larger second part, of the final section of the iconic text by the iconic German writer and thinker. We have already seen how closely Mahler identified with Goethe, to the extent of knowing passages from *Faust* Part II by heart. As Mahler would have been well aware, he wouldn't have been alone in this, at least not amongst educated German-speakers in the first decade of the twentieth century. For many in the larger German world, and particularly in the recently unified German lands, Goethe was the proudest of all the young nation's cultural exhibits. The breadth of Goethe's achievement was awe-inspiring in itself: poetry, novels, dramas, literary and aesthetic criticism, research into botany, theory of colour and, from the age of thirty-three, a career as a highly active and influential statesman at the Ducal Court of Weimar – it must have seemed that there was nothing Goethe couldn't do. He was the type of the *Universalische Mensch*, the 'universal man' – or rather, since the word *Mensch* is supposed to be non-gender specific, 'universal human being'. (*Mensch* remains, however, a masculine noun.) Though Goethe had been dead for nearly eight decades in 1910, his stature and his contemporary 'presentness' was as high and as relevant as ever. For some, Goethe was more a prophet than an artist: hadn't he predicted in *Faust* Part II, with almost forensic precision, the way human society would develop after the Industrial Revolution – an epochal event, it was now argued, with far more important long-term consequences than the French Revolution? (Downplaying French attitudes and innovations had become fashionable in Germany since the newborn country's emphatic victory in the Franco-Prussian War of 1870–71.)

By 1910 Goethe had become a figure of almost religious significance. To take just one example, as Mahler was preparing for the premiere of his *Faust*-centred Eighth Symphony, Rudolf Steiner, the philosopher, mystic and founder of the science (or pseudo-science, if you prefer) of Anthroposophy was making the first designs for his fifteen-hundred-seater Goetheanum – a cathedral-like synthesis of artistic design and sensory effects consecrated, naturally, to the *Universalische Mensch*. At one point in 1910, Stefan Zweig was rendered 'dizzy' by meeting the daughter of Goethe's physician, Dr Vogel. Zweig later developed quite a flair for meeting people who offered a touch of physical contact with 'the heights of the heroic and Olympian world . . . But nothing stirred me so much as the face of that old lady, the last among the living to have met the eye of Goethe himself. And perhaps I, in my turn, am the last who can say today: "I knew someone whose head was touched tenderly by Goethe's hand for a moment."'[6] Nor was this kind of reverence exclusive to the intellectual elite. I remember, on one of my earliest trips to Germany, meeting an old man who delivered, after several beers, an unexpectedly hilarious account of his modestly middle-class family hymning Bismarck to the theme of the finale of Beethoven's 'Eroica' Symphony, while the bust of Goethe beamed approvingly from his place of honour on top of the family piano, just as he did in countless other German-speaking households.

Then there is the text of the first movement, the hymn *Veni, creator spiritus*, composed by Rabanus Maurus, the ninth century Archbishop of Mainz, honoured as 'Praeceptor Germaniae', or 'the teacher of Germany', and thus a key figure in the nationalist story of the emergence of a sense of German cultural identity. Mainz, poised on the east bank of the River Rhine, roughly halfway along the river's German course, was long considered a crucial strategic outpost against attack from the west, specifically from France. When in 1840 the French prime minister, Adolphe Thiers, insisted that France should own the Rhine's left bank, as it had done during Napoleon's reign, the poet Nikolaus Becker responded with what was to become one of the most famous verses in German literature: *Der deutsche Rhein* ('The German Rhine'). This was to become notorious as *Die Wacht am Rhein*, 'The Watch on the Rhine', its enduring popularity much exploited in the twentieth century by Nazi propagandists. Its note is one of jingoistic defiance:

Sie sollen ihn nicht haben,	They shall never have it,
Den freien deutschen Rhein,	The free and German Rhine,
Ob sie wie gier'ge Raben	Though they with ravens' gluttony
Sich heiser danach schrein.	Scream for it till they're hoarse.

Did Mahler buy into all this? He would almost certainly have known Schumann's setting of Becker's poem, and it is quite possible that he had accompanied it during his student days, when he was a member of the so-called Pernerstorfer Circle. This group also included Mahler's lifelong friend and intellectual mentor Siegfried Lipiner – his very name a revealing Jewish/German-nationalist compound. The Pernerstorfer Circle was nationalist in its leaning towards Germany, rather than to the much more ethnically and linguistically mixed Austrian Imperial territories, though what was meant was evidently a 'Greater Germany', in this case not so much a geographical-political aspiration as a cultural ideal that embraced all the German-speaking territories. And that Greater German culture was embodied above all, for these young intellectuals, in the writings of Wagner, Schopenhauer and Nietzsche. Soon after his Vienna Conservatory days Mahler began to distance himself from the ideals of the Pernerstorfer Circle, and in his own mature writings, and the recollections of his friends and colleagues, comments of an overtly political nature are hard to find. The increasingly antisemitic attitudes of some of the Austrian 'German' nationalists would no doubt have influenced that change of attitude; and yet, as Carl Niekerk argues authoritatively in his fascinating essay 'Mahler's Goethe', it was a legacy of Mahler's student nationalist days that he was, throughout his life, oriented particularly towards German culture, and not toward Austrian 'particularism' – the belief that the destiny of the multi-ethnic Austrian Empire was entirely separate from that of 'Germany' either as nationalist dream or political reality. For Mahler there remained, as for Wagner's Hans Sachs, such a thing as *heil'ge deutsche Kunst* – 'Holy German Art'. In the light of that, the invocations of Beethoven's Ninth Symphony and *Missa solemnis*, Bach's *St Matthew Passion* and the Prelude to Wagner's *Die Meistersinger* in Part I of the Eighth Symphony, and the prevalence in the symphony of intricate, muscular and flowing counterpoint, that craft that was elevated to the highest level in both Bach and Wagner, look like a direct response to Sachs's famous injunction:

Verachtet mir die Meister nicht,	Scorn not the Masters,
und ehrt mir ihre Kunst!	and honour their art with me!

For the modern reader, who knows what happened to German and Austrian Jews when the Nazis took possession of the notion of 'Holy German Art' and transformed Hans Sachs's 'Ehrt eure deutschen Meister! (Honour your German Masters!) into one of the most revolting concepts in political history, this may all sound horribly far-fetched. But consider this verdict of Mahler's (non-Jewish) champion Richard Specht:

And he was entirely German: in his spiritual culture, in his objectivity and self-discipline, his submission to the order he accepted, in doing nothing for himself but for the chosen cause – as Richard Wagner described the Germans . . . Not to mention the elements that are rooted in the German land, in the mother soil, in the indigenous folk-songs that permeate his symphonies.[7]

Specht also notes 'Jewish traits' in Mahler, but evidently sees them as in no way contradictory to, or conflicting with his Germanness. In *Vienna and the Jews: A Cultural History, 1867–1938*, Steven Beller identifies a preference for German over Austrian culture and political identity that was prevalent amongst educated and cultivated Viennese Jews in Mahler's day. As Carl Niekerk observes, many of the pioneering Goethe studies were by Jews. He cites George L. Mosse, author of *German Jews Beyond Judaism*, who claims that Goethe's stress on individual freedom, his ambivalent feelings about nationalism, German or otherwise, and his belief in 'Bildung' – education not just of the mind but of the whole human being – made him even more attractive as a cultural icon for assimilated Jews. Niekerk recalls Alma Mahler's description of Siegfried Lipiner as a 'bogus Goethe', and how he resembled a 'haggling Jew' in his manner of speaking. Alma uses the verbs 'goetheln' (to go on about Goethe) and 'mauscheln' – a contemptuous way of dismissing Jews who were felt to mangle the German language. The resemblance between the two words indicates that Alma connected the two in her mind: Jews distorting both the language and the utterances of the great Sage of Weimar. Perhaps there was an element of envy here too – as there often is in antisemitism. From the evidence of her writings and reported conversation, Alma's knowledge of Goethe and of

German literature in general appears to have been significantly less extensive and insightful than Lipiner's, as her husband clearly recognised.

Mahler's choice of texts for his symphonies and songs – Goethe, Nietzsche, Friedrich Rückert, the classic German folk-collection *Des Knaben Wunderhorn* – is highly indicative: all German, iconically German, not Austrian. If Mahler fostered the idea of an ideal German culture, transcending the actual flesh-and-blood phenomenon of modern Germany, represented above all by Goethe, he would have found ample confirmation for this in the writings of Nietzsche. Here is what that philosopher has to say on the subject in *The Case of Wagner*:

One knows Goethe's fate in priggish, old-maidish Germany. He was always offensive to Germans; he had sincere admirers only amongst Jewish women. Schiller, the 'noble' Schiller, who pummelled German ears with long words – he was after their hearts. What did they hold against Goethe? . . . Above all, however, the higher virgins were outraged: every petty court, every kind of 'Wartburg' in Germany crossed itself against Goethe, against the 'unclean spirit' in Goethe.[8]

Could even Wagner, for all his effusive nationalism, have been tragically mistaken about the people he had called upon as his own? Here is what Nietzsche has to say in his final work, *Ecce Homo*, 'Behold the Man':

The origins of this book stem from the weeks of the first Bayreuth Festival; a profound alienation from all that surrounded me there is one of its preconditions . . .

... Where was I? There was nothing I recognised, I hardly even
recognised Wagner. In vain I searched my memories ... What
had happened? – Wagner had been translated into German! The
Wagnerian had become the master of Wagner! – German art! The
German Master! German beer! ... Truly an appalling crowd! ...
Not a single abortion was missing, not even the anti-Semite. – Poor
Wagner! How had he been brought to this! – Better for him to have
fallen in with swine! But among Germans![9]

Remember Mahler's comment that *Parsifal*, begun just after that
first Bayreuth Festival, was 'not a work by Wagner but one by a
Wagnerite'? That sounds like someone who has been reading *Ecce*
Homo. Mahler may not have shared Nietzsche's seething disgust at
modern unified Germany to the last degree, but Nietzsche's notion
that there was something in its greatest art that transcended banal
everyday reality – in Goethe, Beethoven, even in Wagner – would
certainly have spoken to him.

A Holy German Art, a spiritual Germany, far surpassing
the unyielding actuality of the Prussian-dominated 'German
Empire', or of Habsburg Austria? Mahler's fascination with
this ideal Germany must, at least in part, have been rooted in
its sense of 'otherness'. That would certainly have been the case
during his student days in Vienna, when he hymned Goethe,
Schopenhauer, Nietzsche and Wagner along with his comrades
in the Pernerstorfer Circle. The Austrian emperor Franz Joseph
was not keen to encourage any kind of nationalism based on
language or ethnicity. His was an empire that acknowledged
diversity, up to a point, even if it drew the line at encouraging
any kind of ethnic identity politics: how else could one hope
to govern a vast, sprawling territory that included Czechs, Slo-

venes, Magyars, Slovaks, Ruthenians, Serbs, Romanians and, of course, the Jew everywhere?

With this in mind it becomes far easier to understand the reaction of Mahler's younger friend and fellow Jew Arnold Schoenberg to a thoroughly unpleasant experience in the summer of 1921 – a time when, after the German-Austrian defeat in the First World War, nationalistic attitudes had begun to acquire more sinister complexions. Schoenberg had been holidaying with his family at the Austrian resort of Mattsee, near Salzburg, where he apparently experienced a demonstration of antisemitic feeling of a kind he'd never witnessed in public before. He described it, with characteristically bitter humour, in a letter dated 16 July to his friend and former pupil Alban Berg. It took only two days for things to turn nasty:

Toward the end it got very ugly in Mattsee. The people there seemed to despise me as much as if they knew my music. Nothing happened to us beyond that. But it's just as unpleasant outside one's profession as within it – only there one has to accept it.[10]

Was Schoenberg being entirely truthful in his claim that nothing happened beyond expressions of hostility? Mentioning the event thirteen years later, in 1934, he told the American Rabbi Stephen S. Wise that what he had experienced at Mattsee was in effect an act of physical expulsion by a hostile crowd. Schoenberg had already shown himself to be an artist of exceptional courage and determination, exploring terrifying mental hinterlands in such uncompromisingly radical works as the one-act monodrama *Erwartung* ('Anticipation') and the unclassifiable *Pierrot lunaire* ('Moonstruck', or even simply 'Lunatic Pierrot') for 'speech-singer' and chamber ensemble. In searching out the means to express emotions that might have seemed more in place in a Freudian consulting room, Schoenberg had effectively created the new language of 'atonality': music without tonal roots or any sense of final coming-to-rest – the tension of dissonance remains ultimately unresolved. As a result he had already endured powerful hostile reactions, many of them at least coloured by antisemitism. But the experience at Mattsee seems to have struck him to his very core. With the benefit of historical hindsight, Schoenberg's reaction now seems paradoxical to the point of perversity. On one level, understandably, it strengthened his resolve to re-engage with his Jewish identity and inheritance. But on another – and this is where, for the modern reader, the unease begins steadily to mount – it also made Schoenberg more acutely aware of his Germanness, and of his desire to place himself within the great German musical tradition. In his writings of the time he pours scorn on the music of other cultures, contrasting it witheringly with the heaven-scaling power of great German music. When Schoenberg thinks of music, he tells us, the only kind that comes to mind spontaneously is German music (by which he means German and Austrian music, the creations of the 'Greater Germany'). While the music of other peoples may achieve worldly success, through clever, manipulative tricks, true German music strives higher: 'It will always reach for heavens, while worldly superiority only boasts with artifice.'[11] By the following year, Schoenberg was matching even some of his persecutors in the virulence of his xenophobia: all he found in the music of those deplorable Latins, Russians, Hungarians, English and Americans was a pitiful imitation of the richness of German art. Their efforts to be clever, he said, reminded him of the idiocy of circus clowns and drunkards:

one might be amused, at first, or perhaps pitying, but such feelings soon turned to anger and disgust for true German connoisseurs like Schoenberg himself – at times his language positively oozes loathing for these cretinous apes of art.

Some kind of counter-blow was urgently needed. Schoenberg's definitive response to the trauma he had experienced at Mattsee was an act of almost insane heroic defiance. At around the same time he had finally arrived at his most celebrated and notorious innovation: the twelve-tone row. This is the system by which the twelve notes of the chromatic scale are kept in constant rotation, each one 'first amongst equals', bound to each other by repetition, thus creating a musical logic that defies, or at the very least makes redundant, traditional tonal organisation. In that same decisive summer of 1921, Schoenberg announced his invention of this technique to his pupil Josef Rufer with the ringing words, 'I have made a discovery which will ensure the supremacy of German music for the next hundred years.'[12] The tragic irony that statement has subsequently acquired is so multi-faceted that to unpick it would probably require a chapter of its own.

If Mahler ever experienced anything as horrible as what Schoenberg went through at Mattsee, it is not recorded. In any case the combative spirit in which Schoenberg offered the world his twelve-tone system is a long way from that of Mahler's 'gift to the whole nation' – and it is highly unlikely that Schoenberg ever considered any of his twelve-tone compositions 'a great joy-bringer'. But perhaps there was after all one important thing Mahler's Eighth Symphony and Schoenberg's music of the 1920s and early 1930s had in common: they held out to the Germany of their times an image, not of what it was, but of what it could just possibly be.

*

But how many in Mahler's audience would have heard that message – that the image of German culture communicated with such
burning urgency was of something 'holy', transcendent, and not
congruent with the reality of the expanding, ambitious German
Reich in 1910? Guido Adler, in his study *Gustav Mahler*, reports
the reaction of the German dramatist and novelist Gerhart Hauptmann, who asserted that Mahler's genius in particular embodies
'the great traditions of German music . . . He has the daemonic
character and passionately ethical essence of the German masters.'[13] That does sound on balance like an endorsement of the
view that Mahler's Eighth Symphony hymns an ideal German
culture, rather than the reality of modern Germany. However the
story reported in the newspapers (see above, p. 26) of the fight
on the train between the German-speaking Mahler enthusiasts
and his French detractors does suggest that there were those
who read his 'gift to the entire nation' in more obviously nationalistic terms, particularly when it came to engagements with the
Reich's traditional enemy. There were also those who, as we shall
see later, reacted to the Eighth Symphony in ways closer to the
spirit of Alma Mahler's sneer at Siegfried Lipiner's 'goetheln' and
'mauscheln'. And for those from outside Germany – especially
for the French – implications of ideal Goethean internationalism
seem to have fallen on largely deaf ears. Relations between France
and Germany had taken an unsurprising turn for the worst after
France's shock defeat in the Franco-Prussian War of 1870–71. The
final defeat of Napoleon Bonaparte at Waterloo in 1815 had been
humiliating, but in strategic terms it had only seen the French
forced back onto home territory. But the Franco-Prussian War

had ended with the unthinkable: German troops actually march-
ing into Paris, followed by King William of Prussia declaring
himself Emperor of the newly unified Germany at – of all places –
the Palace of Versailles! Resentment against Germany boiled and
frothed in France for generations, and it manifested itself in some
of the expressions of its leading artists on the subject of German
culture. And not just its leading artists: when Mahler conducted
his Second Symphony in Paris earlier in 1910, one member of the
audience apparently shouted 'À bas la musique allemande!' (Down
with German music!). Alma recalled an embarrassing moment
during the performance when she noticed the composers Claude
Debussy, Paul Dukas and Gabriel Pierné heading for the exit in
the middle of the symphony's second movement. Put on the spot
afterwards, the three composers stammered something about the
music being 'too Schubertian' for their tastes: Schubert wasn't just
'too Viennese' for these fastidious Gallic gentlemen, he was even
'too Slav'.[14] Apparently the success of the Second Symphony with
the general public was nowhere near sufficient to compensate
Mahler for the hurt caused by these comments.

Too foreign, too Viennese – too Slav – could it be that this distinguished trio was being a touch evasive here? Was what they
really wanted to say, but drew back from enunciating clearly,
that it was 'too German'? In an article in the *Paris-Journal* a few
months later, Debussy felt the need to make public his reasons
for not attending the premiere of Mahler's Eighth Symphony. For
one thing, he said with obvious irritation, he hadn't been invited,
but in any case, Debussy continued testily, why should the Germans be obliged to understand French music any more than
French music-lovers should understand them? Debussy picks up
on a highly suggestive comment in a recent edition of the Parisian

newspaper *Le Figaro*, which asserted that the choice of Munich for the Eighth Symphony's premiere made sense from a 'political' point of view – imagine what he might have made of Mahler's claim that the symphony was his gift to the German nation! In any case, Debussy continues, the worthy citizens of Munich are indifferent to French art: 'People will come to hear French music only out of politeness. They will applaud, perhaps, with that German courteousness that is so hard to bear.'[15] Even German applause is unbearable for Debussy! But similar doubts were expressed by the much more sympathetically disposed writer Romain Rolland – for whom, as we've seen, Mahler's Schubertianism was one of his most attractive features. Apparently it was hearing – and watching – Mahler conduct Beethoven's Ninth Symphony that had brought it all home to him: 'Above all, I fear Mahler has been sadly hypnotised by ideas about power – ideas that are getting to the head of all German artists today . . . he wants to be Beethoven or Wagner. And he is wrong; for he lacks their balance and gigantic force.'[16]

'Ideas about power' – the unprecedented forces and timescales demanded by Beethoven's 'Choral' Symphony, by Wagner's *Ring*, by Bruckner and Mahler in their symphonies and by Richard Strauss in his operas and symphonic poems, and now Mahler's own employment of substantially enlarged forces when he performed Beethoven's Ninth: for some French ears it was all too symptomatic of the new German lust for power. No matter that French composers had called on vast forces in the days of the French Revolution and Napoleon's first victorious campaigns, or that Berlioz had demanded hundreds of performers for his colossal *Grande Messe des morts* (1837); now it was the Germans' turn to throw their weight around, musically speaking, and the French hated it.

Of course, it wasn't just musically speaking. Nowadays Mahler's assertion to Sibelius that 'the symphony must be like the world. It must embrace everything' is usually quoted without consideration of how it might have sounded then, in 1910. By that time the German word *Welt* ('world') had acquired a new, more ominous significance, as Thomas Mann's son, the historian Golo Mann, points out in *The History of Germany since 1789*. This was the Age of Empire, when the major world powers competed with each other to occupy as much of the world as possible, and to access its economic resources. Germany, a late starter in the great imperial game, was anxious to make up for lost time. This, says Golo Mann, helps explain why the word 'world' was now prefixed to so many German nouns: the world-city Berlin, German world-standing, German world-trade, world politics, world history and, most ominously of all, world power. In 1896, the anniversary of the foundation of the modern German state, the Kaiser congratulated himself and his people in helping build a country that had become much more than simply a German Reich. It had grown, spread its wings and its economic and military tentacles – it had become a *Weltreich*, a 'World Reich': 'Thousands of our countrymen live in far-flung corners of the earth. German goods, German knowledge, German industriousness, cross the ocean. German ships carry goods worth thousands of millions. You, gentlemen, have the important duty of helping me to link this greater-German Reich firmly to ours at home.'[17] With language like that resonating in the background, one can understand how even Emil Gutmann's nickname 'Symphony of a Thousand' could, for some, have taken on disturbing political overtones. Remember the reaction of the French reporter from *Le Monde musical* to what he saw as the typically Germanic military precision with which Mahler's massed forces rose to their feet in Munich. For some of his readers that would have been no joke.

Nevertheless, it is important to stress that in 1910, many in Europe would still have considered a European war 'unthinkable' – or so claims the historian Eric Hobsbawm in his *The Age of Empire: 1875–1914*. Until Otto von Bismarck's dismissal from power in 1890, the German Chancellor, the ultimate master of the game of multilateral diplomatic chess, had devoted himself above all to maintaining peace between Europe's great powers, playing them off against each other with cynical brilliance. Granted, in 1907, the year after Mahler had completed his Eighth Symphony, the so-called 'triple entente' had been signed between, on the one side France, Britain and Russia, on the other Germany and Austria–Hungary, but as Hobsbawm says, the triple entente was 'astonishing' to Britain's enemies and allies alike. In the previous century there had been very little tension between Britain and Prussia – in fact Britain had famously worked together with Prussian forces to bring about the final defeat of Napoleon's armies at the Battle of Waterloo in 1815. Oscar Wilde's Lady Bracknell spoke for many of her class in 1895 when, in *The Importance of Being Earnest*, she observes that 'German sounds a thoroughly respectable language' – quite a concession for a high-class representative of such a notoriously monoglot nation. As Hobsbawm points out, such attitudes in Britain prevailed even for some time after the establishment of the 'super-Prussia' which now called itself the German Empire.[18] France, on the other hand, was the age-old enemy. Long after Napoleon's death, fractious English children were still threatened with visits from a terrifying creature called 'Old Boney'. And while France at the beginning of the twentieth century was no longer capable of aggression on the scale achieved by Revolutionary France, or by the Bourbons in the previous two centuries, friction between France and Britain was on the rise again, now chiefly as a result of competition for the same colonial territories. Things grew more dangerous as Germany, looking covetously at rising British and French imperial power and influence, stridently demanded its own 'place in the sun'. France had long been the hated enemy in Germany too. For centuries the German territories were far more frequently on the receiving end of French aggression than the other way around – until 1870–71, that is. As for Britain? The Kaiser himself was half-English by birth, and throughout his life maintained an intense love–hate feeling for his mother's country. Certainly Britain was a great imperial power; but hadn't the British Empire come about as much by accident as by design? Couldn't German genius and efficiency achieve something far better, if only the loved–hated rival could somehow be induced to step (or be pushed) out of the way? In place of a haphazard acquisition of territories, over a period of centuries (as in the case of the British Empire), it was up to Germany now to show how to do it properly: "'The aim of colonialism", wrote one enthusiast, "is the ruthless and determined enrichment of one's own at the expense of the other, weaker nations."'[19]

Can we really believe Mahler buying into all this – even unconsciously? The selection of Munich as the location for the Eighth Symphony's world premiere may have struck *Le Figaro* as apt from a political point of view, but as far as we can tell from Mahler's own comments it was more a question of expediency – the Musik Festhalle was one of the very few venues in the world that could cope with the huge forces required, to say nothing of the even huger audiences Emil Gutmann anticipated; and even if there had been a suitable location in Vienna, the entrenched anti-Mahler feeling

there would have made it far less attractive. One of the most striking features of Mahler's cultural 'nationalism' – if that is indeed the
word – is how rarely it takes on any kind of political complexion.
If it is a devotion to 'Holy German Art', that devotion, as so often
to things holy, stands in opposition to, not in conformity with, the
'real world'. Naive it may have seemed to many, but Mahler's heart,
as we have seen, was amid nature, especially cut off from the modern world by his beloved Alps, where he could 'live alone, in my
heaven, in my love, in my song', as his exquisite song 'Ich bin der
Welt abhanden gekommen' tells us. One can imagine Mahler identifying completely with the sentiments of Wordsworth's famous
sonnet of 1807, written in protest at the very process of industrialisation Bismarck later commended so forcefully to his own people:

> The world is too much with us; late and soon,
> Getting and spending, we lay waste our powers;—
> Little we see in Nature that is ours;
> We have given our hearts away, a sordid boon!

This is the Mahler who, as a child, reportedly found escape from
a troubled family environment by losing himself for hours (on one
occasion literally) in the woodland around Iglau, who not only
imitated birdsong and the rippling of streams but incorporated
the actual sound of cowbells into his scores, contrasting nature
imagery poignantly with the strident, militarised march of progress in his Sixth Symphony. It is the Mahler who treasured Faust's
great soliloquy in Part I of Goethe's masterpiece:

> You gave me wondrous nature for my kingdom
> The strength to feel her and enjoy her, not

In cold astonishment was I allowed,
But also granted that I gaze
Deep into her heart as a friend's heart.
You lead the dance of all that lives
Before me, and bid me know myself
Brother to silent trees, to air and water.
And when through trees the stormwind roars and creaks,
The giant fir comes crashing down,
And neighbouring boughs and boles are crushed
And the hill booms and thunders with the fall,
You lead me to the safe cave then, and show
Me to myself and the deep wonders, secrets
Of my own heart are opened to me.[20]

This was the man who detested commercialism – the very commercialism that was then heightening the hunger of the great, and would-be great, European powers for 'territory and influence' – and deplored its effects in the world of art. Above all, this was the artist whose veneration for the great German humanistic tradition evidently placed itself at some degrees' distance from the more blatantly nationalistic thinking of Wagner. And in choosing to set the closing words of Goethe's *Faust* in his Eighth Symphony, Carl Niekerk argues, Mahler implicitly laid a claim to his own space within German cultural history. Aware as he was of the various nationalistic trends at work within the culture, even to the extent of being prepared to adopt some of their language and symbols, his own inclination was in a very different direction. However much Mahler admired Wagner, as composer and as conductor, however much he might have contributed to the growing cult of Wagner in Vienna towards the end of the century, and in other countries too,

Wagner's cultural and racial theorising was another matter. Wagner's antisemitism was an issue which, as Niekirk admits, Mahler rarely addressed, but it doesn't require much research to intuit what his feelings on that subject must have been. It is truly fascinating to discover that the composer Goethe considered the best choice to set his *Faust* was Giacomo Meyerbeer, whose Jewishness – and, no doubt, his immense success on the operatic stage – made him the target for some of Wagner's most virulent antisemitic abuse. If Mahler did not know about Goethe's choice of Meyerbeer, he would have known well enough the kind of thinking that lay behind it. It is the kind of thinking, Niekerk rightly says, that can also be found in some of the composer's other intellectual heroes: the Dutch-Jewish philosopher Baruch Spinoza for instance, or (in his higher moments) Friedrich Nietzsche. It is also the kind of thinking that led Brahms, writing to a colleague apropos an early performance of *A German Requiem* (1857–68), to confess that if he had reflected a little longer he would have probably removed the word 'German' and substituted 'Human', which does seem to suggest that for Brahms the two were to some extent interchangeable. If that sounds uncomfortable to modern ears, one should remember what Brahms took to be his own 'German' artistic and intellectual pedigree. The Protestant Reformation had begun in Germany, and it was on German soil that the political might of the Catholic Church had first been successfully challenged. Martin Luther's translation of the Bible (the source of Brahms's text) had at once helped define the still developing German language and marked the beginning of a process by which scripture ceased to be the property of an educated elite and was opened out to the masses. The great Protestant church compositions of Schütz, Bach and Handel, all of which left their mark on the *German Requiem*, had continued this process of democratising the mysteries of faith. Works like Bach's *St Matthew Passion* and Handel's *Messiah* had also brought a new emphasis on the humanity of Christ: a real, suffering human being rather than a mystical symbol. This was fertile ground for the emergence of a more humanistic kind of belief, and eventually of the apparently agnostic, humanistic spirituality of Brahms's *German Requiem*.

Niekerk's conclusion is very much in that spirit. The German–Human – or at least German–Humanist – equation makes sense when one considers what Mahler took to be his own intellectual lineage: As Niekerk writes, 'Spinoza, Goethe, and Nietzsche also stand for a trajectory of German cultural history that is very different from Wagner's. What Mahler envisioned in his works was more modern, more diverse, and much more inclusive than anything Wagner had in mind.'[21] Mahler's approach, claims Niekerk, is symptomatic of a desire to interpret tradition differently, and by implication more critically, thus setting him apart from some of his more conventionally nationalist contemporaries. It may also partly explain, he says, why Mahler is so popular in our more diversity-conscious age.

Given that Spinoza was Dutch by birth, it might have been better to substitute Beethoven's name at the head of that last quotation. In any case, is Niekerk's assertion too glowingly positive? As has already been stated, with this composer it is always worth bearing in mind Beethoven's words: 'Sometimes the opposite is also true.' But the point is that there is evidence for Niekerk's claim, plenty of it, in Mahler's writings and recorded comments. For the contrary position – that Mahler was gesturing, consciously or unconsciously, towards the more ethnically exclusive, territorially aggressive kind of German nationalism – there is none at all, or at least none that I have been able to uncover. Schoenberg's contemptuous cultural exclusivity was completely alien to him. Amongst the composers Mahler included and planned to include in his concert programmes at the New York Philharmonic we encounter the very Latins, Russians, English and Americans whose inadequacy in musical composition Schoenberg was later to find so ridiculous and repulsive. In this central point Niekerk is right: Mahler's cultural world-view was indeed more 'inclusive' than anything Wagner, still less Wagner's nationalist admirers, had in mind.

In any case, the reaction against Mahler, and against his extraordinary success in Munich, had already begun. In some nationalist quarters a rumour had begun to circulate that the Eighth Symphony's ecstatic reaction had been stoked up by wealthy Jewish supporters. A few of the reviews in German and Austrian newspapers imply, or in a few cases openly endorse, this viewpoint. It is depressing to find a composer of the stature of Max Reger, also present at the Munich premiere, adding his voice to this unpleasant chorus. This 'Mahler affair', he grumbles, is becoming a problem. After a side-thrust at the possessors of the stereotypical 'Semitic nose', who naturally only support Mahler because they desperately want to claim one of their own as a great composer, Reger attempts to dignify his plaint with something approaching an aesthetic argument. Mahler's music, he asserts, lacks 'style'. Without style there can be no question of his being a great composer. Echoing Wagner's notorious *Jewishness in Music*, he labels Mahler the Meyerbeer of his day – for Wagner, Giacomo Meyerbeer was the ultimate example of the Jewish would-be artist who steals and synthesises the ideas of others rather than coming up with something truly original. 'They both have the genuine Semitic high intelligence, both employ exaggerated affective devices, and both are absolutely lacking in any sort of style', Reger informs us. Even Mahler's stupendous triumph in Munich is produced as evidence against him: 'As Goethe says: "Woe to the art whose praise is sung on every street corner."'[22]

To modern music-lovers, Reger's claim that Mahler's music lacks a distinctive, authentic style will no doubt be as bizarre as his comment about Semitic noses is grotesque. But it is, alas, horribly symptomatic of a certain kind of thinking – a kind that would increase in intensity and venom after the First World War, and finally become official in Germany after 1933, with catastrophic consequences few in 1910 could have foreseen. However painful it is to consider what was lost when Mahler died the following year, at the age of just fifty – to reflect on what he might have achieved – we may perhaps be thankful that he passed away innocent of what was to take place later in the nation to which he had offered his stupendous 'gift'.

Notes from a Small Island

'My wish for us all, on your fiftieth birthday, is that
you should come back soon to our hated, beloved
Vienna, and stay here.'[23]

For many years Vienna has basked in its status as 'the capital of classical music', a claim repeated today by the city's official tourist website. The list of composers who lived and produced masterpieces there is awe-inspiring: Haydn, Mozart, Beethoven, Schubert, Brahms, Bruckner, Wolf, Mahler, Schoenberg, Berg, Webern – a roll-call of greats stretching from the so-called 'classical era', through various stages of romanticism to the height of twentieth-century modernism. Yet for most of those figures the city was, as Schoenberg says, a home both beloved and hated. For some visitors there has always been the suspicion that, while the Viennese proudly honour their famous dead in the overwhelming number of plaques and memorial tablets the tourist encounters while strolling around the relatively small city centre, most of its inhabitants still prefer the lighter end of their indigenous classical repertoire. The Viennese emigré composer Hans Gál (1890–1987) would have agreed with them. In his book *The Golden Age of Vienna,* Gál lingers affectionately over the enduring tradition of the Viennese waltz, and its great exponents Joseph Lanner, Johann Strauss, and his sons Johann II and Joseph. Those composers' waltzes were sung and whistled all over the city while the great native-born musical genius Franz Schubert remained largely ignored. Well, what would one expect of such a people? 'If the Viennese were careless, pleasure-seeking and frivolous, if they preferred dancing to thinking, a joke to a sermon, the coffee-house to the library, a waltz to a symphony, the waltz tune at least was the most enchanting and graceful ever invented.'

Whatever the average Viennese may claim, says Gál, it was always in music's 'lower sphere' that unpretentious civic pride was truly located. The waltzes, polkas, galops, the Ruritanian old-world charms of Viennese operetta, the Opera Balls, the New Year concerts – somehow the allure of this lavish fantasy world managed to survive, not only the ignominious collapse of the Habsburg dynasty and the advent of the social democratic 'Red Vienna' in 1918, but even the darker experiences of the Second World War. 'If they have created an imaginary city that has never existed, an El Dorado of "Wine, Women and Song", of perpetual lazy happiness and musical comedy, Vienna may regard it as a just punishment for past sins.'[24]

'Pleasure-seeking and frivolous' – despite the traumas and sins of two world wars, something of that remains true of Vienna even in modern times. This is the city that in 1991, the year of the Mozart bicentenary, thought it fit to welcome musical pilgrims at Schwechat Airport with a life-sized effigy of Mozart made entirely of chocolate, surrounded, on the walls, by poster images of the composer proudly holding aloft the confectionery known as *Mozartkugeln* ('Mozart balls'), bearing the slogan 'Österreichs beste Komposition' (Austria's best composition). In any list of typically Viennese concepts, *Gemütlichkeit* – cosiness, relaxed conviviality, warmth, with perhaps a faint background hint of smugness – would have to figure prominently. How much of it is genuinely felt however, and how much a socially convenient mask, is difficult for outsiders to judge, whatever suspicions they may entertain.

Gál, who fled to Britain after the *Anschluss* in 1938, knew well just how great the city's 'sins' could be. Even long before the horrors of the Third Reich, the Austrian writer Hermann Bahr (1863–1934) observed bitterly that, 'The Viennese will forgive anything ... except greatness. It makes them uncomfortable. The very name Vienna . . . appears inseparable from charm, merriment and nonentity. Vienna signifies the opposite of seriousness.'[25] The Viennese, Bahr tells us, have had a long-established tradition of humiliating great artists and thinkers. He mentions Beethoven, the dramatists Franz Grillparzer and Friedrich Hebbel, Bruckner, Hugo Wolf, the painter Ferdinand Waldmüller, Klimt, the physicist Ernst Mach, Burgtheater director Max Burckhard, and of course Mahler. He could have gone on much longer. As one eminent German conductor (now deceased) put it in conversation with me, 'They turned against Beethoven, neglected Schubert, ridiculed Bruckner, persecuted Mahler, drove out Schoenberg –

and they don't even know where Mozart is *buried*!' For the art historian Peter Vergo, documenting the life and works of Klimt and his allies, it is all summed up by the typically Viennese expression *Hetz*, meaning a hunt or a chase, the delight in public brawls or demonstrations, the real motivation concealed behind a mask of moral indignation. Mahler himself had been on the receiving end of this kind of thing. When he once weighed in to stop a member of the audience hissing during a performance of one of Schoenberg's pieces, the gentleman in question responded by telling Mahler bluntly that he hissed his music as well.

It is so easy to think of Vienna in Mahler's day as a kind of modern Athens: a small city swarming with outstanding artists and thinkers, creating a busy intellectual ferment from which so many world-changing ideas would emerge in a remarkably short period of time. But as the Viennese-born writer Otto Friedländer put it trenchantly, Vienna in the first decade of the twentieth century was one of the intellectual hothouses of the world, but try telling that to the Viennese themselves: 'Two or three thousand people write words or think thoughts that will overturn the world of the next generation – Vienna is oblivious.'

At the city's very centre, says Friedländer, is a tiny circle of intelligent beings – writers, academics, journalists, artists, doctors, lawyers, even politicians – whose thoughts will influence the future of civilisation – and in that, it is worth noting, he turned out to be entirely right. These remarkable people are an 'island'. Nothing connects them with the mainland of Vienna and its pleasure-loving citizens. The city vegetates in its 'happy mediocrity',[26] oblivious to the great things being dreamed and perpetrated in its midst.

But there are few things more stimulating to great minds than having something to react against: the grit in the oyster produces the pearl by irritating it. Time and time again we can hear something like this in Mahler's music: in the waltzes, *Ländler* and other sweetly sentimental tunes, culled from the city's ballrooms, cafés and *Heurigen* (wine taverns), invoked in his symphonies with such tenderness and withering irony – 'our hated, beloved Vienna'. The Scherzo third movement of the Second Symphony is perhaps the most spectacular, certainly the most sustained example of this. Waltz characteristics abound: the characteristic tripping three-in-a-bar rhythm, *immer zu* ('on we go') motifs, (Johann) Straussian upward swoops; later trumpets sing out a sweetly lilting tune straight from the Viennese operetta stage, half touching, half repellent. Sounds and colours shift constantly back and forth from the beguiling, the seductive, to the grotesque, and finally to an outburst of savage full-orchestral violence. Mahler wasn't living in Vienna when he wrote the Second Symphony (though he was soon to return), but whether the 'ballroom' he refers to is in Budapest, Hamburg, Berlin, or any of the other cities he stayed in during the early 1890s, we know perfectly well what is being played there. According to the programme Mahler wrote for Max Marschalk, the Scherzo third movement follows a pastoral reverie, in which the symphony's 'hero' seeks escape from the horrors of death – and of life. The attempt is successful, for a while, but then comes the moment when one has to return to chaos and clamour or day-to-day life, at which point 'this ever-moving, never-resting, never-comprehensible bustle of existence becomes horrible to you, like the swaying of figures in a brightly lit ballroom, into which you look from the dark night outside – and from such a great *distance* that you can no longer hear the music.'[27]

Nature may have restored a sense of connectedness to something primal in the symphony's second movement, but that has now gone. Back in the city life now seems meaningless. Mahler, inhabitant of that tiny intellectual and artistic 'island', as Otto Friedländer calls it, looks out on mainland Vienna, wallowing in its own 'happy mediocrity', and reacts with a full-orchestral cry of horror. Significantly, this movement is a much-expanded reworking of a song based on a text from *Des Knaben Wunderhorn*: 'Des Antonius von Padua Fischpredigt' (St Anthony of Padua's sermon to the fishes), composed in 1893. It tells how St Anthony goes to church to preach but, finding it empty, goes to the river instead to preach to the fishes. They listen attentively, some even compliment him, but at the end, 'sie bleiben wie Allen!' (they remain just the same as ever). The song was whimsical, if a little tart at times; its reworking in the symphony transforms it into an existential nightmare.

But of all Mahler's symphonies, the Eighth is the one that contains the least of this kind of thing. There are no waltzes, *Ländler*, gavottes, galops: hardly a whiff of the ballroom, café or wine-tavern – few places in fact where one feels directly challenged to ask whether what one hears is held up for our admiration, loathing, or both. In that respect Vienna is striking in its absence. Also missing are the funeral marches that turn up, in some guise or other, in almost every one of Mahler's previous symphonies, and which will return to haunt the Ninth and Tenth. Mahler's lifelong fascination with death, so evident in his symphonies and songs, is often explained in terms of his own personal experience: the hours spent beside the deathbed of his brother Ernst at the age of thirteen, the suicide of his brother Otto as he was working on the Second Symphony, and later the death of his own daughter Maria ('Putzi') at the age of six and intimations of his own mortality following the diagnosis of his heart lesion that same year.

But in this Mahler in fact reveals himself as a true *Wiener*. Visitors to the city's Zentralfriedhof (central cemetery) can now enter the lavish museum, in which Vienna's almost cult-like devotion to the pomp and seductive pathos of death is revealed on an impressive scale. One can view the stunningly theatrical black costumes worn by the funeral procession leader, representative of the *pompes funèbres* – the opening of the funeral march from Mahler's Fifth Symphony leaps to mind – or the array of ornamental daggers used to pierce the hearts of bodies ready for burial, to ensure that they were really dead. (Mahler's terror of being buried alive was widely shared in the Vienna of his time.) Granted, many British, French and German cities also boasted a grand necropolis, and Mahler's composition of a set of *Kindertotenlieder* ('Songs on the Deaths of Children') probably wouldn't have been seen as very aberrant by the English and American readers who thrilled to the lovingly protracted 'Death of Little Nell' in Charles Dickens' *The Old Curiosity Shop*. Even so, the Viennese cult of *der schöne Tod* ('the beautiful death') is something quite special, and it lingers even today. Newly married couples still routinely take their wedding fiacre for a turn around the Zentralfriedhof before setting off on honeymoon, and traditional bands in the city's *Heurigen* still delight drinkers with André Heller's old hit 'Wenn i amal stirb' (When I come to die), in which the singer fondly imagines the sumptuous funeral that will one day accompany his own commitment to the earth, as if he were picturing a table covered with typically Viennese dishes and drinks.

So we have two important identifiably Viennese features of Mahler's music – one, it seems, born of antipathy (or at least complicated antipathy), the other of a kind of fellow feeling – both of which are apparently missing from the Eighth Symphony. What then are the grounds for talking of a Viennese, or in the larger sense an Austrian Eighth? To reckon with it in the first of those senses, it is necessary to go back to Otto Friedländer's notion of an intellectual 'island' at the heart of a 'slumbering city', to Mahler's description of his sense of 'distance' from the latter, and to his eventual 'cry of disgust'. Mahler was by no means the only Viennese cultural islander to feel this way, or to turn his rage to creative effect. The Viennese artistic movement known as the Secession began as an expression of a very similar kind of alienation and defiance. The act of secession to which the name refers was the resignation in 1897 by a group of Austrian artists from the long-established and predominantly academically conservative Association of Austrian Artists. For these restless, frustrated young men Vienna's official artistic institutions embodied the very hidebound somnolence and escapism from which they wanted to tear themselves free. They took the radical, then scandalous step of forming their own Union of Austrian Artists, with Gustav Klimt as president, and with its own magazine, *Ver Sacrum*, 'Sacred Truth'. The magazine featured drawings and designs in the lavishly decorative, excitingly anti-classical *Jugendstil* ('youthful style') mode, itself indebted to the French *art nouveau* movement, so execrated by the city's traditional-minded artistic pontiffs. *Ver Sacrum* also included writings by some of the most controversial and challenging names in Europe: Hugo von Hofmannsthal, Rainer Maria Rilke, Maurice Maeterlinck, Richard Dehmel, Knut Hamsun. Everything was permissible – or at least that was the message *Ver Sacrum* wanted to convey. There were even (and this was unusual for Vienna in Mahler's day) women contributors, including the writer and historian Ricarda Huch, later nominated seven times for the Nobel Prize for Literature, who emphasised the vital role of such women as Caroline Schelling, Dorothea von Schlegel and Bettina von Arnim in early German romanticism.

For Stefan Zweig, still a teenager in 1897, it was bliss to be alive in such a dawn, and to be young was very heaven. The young, says Zweig, are the keenest barometer when it comes to detecting significant changes in the cultural climate. For him, and others like him, it was clear that along with the old century a whole host of ideas about art were drawing to an end – that some sort of revolution, a Nietzschean Revaluation of Values, was rapidly approaching:

The good, solid masters of our fathers' time – Gottfried Keller in literature, Ibsen in drama, Johannes Brahms in music, Leibl in painting, Eduard von Hartmann in philosophy – had for us all the measured deliberation of the world of security. In spite of their technical and spiritual mastery, they no longer interested us. We felt instinctively that their cold, well-tempered rhythm was not that of our own restless blood, was no longer chiming with the accelerating tempo of the age.[28]

The Secession was the first clear blast of the trumpet from the sleepy old city's tiny island of free thought. The acceleration in momentum that followed was rapid: tension had evidently been accumulating for a very long time. It finally erupted in 1898 at the opening of the first Vienna Secession exhibition, held in the movement's newly built, stylishly provocative Secession Building, displaying, 'to the horror of the old school', all manner of alarming novelties: the French impressionists and pointillists, the tortured expressionism of Edvard Munch, along with challenging figures from the past the old establishment had preferred to ignore, like the German Renaissance painter Matthias Grünewald and the

Spaniards El Greco and Goya. The Secession's liberating effects in attitudes to the visual arts quickly began to spread to other artistic and intellectual fields, music very much included:

We suddenly learnt to see with their eyes, and at the same time heard rhythms and tone colours in music through the work of Mussorgsky, Debussy, Strauss and Schoenberg. In literature, realism broke through with Zola, Strindberg and Hauptmann, the daemonic Slav spirit with Dostoyevsky, and a previously unknown sublimation and refinement of lyrical literary art in the works of Verlaine, Rimbaud and Mallarmé. Nietzsche revolutionised philosophy; a bolder, freer kind of architecture proclaimed, in the face of overloaded neoclassicism, a plainer, more functional style. Suddenly the old, comfortable order had been shattered, its previously accepted norms of the 'aesthetically beautiful' (as Hanslick put it) were called into question, and while the official critics of our solid bourgeois newspapers often expressed horror at the audacious experiments now being made, and sought to damn them with labels like 'decadent' or 'anarchic', we young people threw ourselves enthusiastically into the thunderous waves wherever they foamed most widely.[29]

Zweig's list of thrilling new names, each one a flag thrust in the face of stolid conservatism and mediocrity, includes several that were of central importance to Mahler, and who turn up repeatedly in his recorded conversation, most notably Nietzsche, and 'the daemonic Slav' Dostoyevsky, whom Mahler described to Richard Specht as his 'best friend'. Mahler too could enter into that Bahr-like spirit of championing the new because it was new, even if he didn't quite believe in it wholeheartedly. His valiant public defence of Schoenberg, when the latter's First Chamber Symphony (1906) was subjected to a particularly noisy demonstration of Viennese *Hetz*, has already been mentioned. Mahler wasn't entirely sure he understood where Schoenberg was headed in this work, and he later confessed to being unable to make sense of the score of Schoenberg's Second String Quartet (1907–8), in which tonality – precarious enough in the first three movements – is finally abandoned in the fourth. But that wasn't the point: Schoenberg was courageous, he was honest, he was clearly very talented and, it should be added, he'd been a loyal supporter of Mahler in the teeth of vicious criticism. He in turn had to be supported, and not just in words: Schoenberg, often on the brink of ruin during his Vienna days, was repeatedly helped out financially by Mahler.

Mahler's involvement with the Secession reached its peak at the 1902 Beethoven Exhibition, the movement's fourteenth and its greatest public success. At the heart of the exhibition hall stood Max Klinger's monumental sculpture of Beethoven, while three of its walls were dominated by Klimt's grand *Beethoven Frieze*. And at the grand private view, where Klinger (never resident in Vienna) was received as guest of honour, the music was provided by Gustav Mahler, conducting excerpts from his own arrangement of Beethoven's Ninth Symphony, the orchestration expanded to include eight horns and four trumpets – exactly the same as in the core brass section of his own Eighth Symphony, composed four years later. The exhibition catalogue included a kind of visual programme note, describing the *Beethoven Frieze* as representing the story of humanity's progress from desire to fulfilment. In essence the narrative strongly resembles that of Wagner's programme note for his Dresden performance of Beethoven's Ninth in 1846, though the language has been updated in suitably *Jugendstil* terms. The succession of images on the walls of the exhibition room are described in a manner recalling Wagner's movement-by-movement narrative analysis of Beethoven's symphony. On the first long wall, confronting the spectators as they arrive, they would immediately encounter 'longing for happiness. The sufferings of Weak Humanity . . . the struggle for happiness.' Then on the narrower wall we find 'the Hostile Powers. The giant Typhon, against whom even the Gods battle in vain.' The second long wall presents 'longing for happiness' which 'finds repose in Poetry'. Finally the Arts themselves lead us into the 'Kingdom of the Ideal', where a choir of heavenly angels is depicted singing the finale of Beethoven's 'Choral' symphony: 'Freude, schöner Götter-funken . . . Diesen Kuss der ganzen Welt' ('Joy, beauteous divine spark . . . This kiss for the whole world').[30]

This ecstatic bringing together of the visual arts, music, architecture and philosophical ideas has often been compared to Wagner's notion of the 'synthesis of the arts', the *Gesamtkunstwerk*. But the figure whose sacred image stood at the heart of this temple, and whose music, with Mahler's assistance, flooded the exhibition hall at that inaugural private view, was not Wagner, but Beethoven – the composer Wagner had attempted to turn into a kind of John the Baptist, the inspired prophet of the musical Messiah that was himself. And the work reverentially reflected in exhibit after exhibit, and above all in Klimt's fabulous frieze, was not a Wagnerian music drama, but a symphony. All of this must have been – the cliché is irresistible – music to Mahler's eyes and ears. As he entered Joseph Maria Olbrich's exhibition hall, he would surely have registered the Secessionist motto resplendent in gold letters above the door: 'Der Zeit ihre Kunst, der Kunst ihre Freiheit' (To the age its art, to art its freedom).

And which work of art was it that was now speaking so resound-
ingly to Mahler and his times? What was the artistic centrepiece
of this momentous exhibition? It was a hugely ambitious choral
symphony, composed nearly a century before, but as relevant as
ever – perhaps more so. The response seemed to bear that out:
the exhibition was a major success, with nearly sixty thousand
people attending. The tiny cultural island at the heart of Vienna
– the archipelago of cafés, taverns and private apartments where
the city's alienated, scorned artists and thinkers thrashed out their
manifestos – didn't feel quite so tiny any more. And yet, how many
of those that saw and heard were like the fishes at the end of St
Anthony of Padua's sermon, as described in *Des Knaben Wunderhorn*? 'Die Predit hat g'fallen / sie bleiben wie Allen' (The sermon
has pleased them / but they remain just the same as ever).

While some critics joined the audiences in cheering on Mahler's
performances at the Court Opera and with the Vienna Philharmonic, not least when Mahler brought in the leading Secessionist
Alfred Roller to design the sets for his 1903 production of Wagner's *Tristan und Isolde*, others dissented vigorously, and reactions
to Mahler's own music remained prevailingly indifferent or bitterly hostile. After the Vienna premiere of his Third Symphony
– the work that had scored such a hit at its premiere in the German city of Krefeld, one critic had stated bluntly that Mahler
deserved a term in jail for perpetrating such an outrage. And in
the background was the ominous undercurrent of antisemitism.
In 1895, two years before Mahler's return to Vienna, the politi-
cian Karl Lueger, 'Handsome Karl' as he was widely known, had
led his overtly antisemitic Christian Social Party to victory in the
city's mayoral elections. To his eternal credit, the emperor Franz
Joseph had refused to confirm Lueger's appointment. Franz Joseph

distrusted Lueger and disliked his antisemitism – this was, after all, the same emperor who in 1860, the year of Mahler's birth, had relaxed the laws of abode for Jews (previously tightly regulated), which made it possible for Gustav's father Bernhard to move to Iglau and start his brewery business there. But in 1897, the year of Mahler's 'conversion' to Roman Catholicism, Franz Joseph finally yielded to pressure from several fronts (including the Vatican) and gave Lueger his official position. Naturally Lueger's supporters were no fans of Mahler, either as conductor or composer, and some were vocal in the city's press. As Lueger's popularity grew (his work on improving the city's utilities and social welfare was undeniably highly effective), the appeal of his ideas grew too – as Mahler would have been well aware. It was Lueger who so impressed the young Adolf Hitler, who came to Vienna in 1907, the year Mahler departed for New York. They overlapped by a month, so it is possible that Mahler saw Hitler, selling his watercolours of the city sights, on one of his walks along the Ringstrasse.

So while Mahler may have shared the Secessionists' yearning to send the world a divine kiss of joy, the question remains, which world? Part of the attraction of the German humanist vision outlined in the previous section was that it was 'ideal', as Mahler surely realised, perhaps even in his youthful nationalist days at the Vienna Conservatory. Like his fellow *Wiener*, Franz Schubert, nearly a century earlier, there must often have been times when Mahler felt like crying out 'Schöne Welt, wo bist du?' (Beautiful world, where are you?). If at times he found it in dreams of an ideal, transcendent, Goethean Germanness, there were others when he looked beyond anything in this, in Nietzsche's words, 'all too human' world. If so, Mahler's thoughts and feelings would have found echo throughout Vienna's embattled cultural 'island':

'Faced with scorn and incomprehension', says Peter Vergo, 'the artist's gaze grew more distant, embracing a vision that lay beyond the immediate present – a vision which could be neither perfectly defined nor completely expressed but which, in its scope, its infinite grandeur, transcended the boundaries of this vale of tears.'[31] The writer Berta Zuckerkandl remembered how Klimt responded to press accusations of being a pornographer: the right course of action, Klimt urged, was not to fight back, but to affirm. A friend suggested to Klimt that he take legal action. How long would such an action take, asked Klimt? About two days, came the reply. Wouldn't it be better, Klimt replied, just to spend those two days painting? To the age its art? Perhaps, but perhaps that art could only find its desired freedom in some other, transcendent realm. Writing to his friend and champion, the Dutch conductor Willem Mengelberg, at the end of that staggeringly productive summer of 1906, Mahler reveals that 'I have just completed my Eighth [Symphony] – it is the greatest thing I have done so far . . . Just imagine that the universe is beginning to sound and to ring. It is no longer human voices, but circling planets and suns.'[32]

Just two years later, as Arnold Schoenberg made his desperate plunge into the unknown territory of atonality in his Second String Quartet in 1908, he set words by the German poet Stefan George that similarly turn away from humanity and stretch out toward distant worlds:

Ich fühle luft von anderem planeten.
Mir blassen durch das dunkel die gesichter
Die freundlich eben noch sich zu mir drehten.

I feel breath from another planet.

Palely, through the darkness, faces loom
That once were turned to me in friendship.

Only where Mahler's Eighth Symphony ends in glory, in redemption for the Faustian striver, Schoenberg's far bleaker vision seems
to offer hope only in mystical self-extinction:

Ich bin ein funke nur vom heiligen feuer
Ich bin ein dröhnen nur der heiligen stimme.

I am just a spark of the holy fire
I am just a murmur of the holy voice.[33]

*

Put together the words 'Vienna' and 'eroticism' and images and
thoughts flood to mind: Gustav Klimt's ravishing masterpiece *The
Kiss* (in German *Liebespaar*, 'Lovers'; 1907–8), the worldly-wise
Marschallin and her younger lover climaxing ecstatically to fanfares of whooping horns in Richard Strauss's *Der Rosenkavalier*
(1909–10), or perhaps Sigmund Freud, in his hushed consulting
room in the Berggasse, listening attentively as the wives of prosperous merchants and city officials confessed their most intimate
secrets to him. Florian Illies sums up this erotically charged *Zeitgeist* in his brilliantly kaleidoscopic study *1913: The Year Before the
Storm*. One need only think of the works of Klimt and Schiele.
When one looks at their drawings and paintings, with those long,
sensual lines, is what one is seeing pornography (as some vocal
antagonists claimed) or something closer to the emergent 'New
Objectivity' – or possibly both? Here surely are the luxuriant

curves beloved of the Vienna the psychoanalyst and author Lou Andreas-Salomé dubbed the most erotic city in the world. One of the first things we notice in Klimt's paintings of women, says Illies, is probably the luxurious golden ornament; but in his sketches he encircled their bodies with 'an inimitable line that swept across the page, softly undulating like curls falling loose over a shoulder'. But Schiele went even further into challenging territory in his explorations of the human body – not just of women, but also of his own: 'the forms he depicted were tormented, strained with nerves and martyred, distorted, more sexual than erotic. Where Klimt's work reveals soft skin, Schiele shows nerves and sinews; where Klimt's bodies flow, Schiele's splay, entangle and contort. Klimt's women lure, while Schiele's shock.'[34]

How close this seems to Mahler's own sound-world – or, rather, sound-worlds. Klimt's 'inimitable line . . . softly undulating like curls falling loose over a shoulder' is echoed in later stages of Mahler's great hymn to Eros, 'the creator of the world', in the closing stages of the Eighth Symphony. The string section may lead the lyricism, as it usually does in Mahler, but the enhancement of those lines with celeste, harps, piano and mandolin (silent in the symphony's first part) often feels close to the way Klimt ornaments his paintings with gold and precious stones. The hushed instrumental section before the final chorus, the passage that so enchanted Anton Webern, could have been created by a composer trying to realise the ravishing yet delicately precise sensuality of *The Kiss*, or of parts of the *Beethoven Frieze*, in music. Something of Mahler's 'Klimt' sound palate lingers, in a somewhat more attenuated form, in the sublime 'song-symphony', *Das Lied von der Erde*, composed after Mahler's two great convulsive shocks of 1907 – the death of Maria and the diagnosis of his heart condition. But then, in the Ninth Symphony (1909–10), we find something closer to Schiele's 'entangled and contorted' linear thinking, 'martyred, distorted, more sexual than erotic', especially in the *Rondo-Burleske* third movement, which Mahler dedicated sarcastically 'to my brothers in Apollo' – the Viennese critics who had mocked him for his alleged contrapuntal incompetence. Eros as god in the Eighth Symphony has become Eros as demon in the Ninth. It was in 1910, too, that Schiele began his radical experimentation with the naked human body, sparking an immediate critical uproar.

And here is another paradoxical aspect of Vienna, not often made explicit in popular portrayals of the city as an easy-going paradise (at least for men) of 'wine, women and song'. Mahler's 'hated, beloved' home city could also be remarkably prudish, especially when it came to its treatment of women. For Stefan Zweig, the prevailing attitude was 'doubly mendacious'. On the one hand it averted its gaze from the sexual exploits of young men, or even winked encouragement to them – nothing wrong with 'sowing a few wild oats'. But it was a very different matter when it came to women:

That a man could feel and should be allowed to feel certain urges was silently endorsed by convention. But to concede that Creation, for the fulfilment of its eternal plan, required that the female element should also be subject to them, would have offended against the whole notion of the 'Sanctity of Women'. Before Freud, it was accepted as a self-evident truth that a woman had no sexual urges until such were awakened in her by a man, although of course that was only officially permitted in marriage.[35]

Women – and particularly young girls – had therefore to be protected from anything suggestive of 'certain urges'. Girls from middle- or upper-class families were never left alone. They were escorted everywhere, and at home had governesses to police their every private moment, to supervise their reading matter, to ensure that, under all circumstances in which another human being might be present, as little as possible of their bodies would be exposed to scrutiny – or even to fresh air. Purity was the watchword, and even in the immediate preparation for a girl's wedding night, it was very likely that nothing at all would be said to her about what would be expected of her once the bedroom doors were closed. Zweig remembered an aunt who, at one in the morning on her wedding night, turned up at her parents' apartment insisting that she never wanted to set eyes on her husband again. Why, the monster had actually tried to take her clothes off! It's the sort of anecdote one can imagine eliciting hearty guffaws at a smoke-fogged, Schnapps-reeking, all-male *gemütlich* gathering. But for girls brought up in such enforced chastity, suddenly to be pitched into the world of men and sex in such a manner must have been traumatic. Whatever one thinks of psychoanalytical doctrine, the casebooks of Freud and his colleagues and disciples testify again and again to the lasting traumatic effects of such shock encounters. In the literature in German that appeared in Mahler's lifetime, resonant female voices are hard to find: there is no George Eliot or Virginia Woolf, no Edith Wharton or Emily Dickinson; even male writers capable of sustained compassionate insight into the female predicament – equivalents of Norway's Henrik Ibsen or America's Henry James – are rare. Nevertheless, perhaps the most poignant and disturbing account of the kind of potentially devastating experience Zweig describes is to be found in a novella by Arthur Schnitzler, *Fräulein Else* (1924). For all his priapic, Casanova-like tendencies, Schnitzler shows surprising empathy in his description of the tragic consequences of the sudden, violent destruction of innocence. How striking though that this should have appeared well after the downfall of imperial Vienna, when the milieu Zweig describes so memorably had begun to change.

The paradox is that, as Zweig says, for all the adults' efforts to shield their daughters from sex, the very atmosphere of Vienna in particular was charged with a dangerously infectious eroticism. This was a Roman Catholic city, once capital of the self-styled Holy Roman Empire, and the city's churches were full of the kind of half-disguised, half-celebrated sensual imagery that made Northern Protestant visitors turn away in righteous horror: breast-feeding Madonnas, male and female saints undergoing all manner of scantily clad tortures and martyrdoms with looks of orgasmic transfiguration on their faces. The whole spirit of rococo devotional art was charged with that spirit of barely sublimated eroticism that sings out so beautifully and shamelessly in the 'Et incarnatus' of Mozart's Mass in C minor, and which blazes out in some of the solo sections in Part II of the Eighth Symphony. The words of Pater Ecstaticus – the solo that gave Mahler his nickname *Ewige Wonnebrand* ('eternal flame of joy') – could have come straight from the mouth of one those agonisingly contorted plaster saints. The breast's 'seething pain' is the token of its 'foaming Divine bliss' – 'Arrows, pierce though me, Lances, subdue me, Cudgels, smash me, Lightning, shoot through me!' – all so that 'everything worthless' might fade into nothingness, and the 'everlasting star' might shine through, 'Seed of Eternal Love!' The luxurious pain and willed humiliation of the novel *Venus im Pelz* ('Venus in Furs',

1870) by Leopold von Sacher-Masoch – from whom the term 'masochism' derives – is barely a martyr's breath away.

It wasn't just in the churches: Eros might be waiting in other kinds of public spaces. Take Vienna's most famous concert venue, the Great Hall of the Wiener Musikverein, erected in the 1860s as part of Franz Joseph's sweeping urban reconstruction plans. Its decor is the embodiment of Zweig's 'double mendacity': a description of this forms a highpoint in Simon Winder's ebullient and thought-provoking *Danubia: A Personal History of Habsburg Europe*. There will be some visitors to the famous Musikverein who will find comfort in Winder's description of its much-celebrated concert hall as 'a temple to the bad taste of the 1860s'. Yes, of course the acoustics are wonderful, and the sense of musical history (*how* many great works have had their premieres in this one room?) can induce a feeling of quasi-religious reverence. But what about the decor – and in particular those ranks of nude female caryatids lined up along the walls? The identical, impassive, doll-like faces are certainly unnerving, but what really stand out – in both senses of the phrase – are the caryatids' breasts. It would be interesting, Winder muses, to see the minutes of the meeting of the working committee for the design of the Musikverein at which those breasts must have been discussed: 'Presumably, once the reckless and by no means in-the-bag decision to have nude female caryatids lining a public building had been taken, there must have been a number of awkward debates about the breasts, with different factions arguing for different levels of realism, heft and enjoyableness, and concerns raised about how much they may be a distraction at Brahms's next recital.'[36] No doubt embarrassed prudery played a part, which might explain the strange conical shapes of the caryatids' mammaries; but there they were, in shocking numbers, a source of anxious distraction for the

governesses and their young charges, and of no doubt more lubri-
cious speculations for the male concertgoers.

In the face of all this, Mahler's declared determination to acknowledge (in Stefan Zweig's words) 'that for its eternal purposes creation
required the feminine as well as the masculine principle' looks
increasingly like an act of provocation – a gauntlet thrown down at
the feet of conventional Viennese morality. If so, it was an attitude
and an aim he shared with the Secessionists. The press and public
officialdom might accuse Klimt and his fellows of being pornog-
raphers, but many of these artists saw themselves as engaged in
a war of liberation. The poet Peter Altenberg wrote that Klimt's
female nudes seemed to him an act of defiant liberation, expressing a determination to throw off the bondage of sexual repression.
Such open acknowledgement that female sexuality even existed
was a major step forward in a society determined to avert its gaze
from such dangerous, destabilising possibilities. And yet in so much
of the writing of the Secessionists, and of their Viennese literary
kindred spirits, and in almost everything Mahler wrote about his
Eighth Symphony, the spirit of Goethe's *Ewig-Weibliche* hovers,
half-inspiring, half-troubling. In her essay 'Figurations of the
Feminine in Goethe's *Faust*', Ellis Dye takes issue with the German
scholar Gail K. Hart and her relatively positive reading of the *Ewig-
Weibliche* as 'ultimately a feminised projection of [Faust] himself'.
It is, says Dye, 'rather, an imposition of male concepts on women'.
Goethe's *Faust*, she continues, tells the reader nothing about what
it means to be female, only what the notion of 'femaleness' means
to men: 'Indeed it would take no great leap of the imagination to
think of Goethe's drama as the story of a needy male conscious-
ness addressed to a *female* audience.'[37] The use of the word 'needy'
is telling there. And it would take even less of a leap of the imagina-

tion to think of Mahler's Eighth Symphony in those same terms. By September 1910, as we've already seen, Mahler had convinced himself that the symphony was addressed to one very particular female audience, and for reasons of the most desperate need. There are also good reasons for taking Gail K. Hart's notion of the *Ewig-Weibliche* as a 'feminised projection' of its creator seriously in relation to the Eighth Symphony. Both points will be examined at greater length when we consider Mahler's consultation with Sigmund Freud in 1910. Discussion of Vienna and the erotic inevitably leads to Freud and to the newly emerging 'science' of psychoanalysis. How much Freud's ideas were discussed and approved in the city by 1910 is hard to gauge, but some – even on that narrow cultural island – had their doubts. As the brilliant and fiercely independent-minded satirist Karl Kraus (1874–1943) observed, it all looked suspiciously like voyeurism disguised as scientific rationalism: the psycholanalysts are ready to explain everything in the world in terms of sexual urges – except, that is, for their own profession! Karl Pringsheim, brother of Thomas Mann's wife Katia, worked with Mahler as repetiteur at the Vienna Opera. He remembered a conversation with the composer the year after the completion of the Eighth Symphony. Some time in the late summer of 1907 Pringsheim spent an evening with the Mahlers, during which he brought up the name of Freud. Mahler's reaction was a sudden silence. Psychoanalysis was clearly not a subject on which this normally voluble and highly articulate man wished to expand. All he did was make a dismissive gesture, accompanied by the words, 'Freud, he tries to cure or solve everything from a certain aspect.'[38] That 'certain aspect' was not to be named, especially not in Alma's presence, Pringsheim concluded.

If so, this suggests that Mahler knew worryingly little about the mind of his own wife, whose private diaries were remarkably frank about her own sexual feelings and experiences. And just three years later, in June 1910, Mahler was to write ecstatically to Alma about the role of Eros, the 'creator of the world', in artistic creation. Was it just a matter of wording? Or had Mahler's own thinking begun to shift in Freud's direction? As Mahler indicates in that letter to Alma about the Eighth Symphony, the notion that erotic impulses might be 'sublimated' – directed away from instant gratification towards 'higher' goals – had been foreshadowed by Plato in his *Symposium*. Nietzsche too had explored the notion, in the process asking the valid question of whether an impulse should still be called 'sexual' if it no longer had the sex act itself as its goal. Was it something intrinsic to the urge that defined it as sexual, or was it the nature of its object? Nietzsche's answer was that the true basic urge in human beings was one of 'will to power'. But Freud disagreed. The sexual urge was fundamental, but civilisation – the peaceful, mutually co-operative co-existence of human beings within defined social and ethical limits – demanded that such impulses be restrained. For Freud, sublimation was a vitally important safety valve, deflecting primary animal instincts into acts of value to society as a whole. It was an outstanding feature of human cultural development, keeping dangerous instinctual urges at bay, but at the same time making possible their redirection into creative activity, expressing itself in works of science, art and ideology, all essential to civilised life. That does sound close to Mahler's own thinking, at least as expressed in that letter to Alma. One can find similar notions, openly or covertly expressed, in the writings of several of the Secessionists, and of writers like Stefan Zweig and Arthur Schnitzler. Intellectual Vienna, it seems, was buzzing with this kind of talk: it was a central strand in the 'revolution' Stefan Zweig described above. For millennia, God or gods had been the inspiration for great art. If, as Nietzsche had proclaimed, God was dead, could a humanised, or even a mystical Eros take His place? If so, then Mahler clearly saw – or came to see – the Eighth Symphony as his earth-shaking advent hymn.

*

But Vienna is not Austria, any more than Paris is France, or London Britain – or indeed than Mahler's newly adopted professional home of New York is America. However insular the attitudes of these cities' inhabitants might seem to outsiders, Mahler for one certainly turned his gaze outside. As a student he once claimed that he learned more from walking in the Vienna woods than from any lectures at the Conservatory. When it came to composing, Vienna may have been good enough for revising, contrapuntally enriching, orchestrating the work he had done during his precious few months of summer holiday, but it was away from the city that the bulk of the work was done, amidst those very mountain gorges, forests, cliffs and wide open wildernesses Goethe had listed in his stage direction for the final scene of *Faust*, which Mahler had reverently reproduced in his score. 'Hier ist die Aussicht frei, der Geist erhoben' (here the view is unrestricted, the spirit lifted up) sings Doctor Marianus at the beginning of his first solo. Mahler who, as Ernst Decsey tells us, knew great chunks of *Faust* Part II by heart, must have remembered those words as he stood amongst the high Alpine pastures he loved so intensely.

At the opening of Part II the features of the musical landscape are unmistakably Austrian. The violins' hushed high opening tremolo (after the initial *sforzando* jab) is a clear echo of the nebulous string tremolos that open five of Bruckner's symphonies, or which shimmer quietly in the background in those points of stillness where Bruckner seems to pause, draw breath and drink in space around him. To many Bruckner-lovers they suggest huge vistas, such as one might enjoy all the more after a long, strenuous climb. In one of the most beautiful of these, at the heart of the first movement of Bruckner's Eighth Symphony, a sense of depth is added by the deep, quiet brass tones, contrasting strongly with the ethereal high strings – exactly the kind of potently evocative texture we hear at several points in the orchestral introduction to Part II of Mahler's Eighth. When Richard Strauss wanted to recreate the sense of awe-inspiring space and vertiginous height in the section of his *Alpine Symphony* entitled 'On the Summit', he similarly drew on Bruckner for inspiration. Bruckner's influence can also be heard in the carefully measured, steady build-up of the Eighth Symphony's magnificent final crescendo. This, like the Schubertian lyrical momentum, borne forward on flowing song-like accompaniments, in the solo sections in the symphony's second part, is quite different from the dramatic 'progression by contraries' dialectic that prevails in Beethoven's symphonies and in Part I of Mahler's Eighth. Given the inevitability and frequency with which Schubert's and Bruckner's names come to mind in Part II, it is tempting to think of this as representing a more Austrian – or at least more Austrian romantic – kind of symphonic thinking, steeped in the contemplation of nature. The kind of German, Hegelian purposefulness – in which everything is justified by, rationalised by, the goal that will inevitably be attained – seems rather less pressing here. The Germans, wrote Nietzsche in *Beyond Good and Evil*, 'would be Hegelians even if there had never been a Hegel, in so far as we (different in this from the Latin nations) instinctively attribute to "becoming", to "developing", a deeper meaning and a richer value than to that which "is" – we

can hardly believe that the notion "being" is justified'. And earlier, more aphoristically, Nietzsche states bluntly that, 'a German
is not, he *becomes*, he "develops"'. But there are moments in the
second part of Mahler's Eighth Symphony – in marked contrast
to Part I – where the music does seem, if only for a few moments,
content just to 'be': in that Brucknerian Alpine pastoral opening,
before the sense of expectancy begins to mount; in the Mater Gloriosa's rapt 'Come! Come! Raise yourself to higher spheres!'; and
in that moment of heavenly stillness, with those touchingly childlike piccolo and clarinet solos, just before movement resumes in
the final Chorus Mysticus. In such moments it can seem that 'the
unfulfillable, / Here becomes real' (Das Unzulängliche, / Hier
wird's Ereignis), if only for a few fleeting moments.

'Everywhere an Intruder'

As has already been observed, most of Mahler's symphonies
contain quotations from, or allusions to, songs. Sometimes they
are Mahler's own songs, sometimes those of others. Many claims
have been made as to possible sources, with varying degrees of
plausibility, and great swathes of inference have been drawn from
them. For those who like tracking down such things, the Eighth
Symphony has often proved disappointing – certainly when compared to, say, the Fifth Symphony. But there is one very striking
reference to a song in the Eighth Symphony's second part, and
it occurs at a crucial moment: the hushed beginning of the final
Chorus Mysticus. The soprano motif, along with its harmonisa-
tion, in the first two bars, is a relative-major transformation of
the opening theme of the Adagio section from Schubert's Fantasia in C, 'The Wanderer', D760, for solo piano. Transpose the

Schubert down just a semitone from C sharp minor to C minor
and the resemblance becomes patent:

Schubert: Wanderer Fantasy   Mahler: Symphony No 8
(Transposed to C minor)   Chorus mysticus

Mahler would have known, and almost certainly played, the
'Wanderer' Fantasy during his student days at the Vienna Conservatory. It was one of Schubert's most popular instrumental pieces at
the time – significantly more so than the three great piano sonatas
composed in Schubert's last year. Mahler's playing of Schubert at
that time was apparently much admired. But the theme, as presented at the beginning of Schubert's slow movement, is itself a
reference (and how Mahler must have enjoyed that!) to one of his
own songs: 'Der Wanderer' (The Wanderer), also very popular
in Mahler's time, though somewhat less so today. The landscape
from which the song's narrator emerges is the very mountain wilderness in which Part II of Mahler's Eighth Symphony begins. But
the scenery he arrives at, physically and emotionally, when the
motif in Ex 6.1(b) declares itself could hardly be less like that of
Goethe's Heaven:

> *Die Sonne dünkt mich hier so kalt,*
> *Die Blüte welk, das Leben alt,*
> *Und was die reden, leerer Schall,*
> *Ich bin ein Fremdling überall.*

The sun is so cold to me here,
The blossom is faded, and life grows old,
And what men say to me sounds empty,
I am a stranger everywhere.

I am a stranger, an alien, an intruder everywhere – it is more than likely that Mahler would have had those words at least at the back of his mind when he told Alma that he was 'thrice homeless . . . everywhere an intruder'. It isn't simply a matter of quotation: the progress of the motif outlined in Ex 6.1 (b) through Part II of the Eighth Symphony can also be seen as symptomatic. Writing about this work in the Simon and Schuster *Companion to the Symphony* in 1992, this writer took Mahler to task for his treatment of this (and another of the symphony's leading themes) in the second part. Self-citation is almost always a vice, but in this case, rather than put another commentator in the firing range, I prefer to admit that I too can get it monumentally wrong. The problem, I alleged, was that the themes didn't lend themselves easily to sequential modification – they clung too resolutely to their own identity. The kinds of expressive and dramatic transformation that were so crucial to the musical narratives of the Fifth and Ninth Symphonies were therefore largely absent. This was the reason, I claimed, why the Eighth Symphony's final climax could for some listeners (my listener poll was hardly exhaustive) seem less convincing in context than when the last ten minutes or so were heard – say on a recording – on their own. It was not just that there had been too much of the two leading motifs, I concluded, but that their effect had grown stale through the lack of meaningful transformation.

It is hard now to think of a better justification of Samuel Johnson's remark that, when assessing one's own work immediately after completing it, if something strikes the author as particularly fine, the best policy is to delete it. The above, one might justly say, is what comes from wallowing in individual CD tracks rather than listening to the whole work. It is also obvious to me now that in wanting Part II of the Eighth Symphony to be more like the Fifth and Ninth Symphonies, I was simply incapable of letting it speak for itself. The symphony's first part may be a thrilling drama of becoming – of the very purposefulness characterised as 'German' by Nietzsche – but the second is a different creature entirely. What happens to the motif Ex. 6.1(b) is far closer to the 'wandering' journey undergone by Ex. 6.1(a) in Schubert's Fantasia. In Part II of the Eighth Symphony Mahler reveals the depth of his kinship to Schubert, so tellingly identified by Romain Rolland. Schubert's Fantasia begins in what seems to be a heroic, Beethovenian mode – Beethoven's 'Waldstein' Sonata, op. 53, is almost certainly the primary model. But soon the heroic drive is abandoned, in favour of something more lyrical, contemplative, sustained by the kind of continuous rippling accompaniment one finds in so many of Schubert's songs, or in what Mahler himself called the 'giant guitar' figurations given to piano and harp during Doctor Marianus's solo, just before the Chorus Mysticus. When the musicologist Alfred Einstein published his pioneering study of Schubert in 1951, it was still common for critics to reproach Schubert for this kind of dereliction of romantic-heroic duty. What was the purpose, the goal of all this? Where was the true, Beethovenian development? What had happened to 'becoming'? Einstein responded with the kind of insight that was all too rare in those days – fortunately it is much less so today. Such critics had accused Schubert's last three sonatas of doing what the 'Wanderer' Fantasy was also said to have done: abandoning the cause in favour of aimless daydreaming, 'wandering' in the pejorative sense. Not so, said Einstein: it wasn't that Schubert *couldn't* create development. (There is enough proof that he could in works like the 'Great' C major Symphony and the 'Death and the Maiden' Quartet.) It was that he had something quite different in mind – something just as valid artistically. Take, for example, the A major Piano Sonata, D959: 'everything that could be called "development" finds its way into the exposition, and in place of the development proper Schubert spins a dreamy, ballad-like web of sound, the very existence of which is its own best justification.'[39]

'A dreamy, ballad-like web of sound' – that is exactly the kind of sound that accompanies the soul of Faust on the final stages of its journey to the 'higher spheres'. For English listeners, the musical momentum here may be strongly reminiscent of the words sung by the departed Soul in Part Two of Elgar's *The Dream of Gerontius*, as he begins his progress towards the throne of God:

> . . . A uniform
> And gentle pressure tells me that I am not
> Self-moving, but borne forward on my way.

It is this sense of a steady current, sustained in the background even when the surface appears agitated, which helps explain why for many, like the musicologist and composer Harold Truscott, the more one gets to know the Eighth Symphony, the less time it seemed to take to get to its exultant end: the symphony itself seemed to grow shorter. Even the philosopher Theodor Adorno, notoriously agnostic when it came to the Eighth Symphony, conceded that its second part is 'endowed with a mighty, evolving subterranean flow'.[40]

Of course the Wanderer is a familiar romantic trope. The iconic image is the famous painting by Caspar David Friedrich, *Der Wanderer über dem Nebelmeer* ('The Wanderer above the Sea of Mist', 1818), which depicts a young man, his back to the viewer, stick grasped in his right hand, standing high up in precisely the kind of rocky mountain landscape Mahler loved, and which Goethe described in his scenic stage direction. It is the landscape too from which Schubert's anti-hero emerges at the beginning of the song 'Der Wanderer'. Mahler would also have been well aware of the link, in the works of many German romantic writers and composers, between this image and the legendary figure of the 'Wandering Jew', who according to the Christian tradition taunted Jesus on the way to his crucifixion and was doomed to walk the earth without rest until the Second Coming, 'everywhere an intruder'. The 'dreamy, ballad-like web of sound' is also the kind of texture that accompanies one of Schubert's most famous wanderers, the young miller in the song cycle *Die schöne Müllerin* ('The Fair Maid of the Mill') as he strides forth in conversation with his friend, the murmuring brook. In Part II of the symphony, the first solo for Gretchen (Una Poenitentium) is introduced with a walking and rippling texture that vividly recalls some of the miller's earlier songs. The use of the mandolin (its first entry in the symphony) is telling here – in Mahler's next work, *Das Lied von der Erde*, the instrument is directly identified with the sound of a brook, whose current carries the song towards its final image of blissful extinction. Mahler's identification with Schubert's miller, and with his more darkly alienated cousin, the anti-hero of Schubert's *Winterreise* ('Winter Journey'), is made explicit in his own song cycle *Lieder eines fahrenden Gesellen* ('Songs of a Wayfarer'), which also tells of a young man rejected in love, progressively estranged from nature, who eventually realises that relief from his pain can be found only in death. But at this point we need to pause for a moment. Surely the fate of Schubert's wanderers is, on the face of it, entirely different from that of the soul of Faust? 'There, where you are not, there is happiness,' is the final revelation in Schubert's song 'Der Wanderer'. Faust however is released from constant striving, to be borne aloft into the arms of the Eternal Mother-Goddess. Has Mahler somehow contrived to give the Wanderer a happy ending?

There are reasons to be doubtful. Any commentator on music would do well to bear in mind the acute observation of the philosopher Ernst Bloch: that when we listen to music, what we really hear is ourselves. But remember the words of Lilli Lehmann, responding to the Eighth Symphony's first performance: 'The second part of the symphony . . . touched me painfully. Was it he, his music, his appearance, a premonition of death, Goethe's words . . . ?' That Lehmann is honest enough to interrogate herself as to the cause of her reaction gives her words added credibility. Others have had similar feelings about this music, not just about the sombre orchestral introduction or Pater Profundus's agonised solo, but even about the seemingly triumphant ending. Writing about the final scene of Goethe's play, Ellis Dye is reminded of the outcome of *Die schöne Müllerin*, where it is the brook to which the miller boy returns in death, and that sings one of the most tender lullabies in all music over his body. There is after all something rather eerie about the conclusion of *Faust* Part II – something that comes into focus if one compares Goethe's Heavenly apotheosis with the second part of *The Dream of Gerontius*. Few, one imagines, would claim that John Henry Newman was as fine a poet or as profound a thinker as Goethe. But one of the things that makes *The Dream of Gerontius* so compelling in its later stages is that the Soul's adventures continue, dramatically, even after he has departed this world. We hear, and feel, his reaction to his first meeting with his guardian angel, to the raging of the demons, to the hymning of the angelic choirs circling the divine throne, and to the shattering split-second vision of God Himself. Faust, on the other hand, speaks not a word. He has not done so since the moment of his death, two scenes earlier. All we have is a description of his reawakening – or, rather, the awakening of Faust's 'immortal essence' (*Faustens Unsterbliches*) – by his former lover, Gretchen, now named as Una Poenitentium – the second soprano in Mahler's setting. This 'new arrival', she tells us, is hardly aware of where, or even what he is:

> See how he breaks his earthly bands
> And shakes off the old husk,
> And from the ethereal garment
> The strength of earliest youth comes forth!
> Allow me to enlighten him:
> The new day dazzles him!

The poetry is beautiful, but there is something unreal about all of this. Are we seriously meant to believe that this 'ethereal' newborn spirit is the same driven, morally questionable being whose varied, colourful, sometimes troubling exploits Goethe has charted through *Faust* Part I and the greater part of Part II? It could be argued that Gretchen was more Faust's victim than his willing lover, given the part diabolical trickery played in her seduction. (Mephistopheles tells Faust that she is a 'very innocent little thing'.) If to all intents and purposes that Faust is truly dead in the concluding scene of Part II, is it really possible to believe that the old restless, continually striving Faust hasn't died with him? Is there perhaps something in Mahler's music that reflects, even enhances the sense of loss, or of doubt, that so troubled Lilli Lehmann? Perhaps, as Theodor Adorno implies, the massive insistency of the symphony's closing moments contains an element of pathos. Perhaps, in Shakespeare's words, it 'protests too much'. 'Sometimes', in those very Mahlerian words of Beethoven, 'the opposite is also true.' Or, we could take another of Mahler's artistic and philosophical idols, Fyodor Dostoyevsky. Dostoyevsky could with justice be described as a partly converted Christian. But – and this was evidently a significant element in his appeal for Mahler – he was also capable of confronting and acknowledging his own doubts, as a letter to a friend from 1861 demonstrates. There is, says Dostoyevsky, a kind of believer who, despite his seeming assurance and his energetic attempts to convert others, is privately consumed with doubts. Eventually someone realises this and confronts him: why this raging, impassioned conviction in one who doubts his own assertions? The reason, Dostoyevsky confesses, is 'a persistent urge to convert himself'.[41] If others can be converted, and thus give their assent to the doubter's 'beliefs', perhaps he will even come to believe in them truly in his own heart.

'A persistent urge to convert himself' – how often do we hear that in Mahler's music? Several musicians and commentators have heard exactly that in the apparently affirmative, Brucknerian conclusion of the Fifth Symphony. Deryck Cooke found the Fifth's darkness–light opposition 'schizophrenic', while the triumphant return at the end of the finale of the chorale, formerly associated with tragic failure, could in itself be seen as emphasising, rather

than reconciling, the 'dangerously disparate' elements in the symphony.[42] When it comes to the matter of dangerous disparity, Alma
is characteristically blunt. She remembers how, towards the end of
the couple's summer holiday in 1902, Mahler played through the
newly completed Fifth Symphony on the piano. As this was the
first time he had played a new work to her, Mahler insisted on
making something of a ceremony out of it. The couple climbed
up to his composing hut arm in arm, with measured solemnity.
When Mahler had finished, Alma was full of praise for the music
– all except for one important detail: the concluding return in triumph of the chorale. She wasn't sure about it, she told him. It was
too hymn-like, and – one can imagine Mahler's astonishment at
this – 'boring'. 'Yes, but Bruckner –' he retaliated. Bruckner had
ended his Fifth Symphony with a magnificent chorale sounding,
like the chorale in Mahler's own Fifth, on full brass through cascading string figurations. 'He yes,' Alma replied; 'but you no,' and
she tells us that as they made their way back down to the house she
attempted to explain to him why his nature was so radically different from Bruckner's: 'I was touching here on a rift in his being
which often brought him into serious conflict with himself.'[43]

Can we perhaps hear something of the 'rift in his being' in the
'whispered' opening of the Eighth Symphony's Chorus Mysticus
– the moment when Mahler recalls the desolation of Schubert's
'Der Wanderer' and the words he clearly associated with himself?
As the Wanderer motif yields rapturously to the embrace of the
Ewig-Weibliche, and the bass line falls languorously, are the arms
that encircle him those of eternal love, or schöner Tod, 'beautiful
Death'? In fact there is no need to speak of rifts here. The notion
that the face of Eros can also be the face of Death is an old one,
much explored by German romantics: think of Schubert's famous

song 'Der Tod und das Mädchen', the inspiration for his voluptuously sombre String Quartet in D minor, D810. Freud might
not have published his thoughts on Eros and Thanatos (death) as
the two complementary drives in the human psyche – the creative life instinct and the destructive death instinct – until 1920,
but the Russian-born psychoanalyst Sabina Spielrein had developed her own thoughts on the subject in her significantly entitled
essay 'Destruction as the Cause of Coming into Being' as early as
1912, two years after the premiere of Mahler's Eighth Symphony.
In the world of repertoire opera in which Mahler laboured for so
much of his mature life, the coupling of love and death is virtually routine. And of course Mahler would have had before him
the towering example of Wagner's erotic masterpiece *Tristan und
Isolde*, in whose oceanic concluding *Liebestod* ('Love's Death', or
'Love-Death') extinction of the self, not sexual gratification, is presented as the only true resolution of the emotional longing and
physical desire of love.

For Adorno, and for Alma Mahler, the possibility that Mahler's
affirmation may have been anything other than whole-hearted was
an aesthetic weakness. But there are those, this writer included,
for whom the presence of such ambiguity only makes the ending
of the Eighth Symphony all the more intensely moving – more
so than that of the Fifth. And when one looks at the works that
followed the Eighth Symphony, and considers what happens to its
ecstatic concluding 'Ewig! Ewig!' in *Das Lied von der Erde* (1907–
9), and to the motifs associated with those words in the Ninth
Symphony (1909–10), Lilli Lehmann's 'premonition of death' reads
increasingly as a profound and, for its time, rare insight. We must
now look at those works in the context of the events that shaped
them – or, perhaps, heightened traits already present in Mahler

and his music. Whatever the case, in 1907, the year after the completion of Mahler's 'joy-bringing' Eighth Symphony, his life was to change irrevocably.

7

The Shadow Falls

Three Blows of Fate?

From the vantage point of 1910, the year 1907 looks like a dramatic faultline in both Mahler's life and work. According to Alma, Mahler had even sensed what was coming in the depths of his prophetic soul, and foreshadowed it in his 'tragic' Sixth Symphony. In the original version of the Sixth's finale there were three 'hammer blows of fate' – literal hammer blows: Mahler indicates 'Hammer' in the score, and asks the percussionist to produce a 'short, forceful, but dull-sounding thud, *not* metallic (like an axe-blow)'. Alma gives an alluringly sinister explanation. In the last movement of the Sixth Symphony, she tells us, Mahler portrayed himself and his own downfall – though he always described the tragedy as occurring to an unnamed 'hero': 'It is the hero, on whom fall three blows of fate, that last of which fells him as a tree is felled.'[1] In this, she continues, Mahler prophesied his own fate in music. On him too three blows of fate were to fall, and the last of these was to destroy him. Alma's interpretation has created an aura of almost supernatural mystery around the Sixth Symphony. It was in the summer of 1907, she tells us, that those three blows fell. First his daughter Maria, his adored 'Putzi', died of scarlet fever; almost immediately afterwards he was diagnosed with a potentially fatal lesion of the heart; then, in August, political and professional intrigues and campaigning forced him to resign his post at the Vienna Opera, leaving him a broken man.

It is a good story, and as such it has probably helped a great many newcomers (this writer very much included) to find their ways into this hugely complex, forbiddingly dark and intense symphony. Good stories can often be significantly more effective than musicological analyses in opening up challenging works to apprehensive potential listeners. But there are good reasons to view Alma's account with caution, especially when it comes to blow number three. Although Mahler had experienced some pretty vicious attacks from certain quarters of the press, there were equally impassioned expressions of support from journalists, public figures and members of Mahler's own staff. When the newspaper *Die Zeit* lampooned him in a series of cartoons, a declaration of support for him was published, with a breathtakingly impressive list of signatures from prominent Viennese artists, intellectuals and movers and shakers in the city's musical life. Clearly many were keen, some almost desperate, for him to stay: when a substantial party gathered – apparently spontaneously – to watch him depart for New York in December 1907, some were in tears. But as Jonathan Carr argues persuasively in his book *The Real Mahler*, the composer himself was keen to go. Repertory opera was done with, Alma recalls Mahler saying to her during their journey. What a good thing he wouldn't be around to witness its decline, or to go on pretending that he could make bricks without straw. That could of course be bitterness speaking, but there were signs Mahler had been thinking in similar terms for some time: see for instance his comment to Bernhard Paumgartner, made the year before at the Salzburg Mozart Festival. That same year Mahler had been on the receiving end of a characteristically blunt exhortation from Richard Strauss, whose opera *Salome* had been turned down by the censors at the Vienna Opera on the grounds of obscenity:

what was he doing wearing himself out in such a pigsty, Strauss urged? If what Mahler really wanted was to compose, he shouldn't go on squandering his energy like this. Even the Vienna Court Opera wasn't worth all that labour and pain. Forget the prestige, Strauss told him, and give yourself some creative space. Moreover, as Cainer points out in impressive detail, the offer from New York – to conduct at the Metropolitan Opera – was very attractive for a number of reasons: a far less demanding timetable, splendid facilities, a potential galaxy of stars to draw upon, and a fee more than double Mahler's *total* annual earnings in Vienna. This was hardly a blow of fate – it was a hugely attractive and timely opportunity.

It was timely too because both the Mahlers were soon to be in dire need of a change of scene. While negotiations were under way Mahler set off, as usual, for his Alpine summer holiday. But only a few days after his arrival at the lakeside villa in Maiernigg, Putzi went down with a horrible cocktail of scarlet fever and diphtheria. When the swelling in her throat threatened to suffocate her, a tracheotomy was attempted (almost certainly without any form of anaesthetic), which must have been horrendous for her parents to watch – Alma tells us she fled weeping to the lakeside. Putzi lasted another day, then died. Alma reports Mahler running crazily around the house, sobbing convulsively. The horrors continued: Alma's mother, Anna Moll, had some sort of seizure, and Alma herself fell into a faint. A doctor was summoned, and he expressed serious concern for Alma's own heart – complete rest was ordered. What Alma tells us next has become legendary. Apparently Mahler thought it would lighten the mood if he asked for an examination too, and lay down on the sofa. The doctor, whose name was Blumenthal, examined Mahler thoroughly, then in mock-cheery tones (or at least that's how Alma reported it) remarked, 'Well, you've no cause to be proud of a heart like that.' 'This verdict', she tells us categorically, 'marked the beginning of the end for Mahler.'[2]

But was this the blow of fate Alma leads us to believe? Mahler went straight to Vienna to consult a well-known specialist, Professor Friedrich Kovacs, who diagnosed hereditary valve defects on both sides of the heart, though these were 'compensated' – in other words the heart had to some extent developed strengths of its own to balance these weaknesses, perhaps as a result of Mahler's vigorous exercise regime. It is true that Professor Kovacs did recommend Mahler to take things easier, at least for the immediate future, though whether that meant quite the rigorous abstention from anything but the simplest exercise Alma relates is hard to tell. Professor Kovacs' diagnosis implies that the heart ought, with a little care, to be able to carry on its duties more or less as before. At the end of August Mahler saw another specialist who, or so he reported to Alma, told him that he could go on living a perfectly normal life, professionally speaking, so long as he avoided over-exerting himself – a remark that suggests that this doctor, however qualified he may have been in his own field, was no great judge of character. Mahler adds that as a result he has lost his anxiety about conducting. Another letter, written to Alma a short while later, seems to indicate that he is now more worried about her heart than he is about his own. Nevertheless, Alma's story of the three prophetic hammer-blows in the Sixth Symphony, and of their fulfilment in 1907, the year after the symphony's far from successful first performance, has been a gift to the myth-makers. And it has deeply coloured reactions to the three masterpieces he produced between the completion of the Eighth Symphony and its sensationally successful premiere in 1910: the 'song-symphony'

Das Lied von der Erde, the Ninth and the incomplete Tenth Symphonies. Bruno Walter – one of the greatest of Mahler interpreters and a friend whose opinions on Mahler are always worth taking seriously – remembered his reaction after Mahler handed him the manuscript of *Das Lied von der Erde*. This, says Walter, was the first time Mahler had held back from playing a new work to him, which he interpreted as a sign that Mahler was concerned about the effect the music might have upon his own fragile constitution. Instead, Walter discovered the music for himself, and in doing so he was profoundly moved by 'that uniquely passionate, bitter, yet resigned, and benedictory sound of farewell and departure, that last confession of one upon whom rested the finger of death'.[3]

Walter goes on to tell us that the Ninth Symphony too is permeated with 'a sanctified feeling of departure' and dominated by 'the shadow of death'. It is also apparently from Bruno Walter that the story derives of Mahler anxiously checking his own pulse – the story that led the conductor Leonard Bernstein to compare the strange syncopated rhythmic pattern that haunts the first movement of the Ninth to the composer's own faltering heartbeat. Mahler's biographer Michael Kennedy speculated that perhaps the impact of the heart diagnosis didn't actually register until the following summer, when Mahler set off with Alma for his customary composing holiday. Understandably there was no thought of returning to Maiernigg, with all its horrendous recent associations. Instead the couple rented a farmhouse in the village of Toblach, in what is now the Italian Dolomites. Kennedy cites in evidence a letter Mahler wrote to Walter; it does suggest that Mahler's attitude to his own health had shifted since those guardedly optimistic declarations of 1907: 'I must alter my whole way of life. You cannot imagine how painful it is to me.'[4]

For most of his life, Mahler tells Walter, he has sought solace and strength in strenuous exercise, walking through forests and across mountains, discovering his ideas – as Nietzsche did before him – in nature. Returning to his desk to write them down was not the real creative exercise: it was more like that of a peasant farmer bringing in his harvest from the fields. He had also found, as many troubled souls do, that anxieties could be dispelled by a long walk or climb, or later by cycling. With all that taken from him, forced into solitude and immobility, he had nothing to distract him from or dispel his worries, especially when it came to his own physical condition.

Yet the following year, probably after having finished the sketch score of *Das Lied von der Erde*, Mahler wrote to Walter again in very different terms: 'I have been very industrious (which tells you that I have "acclimatised" quite well) . . . I think this is probably the most personal [work] I have created so far.'[5]

Nor should we forget that this is the same Mahler who described himself as being 'in excellent health' in 1908, and who in 1909 signed up for a busy three-year programme as conductor of the New York Philharmonic Orchestra, and who immediately set out looking for new repertoire to perform. None of this sounds like the behaviour of a man who has decided that he is not long for this world.

'Sometimes the opposite is also true': it is possible that during this period Mahler swung (as he so often had in the past) between optimism and something closer to despair. It is also possible that, if Mahler did develop anxiety about his heart, this may have had another cause. Psychologists and psychotherapists of many different persuasions have noted how often sufferers from acute grief will develop obsessive preoccupations, fixate anxiously on something that makes little or no sense to those closest to them. It is as though the mind is trying to blot out thoughts of unbearable loss by transferring its painfully negative feelings to some other, possibly more manageable object. Even if this kind of transference or projection doesn't occur, there is nothing like the death of someone very close to us to remind us of our own fragility as human beings. There are plenty of good reasons for sensing the touch of 'the finger of death' in Mahler's Ninth Symphony and *Das Lied von der Erde*. But if so, whose death? The biggest problem with Alma's 'three blows of fate' story is that two of these 'blows', Mahler's 'compensated' heart defect and his departure from the Vienna Court Opera, surely shrink to insignificance beside the shattering impact of the death of Putzi.

It is also possible that there was a hidden agenda behind Alma's myth-making: that by focusing our attention on the events of 1907 she was trying to create a kind of smokescreen. Why she might have wanted to do that should become clearer when we look more closely at the crisis of summer 1910. But before that – and before we examine the work Mahler was engaged on during that cataclysmic summer, the Tenth Symphony – we should consider those two masterpieces in which Bruno Walter heard 'farewell and departure', the Ninth Symphony and *Das Lied von der Erde*. Are there other ways to represent what this music might have to tell us – or at the very least to open up new possibilities in considering what kind of 'farewell' they may represent? And what do these two works tell us about the evolution of Mahler's thinking and feeling after the colossal, yet complicated, affirmation of the Eighth Symphony?

'The Lonely One in Autumn'

'Ewig! Ewig!' (Eternally! Eternally!) the male voices declaim ecstatically in the huge final crescendo of the Eighth Symphony. 'Ewig' is also the last word intoned by the contralto soloist in the long drawn-out decrescendo that ends *Das Lied von der Erde*. Once again the word is repeated, this time to a stepwise falling pattern, E–D, D–C, 'ewig, ewig'. But musically and emotionally it couldn't be much less like the symphony's thunderous, solidly E flat major ending. The textures are breathtakingly delicate, the harmonies poignantly ambiguous, and the singer's final 'ewig . . .' seems to melt into the last fading orchestral sounds – *Gänzlich ersterbend*, as Mahler requests in the score: 'completely dying away'.

Alma tells us only that it was 'an old consumptive friend of my father's, who transferred all the love he had for him to Mahler', who gave the composer a copy of a book entitled *The Chinese Flute*. The gentleman whom Alma mysteriously fails to name was Theobald Pollack, and his gift was to have far-reaching consequences. *The Chinese Flute* was a collection of verses based on Tang Dynasty poetry, adapted into German by the writer Hans Bethge (1876–1946) and published in 1907. It is important to stress 'adapted', as Bethge was not fluent in Chinese, and he based his versions of the ancient texts on already existing translations by other scholars. But the beauty of his German renderings gained them wide appeal, and an impressive array of composers was soon to follow Mahler's example in setting them to music: prominent amongst them were Arnold Schoenberg, Anton Webern, Richard Strauss, Karol Szymanowski, Hanns Eisler, Ernst Krenek and Bohuslav Martinů. Interest in the art and poetry of the Far East had grown considerably in Vienna in the first decade of the twentieth century. Mahler himself had shown little interest in Eastern literature before 1907, but his intense admiration for the philosopher Arthur Schopenhauer may well have prepared the ground. Schopenhauer was one of the first major thinkers in the German-speaking world to look seriously and thoroughly at

Hindu and Buddhist thought, and the quietist, world-renouncing tendency in his own philosophy owes a great deal to what he found in classical Indian scriptures. There is no talk of Nirvana in the poetry Mahler took from *The Chinese Flute*, but there is a poignant, at times very Schopenhauerian–Buddhist sense of the vanity of human wishes and desires, and of the transience and ultimate insignificance of human existence. At times the words protest at the pitifulness of our lot, at others they cry out with an almost painful longing for the ungraspable beauty of life on the earth, but in the background, running through the cycle of six songs in *Das Lied von der Erde*, is a growing sense that the only real answer lies in resignation. In Part I of *Faust*, Goethe had identified the goal of his hero's striving and searching in these lines:

Werd ich zum Augenblicke sagen: If I could say to the moment:
Verweile doch! Du bist so schön!   Stay, you are altogether lovely!

Like the *Faust*-inspired Eighth Symphony, *Das Lied von der Erde* also ends with a vision of eternity. The words Mahler added to the verses of Wang-Sei tell of the endlessly recurring cycle of nature:

Die liebe Erde allüberall
Blüht auf im Lenz und grünt aufs neu!
Allüberall und ewig blauen licht die Fernen!
Ewig . . . ewig . . .

The lovely earth everywhere
Blossoms in spring and grows green yet again!
Everywhere and eternally shines the blue, far-distant light!
Eternally . . . eternally . . .

But for the human observer, for Mahler himself, there is to be no lasting participation in this eternal recurrence. In the closing words of Wang-Sei's poem, just before that blissful final vision:

> *Ich suche Ruhe für mein einsam Herz!*
> *Ich wandle nach der Heimat, meiner Stätte!*
> *Ich werde niemals in die Ferne schweifen.*
> *Still ist mein Herz und harret seiner Stunde!*

> I seek rest for my lonely heart!
> I journey to the homeland, to my appointed place!
> I will never again wander into the far distance.
> My heart is still and awaits its hour!

If this is another version of Mahler's Wanderer swooning blissfully into the arms of the *Ewig-Weibliche*, this time hers is unmistakably the face of extinction, of *der schöne Tod*.

That final movement of *Das Lied von der Erde* is entitled 'Der Abschied' (The Parting). What more is there is to say? Surely this is all the confirmation we need that Bruno Walter was right, and that this 'Song of the Earth' is in essence a farewell to the Earth Mahler loved so intensely? Except that, as so often with Mahler, on closer inspection the truth turns out to be more complicated. Two of the songs – 'Von der Jugend' (Of Youth, no. 3) and 'Von der Schönheit' (Of Beauty, no. 4) – are much more celebratory: the faster central section of 'Von der Schönheit' brings us much closer to the joyous images of childhood merry-making captured in the first movement of the Fourth Symphony. And then there are the two drinking songs: 'Das Trinklied vom Jammer der Erde' (The Drinking Song of Earth's Misery, no. 1) and 'Der Trunkene im Frühling'

(The Drunkard in Spring, no. 5). Though they are well separated by the three intervening numbers, these two movements could have been engineered to demonstrate that, with Mahler, the whole truth is often to be found in the polarity of opposites. They are also an important reminder that the 'personality' apparently revealed in Mahler's music isn't always a straightforward reflection of the man himself. It can sometimes seem that the close relationship between Mahler's life and work is the ultimate refutation of T. S. Eliot's assertion that the individual suffering human being should never be confused with the creative mind itself. But as one listens to these two vividly realised portraits of alcoholic self-abandonment one should bear in mind that there are no records of Mahler himself getting even slightly drunk. In the pleasures of the table, as in almost every other aspect of his day-to-day life, Mahler was remarkably self-disciplined. In fact he could be held up as a prime exemplar of Gustave Flaubert's motto, 'Be regular and orderly in your life, so that you may be violent and original in your work.'

The first song, 'Der Trinklied vom Jammer der Erde' is certainly 'violent and original' – a convulsive cry of grief, punctuated by moments of fleeting, agonised tenderness, and by a thrice-intoned refrain that seems to rise from depths unglimpsed in the Eighth Symphony: 'Dunkel ist das Leben, ist der Tod!' (Dark is life, is death!). But the fifth, 'Der Trunkene im Frühling', is pure glee-ful exuberance, beginning with a verse one can imagine emerging lustily from the garden of a Viennese *Heurige*:

Wenn nur ein Traum das Leben ist,	If life itself is but a dream,
Warum denn Müh' und Plag?	Why than should care dismay?
Ich trinke, bis ich nicht merh kann,	I'll drink till I can drink no more,
Den ganzen lieben Tag!	The glorious livelong day!

There is however one movement in *Das Lied von der Erde* in which, it has been claimed, Mahler's anxiety about his own health can be discerned quite clearly: the desolate 'Der Einsame im Herbst' (The Lonely One in Autumn, no. 2). Some of the sparest textures Mahler ever created accompany a lament that often seems more wintry than autumnal. And at the beginning of the third stanza come the two lines that seem to clinch the argument:

> *Mein Herz ist müde. Meine kleine Lampe*
> *Erlosch mit Knistern, es gemahnt mich an den Schlaf.*

> My heart is weary. My little lamp
> Goes out with a splutter; it makes me think of sleep.

There follows a great cry of grief: 'Sonne der Liebe, willst du nie mehr scheinen, Um meinen bittern Tränen mild aufzutrocknen?' (Sun of love, will you never again shine, And tenderly dry my bitter tears?). But the mention of the 'little lamp' is accompanied by textures that – for this listener at least – recall those of Mahler's song cycle *Kindertotenlieder* ('Songs of the Deaths of Children'). In itself, that's hardly conclusive evidence, but it could be at least a hint. Take away the myths, the retrospective knowledge that Mahler only had two years to live when he finished *Das Lied von der Erde*, read the words and listen to the music afresh, and it could be that the singer has another reason for his terrible loneliness: the little lamp could also be Putzi. In which case the sense of loneliness conveyed so acutely in this song has its roots in something deeper than self-protective withdrawal from the world.

*

In any case, none of this is really new. Throughout his composing career Mahler returned to the themes of death and loss again and again. As a child, he told a close confidante, the violinist Natalie Bauer-Lechner, he had written a piano piece in which a funeral march was followed by a polka! It is hard to say whether this is an early symptom of the 'rift in his being' identified by Alma, or merely an indication that young Gustav was familiar with the 'Dumka', a Slavic folk form in which melancholic lyricism alternates with high-spirited dance. Either way it is as utterly characteristic of Mahler as the polar contrast between 'Das Trinklied vom Jammer der Erde' and 'Der Trunkene im Frühling' in *Das Lied von der Erde*. The First Symphony may end in a loud hymn of triumph, but the song-cycle it extensively references, *Lieder eines fahrenden Gesellen*, ends with another lonely, alienated Wanderer seeking relief in a reconciliation with nature, and with it, death. The repeated 'Alles! Alles!' (Everything! Everything!) in the closing moments of the last song sounds eerily prophetic of the 'ewig, ewig' in the last dying moments of *Das Lied von der Erde*. Deryck Cooke, one of the wisest and most balanced of all Mahler commentators, cites a letter written by Mahler to a friend in 1879, when he was just nineteen. It reads like an adolescent sketch for the emotional journey of 'Der Abschied': 'Oh my beloved earth, when, oh when, will you take the forsaken one to your breast? . . . Oh care for the lonely one, the restless one, Universal Mother!'[6]

Granted there is, as Cooke concedes, an element of conventional romantic attitudinising here; but the more one knows about Mahler the harder it is to disagree with him that the sentiments expressed are 'genuine enough'. Let us not forget that this is also a young man who had already witnessed the premature deaths of several of his siblings, who was to be profoundly shocked by the suicide of his brother Otto in 1895 and then – almost certainly the hardest blow of all – by the horrible death of his beloved infant daughter. That last blow may have brought Mahler's lifelong pre-occupation with irreparable loss into sharper focus, but in doing so it would only have heightened what was, to a certain extent, already there.

But Bruno Walter calls another work to witness: the Ninth Symphony. And here the claim that Mahler is speaking of 'farewell and departure' can be felt to ring even truer.

'Up on the Heights'

> . . . the expression of an exceptional fondness for
> this earth, the longing to live in peace on it, to enjoy
> nature to its depths before death comes. For he comes
> irresistibly. The whole movement is permeated with
> premonitions of death.[7]

Alban Berg's description of the first movement of Mahler's Ninth Symphony has been quoted so often in connection with this work that it has acquired a status close to that of holy writ. When Berg wrote of the presence of death in the Ninth Symphony, he wasn't simply giving voice to a fanciful personal interpretation; the music is full of details that support his words. One of Mahler's eeriest funeral marches haunts this music, and its sinister tread seems to grow directly from the weirdly faltering syncopated rhythm spelt out by cellos and low horn in the symphony's opening bars – the motif Leonard Bernstein compared to Mahler's erratic heart-beat. From very early on – almost from the first bars – the first movement is dominated by a two-note falling figure, like a sigh. We have heard this figure before: it is the same stepwise falling two-note figure to which the contralto sings the final 'ewig' in the 'completely dying away' final moments of *Das Lied von der Erde*.

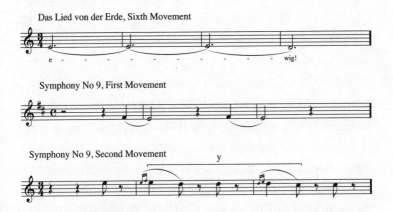

Das Lied von der Erde, Sixth Movement

Symphony No 9, First Movement

Symphony No 9, Second Movement

In the following three movements this figure returns, sometimes as originally heard, sometimes falling again by two more steps (Ex. 7.1). But it is in the finale that the three-step descent becomes decisive. Now it clearly spells out the leading motif from Beethoven's Piano Sonata op. 81a, known as 'Das Lebewohl' (The Farewell), the work the teenage Mahler had played at his audition for the Vienna Conservatoire, in the process greatly impressing his future professor, Julius Epstein. Beethoven marked his motif 'Le-be-wohl': Mahler not only follows Beethoven's pattern; he also echoes Beethoven's wonderful harmonic surprise in the eighth bar of his sonata.

Beethoven: Piano Sonata Op 81a   Op 81a, bars 7-8
First Movement

Mahler: Symphony No 9, Fourth Movement

Mahler's finale is an Adagio. In placing the slow movement last, Mahler may have been thinking of Tchaikovsky's 'Pathétique' Symphony, or perhaps of Bruckner's unfinished Ninth – both works are overshadowed by thoughts of death. The intensely expressive rising figure for violins that begins this movement strongly recalls the opening of Bruckner's Adagio, the last movement he lived to complete. But what Mahler achieves is utterly personal. The first theme, on full strings, not only spells out Beethoven's 'farewell' theme in full, there's also a striking echo of the Victorian funeral hymn 'Abide with Me'. The resemblance may be coincidental, but it is also possible that Mahler heard the hymn on one of his visits to New York – perhaps while observing the funeral for a young fireman that, according to Alma, stirred him so deeply, and which was to leave its black imprint on the Tenth Symphony (see below p. 263). This richly sonorous music for full strings alternates with weirdly skeletal sounds: first hushed violins and low bassoon (a very Tchaikovskian sound) then, even more chillingly, high violins ('without expression'), low cellos and a sepulchral contrabassoon. Eventually the 'farewell' theme builds to a massive, desperate climax, which seems to be striving for the transcendent glory of the Eighth Symphony: at one point the horns even cry out the men's 'Ewig! Ewig!' motif from the Eighth's final crescendo. The striving is in vain, however – there is something desperate about the horns'

attempt to recapture the Eighth Symphony's affirmation, and the rich textures gradually thin out into the near-emptiness of the final bars. The silences between the slow, quiet phrases are almost unbearably poignant, like the pauses between the final breaths of a loved one who is dying. The dynamics fade from *pp* (*pianissimo*) to *ppp* (*pianississimo*) and *pppp* (*pianissississimo*), and even the final chord is marked *ersterbend*, 'dying away'.

But just before the end is a highly significant quotation. Softly, the violins echo the last heart-rending crescendo from the fourth of Mahler's *Kindertotenlieder*: 'Oft denk' ich, sie sind nur ausgegangen!' (Often I think they're just out walking), where the singer relates a common experience for those dealing with unbearable loss: the delusion that the loved one is still there – somewhere. The violins recall the music that accompanies the singer's agonised cry:

> *Wir holen sie ein auf jenen Höh'n*
> *im Sonnenschein! Der Tag ist schön auf jene Höh'n!*

> We'll soon catch up with them on the heights
> In the sunshine! The day is beautiful up on the heights!

The words, by the poet Friedrich Rückert, capture a phenomenon familiar to anyone who has spent time amongst the Alps, one Mahler himself would have experienced many times. Often, long after dusk has fallen in the deep, steep-sided valleys, the sunlight is still quite clear in the high pastures and on the snow and ice. To look up out of the growing darkness towards those still-illuminated heights can be like gazing into another, far serener world, from the world of deepening dusk into an enduring, perhaps perpetual day. But is Mahler expressing a hope, a belief that he will soon join his own lost daughter 'up on the heights', or is he recapturing the desperation of the bereaved parent, helplessly trying to cling to a fading delusion?

No one could seriously doubt that mortality is being confronted here, and in *Das Lied von der Erde*, and with an impassioned urgency unmatched in anything Mahler had written before. What is at issue however is the still widely popular notion that in these two works Mahler anticipated his own end, naturally or supernaturally, eight months after the premiere of his Eighth Symphony. While this reading has proved enormously popular with Mahler-lovers, it has also given rise to the idea amongst Mahler-phobics that the Ninth Symphony and *Das Lied von der Erde* have nothing deeper to offer than 'a heartbroken egocentric leave-taking', as Michael Kennedy puts it. (Kennedy himself took a very different view of both works.) The ultimate argument against that is to be found in the work Mahler was writing – and came very close to finishing in sketch score – in the year 1910, his Symphony no. 10. In a short while we will take a closer look at this astonishing work, glorious and shatteringly eloquent even in the not-quite-finished state in which its composer left it. But before that, we must consider the events of the summer of 1910, events that were to leave their mark, not just on the music, but on the very manuscript of the Tenth Symphony.

8

'To Live for You, To Die for You'

The Fourth Blow

There must have been times when it was hard being Mrs Gustav Mahler – or 'Frau Direktor Mahler', as Alma would have been addressed in polite Viennese circles during her husband's tenure at the Court Opera. Granted, status was one of the things she craved, and being married to one of the city's leading artistic celebrities – a man people pointed out to each other as he walked the streets of Vienna – fulfilled that need in abundance. But it had its downsides, plenty of them. Living with the man Ethel Smyth described as 'a bomb cased in razor-edges' would have been wearing enough. But for a great deal of her married life Alma would hardly have seen her husband: when he wasn't taken up with his many duties at the opera, he would have been busy working on his scores, or throwing himself into his vigorous solitary exercise programmes, or reading voraciously. Even when he wasn't, he would often have been spiritually absent: 'alone in my heaven, in my love, in my song', in the words of the exquisite song 'Ich bin der Welt abhanden gekommen' – the same words he invoked in his orchestral 'love song' to her, the famous Adagietto from the Fifth Symphony. A man who could sing so sweetly of being 'alone' in his love clearly had a lot to learn about the laborious give-and-take of real-world marital relations. It is also patently obvious from Alma's diaries that she was a woman with strong physical needs – needs that Mahler wasn't ideally equipped to satisfy. Apparently Mahler had acquired a reputation as a bit of a Lothario by the time he met Alma, yet Alma herself records finding him sexually 'inexperienced' in the early days of their marriage. There is a particularly painful account in Alma's diaries of the couple's first failed attempt at sex, and reading between the lines it is reasonably clear that Mahler sometimes suffered from impotence, as quite a few artistic men have when in the throes of creation. The English composer William Walton's impotence in the early stages of work on his First Symphony was a major contributor to the catastrophic breakdown of his relationship with the Baroness Imma Doernberg – though without the trauma of that breakdown Walton's symphony might never have evolved into the magnificent cathartic statement it is. Alma's lover before Mahler, the composer and conductor Alexander Zemlinsky, had apparently been more expert when it came to pleasing her, even if (as Alma candidly admits) she allowed him every intimacy except for the ultimate one. But Mahler was more of a catch, and as a result Zemlinsky suffered a rejection that was to leave its mark on him, and on his music, for many years to come.

But Zemlinsky did something else for Alma: he encouraged her composing. Mahler took a very different attitude. In December 1901, three months before their wedding, Alma received an unusually long letter from Mahler, a letter whose tone is more that of a stern Victorian father addressing a potentially errant child than of a lover. 'A husband and a wife who are both composers: how do you envisage that?' he expostulates. One can imagine Alma's feelings when she came to the sentence, 'But from now on you have only *one* profession: *to make me happy!*'[1]

This isn't a throwaway: Mahler dwells on this thought at length and interrogates Alma about it. Does she fully understand what she's taking on? His is the role of the composer, the breadwinner; hers is that of the loving wife, the sympathetic and supportive partner. Can she be satisfied with that? He knows that he is asking a great deal of her, he concedes, but he not only can but must do so, and she will soon realise how much he has to offer in return.

It cannot be said that Mahler did not warn her. And yet, having read all this, Alma did marry him, give up her own composition and, it seems, make some effort to be the sympathetic comrade he demanded. Given all this, and given Alma's own passionate and highly creative nature (*Memories and Letters* alone is proof of that), it was perhaps remarkable that the relationship lasted as long as it did. Marriages amongst the Viennese artistic intelligentsia could be rather less durable than they were amongst the city's respectable bourgeoisie or working classes. Arnold Schoenberg's marriage to Zemlinsky's sister Mathilde nearly broke down completely when she left him (and the two children) for the painter Richard Gerstl in 1908.

It is important to try to see things from Alma's point of view because in recent years, after the initial sweeping success of her *Memories and Letters*, there has been an increasing tendency to cast her as the villain in the story, or at the very least to see her as the ultimate unreliable witness. She has been accused of collecting celebrity husbands and lovers like a trophy-hunter, and of re-adopting Mahler's surname as her own when she realised in old age that in terms of posterity he was probably the best bet. A lot of negative comments have been made about her suitability as a mother, evidently with some justice. It is hard to argue that her shock and horror at the death of Putzi were anything other than genuine, but if so there is evidence that her reaction was of the kind psychotherapists describe as 'complicated grief'. Bruno Walter noted that, for all her tears, Alma seemed to take the loss of her child better than Mahler did. In her diaries, Alma admits half-guiltily that on at least one occasion she had wished Putzi dead. Nearly thirty years after Putzi's death, in 1935, Alma's daughter by Walter Gropius, Manon, lay dying at the age of just eighteen. Her last recorded words to her mother are painful to read: 'You'll get over it, Mummy, as you get over everything – I mean . . . as everyone gets over everything.'[2]

Nevertheless, there is little question that by the summer of 1910, when Mahler set off to compose at his new retreat at Toblach in the Dolomites, Alma was suffering from fairly serious depression. 'The wear and tear of being driven on without respite by a spirit so intense as his had brought me to a complete breakdown,' she tells us, and it is easy enough to believe. She went to stay at a sana-torium in the Alpine spa resort of Tobelbad, some two hundred miles from Toblach. In *Memories and Letters* she tells us that her life in Tobelbad was 'utterly solitary', and she was left more or less to her own devices. Eventually she became so low that the director of the sanatorium intervened and decided to set Alma up with company for her walks – the younger the better, it seems: 'There was an architect, X, whom I found particularly sympathetic, and I soon had little doubt that he was in love with me and hoping I might return his love. So I left.'[3]

When Alma's memoir *And the Bridge is Love* came out, twenty years later, she was less coy about naming her admirer: he was the twenty-seven-year-old Walter Gropius, then taking his first steps on a stellar career as one of the century's most original and influential architects. He would also be, between 1915 and 1920, Alma's second husband. The version of the story related in *And the Bridge is Love* is slightly different: Alma now meets Gropius on the dance-floor, not out on therapeutic country walks. But the upshot is still the same: Alma welcomes Gropius's friendship and admiration, but manages to convey to her young admirer that she does not wish to take their relationship any further. She had no wish at all, she tells us in *Memories and Letters*, to exchange her old life for a new one.

It was only when Alma and Gropius's correspondence was first published in the 1980s that the truth finally came out, though a few had long suspected it. The pair had become lovers during Alma's stay at Tobelbad, and after Alma left for Toblach they began exchanging passionate letters. Some were sent to the local post office, but a special few appear to have been sent directly to the farmhouse in Toblach – and that, it seems, is what precipitated the catastrophe. Alma's version of events has been widely questioned. She tells us that Gropius sent her a letter telling her that he could not live without her, and that she must leave Mahler and join him at once. But, says Alma, he made a serious mistake: instead of addressing the letter to her, he wrote 'Herr Direktor Mahler' (or, more correctly, in the dative case, 'Herrn Direktor Mahler') on the envelope. It seems to strain credulity, and several English-speaking writers have been very sceptical about it; but the plain fact is that a letter sent formally to Alma – in this case presumably to disguise the true nature of its contents – would have been addressed to '*Frau* Direktor Mahler'. It could easily have been a slip, but if so it was almost certainly a Freudian one. Unconsciously at least, Gropius wanted to force the issue. The effect was devastating. Alma tells us that Mahler was sitting at the piano when he opened the letter. Suddenly his expression changed and he spluttered out a question – what was this? The discovery provoked a tirade, but not from Mahler – from Alma herself:

And now – at last – I was able to tell him all. I told him I had
longed for his love year after year and that he, in his fanatical
concentration on his own life, had simply overlooked me. As I
spoke, he felt for the first time that something is owed to the person
with whom one's life has once been linked. He suddenly felt a sense
of guilt.[4]

In a play about a problem marriage it would make a stirring
climax, perhaps to be followed by a still more moving reconciliation. And at first Alma seems to be telling us that that is what
actually happened. After both had opened their hearts, Alma felt
as strongly as she had ever done before that she could never leave
Mahler. When she told him so, his face was transfigured, and from
that moment on he could not bear to be parted from her, even for
a second. But with Alma Mahler, as much as with her husband,
the opposite can also be true. One of the things that makes her
writing so fascinating is that her inner contradictions, the rifts in
her own being, cannot help revealing themselves, whatever her
own conscious intentions. A paragraph later Alma tells us that
her 'boundless love had lost by degrees some of its strength and
warmth', and a couple of sentences after that, 'I knew that my marriage was no marriage and that my own life was utterly unfulfilled.
I concealed all this from him,' (she has just told us that she did
exactly the reverse!) 'and although he knew it as well as I did we
played out the comedy to the end, to spare his feelings.' And in
the middle of that paragraph, after having implied that she and
Gropius had never got further than a passionate but chaste friendship, she makes the highly suggestive admission that her 'eyes had
been opened by the impetuous assaults of a youthful lover'. The
confusion, the contradictions that emerge in this relatively short

passage suggest strongly that Alma's feelings were still highly conflicted when she wrote this account, thirty years after the event.
Freud, one imagines, would have had a splendid time unpicking
this tangle in his consulting room.

What happened next has to be pieced together from a variety
of sources. Add in Alma's correspondence with Gropius, plus her
autobiography *My Life, My Loves* (1958), and a reasonably firm
story emerges. Goaded by the lack of a response from Alma, Gropius came to Toblach, where Alma apparently happened to catch
sight of him hiding under a bridge while she and Mahler were out
driving. It seems he had even attempted to present himself at the
farmhouse to demand a resolution of the issue, but that he'd lost
heart and fled when a dog ran out at him. Alma confessed the
truth to Mahler, who set off to find Gropius in the growing dark
and then led him back to the house with a lantern. Mahler then
summoned Alma and left her alone with Gropius, but after only
a few minutes, she tells us, she became so anxious about him that
she went to his room, where she found him pacing back and forth,
reading the Bible by candlelight. According to both *My Life and
Loves* and *Memories and Letters* Mahler assured her that he had
faith in her to reach the right decision. That decision, she now
relates, was not so much to 'play out the comedy to the end' as to
decide that there was no question for her of life without Mahler:
certainly not with another man. The next day Gropius was seen
off at the railway station, and that was that – at least for as long as
Mahler remained alive.

But as we have already seen, the lovers' correspondence tells
another story. And even from Alma's own accounts we can infer
that Mahler himself more than half suspected it. The chronology
isn't clear: Alma seems to flit back and forth somewhat (possibly

another symptom of guilty emotional confusion), but Mahler's traumatised state of mind appears to have endured for some while. The couple slept in separate rooms (as many prosperous married couples did at that time), but now Mahler demanded, like a child terrified of the dark, that the door connecting them be left open. Alma recalls frequently waking during the night to find Mahler standing, ghost-like, by her bedside in the dark. She also remembers finding him in his studio lying on the floor, weeping in terror that he might lose her. Being close to the earth was comforting. *Die liebe Erde* again! If Alma could not be Mahler's redemptive *Ewig-Weibliche*, perhaps dear Mother Earth could.

There was one other possible course of redemptive action: composition. Even after the terrible shock of the discovery of Alma's liaison with Gropius, Mahler continued working on the score he had begun at the start of that summer holiday in 1910: Symphony no. 10. By the end of that holiday he had apparently finished the sketch score – exactly what state of being that represents will be examined below. The music of the Tenth Symphony, and the manuscript itself, are the ultimate witnesses to Mahler's spiritual journey in this, his last full year. But before we look at that astonishing, so very nearly completed masterpiece in detail, there is another possible inference to be drawn from the above account of the summer of 1910. It is one that would help explain the contradictions, ambiguities and evasions in Alma's versions of events; it would also throw light on her highly contentious story of the three fatal 'blows of fate' that struck Mahler in 1907. The real hammer blow of fate that felled Mahler 'as a tree is felled' – i.e. slowly at first, but with steadily increasing momentum – was not his departure from the Vienna Court Opera, nor the diagnosis of a valvular heart defect, perhaps not even the death of Putzi, but the shattering discovery that his *Ewig-Weibliche* might be about to abandon him.

'One Great Song': The Tenth Symphony

In his study of Franz Kafka, the critic Erich Heller writes of Kafka's terrifying 'enslavement' to his writing table. Heller quotes a letter from Kafka to his close friend Max Brod: 'He must never move away from it, must hold on to it with all his might, if he does not want to fall into madness.'[5] Looking at the manuscript sketches for the Tenth Symphony, it is hard to fend off the growing impression that composing this music performed a very similar function for Mahler. On significant pages of the last two movements we find what look like desperate exclamations, to God, to Alma, even apparently to the Devil, written in the same uncharacteristically shaky hand in which Mahler dashed off his letter to Emil Hertzka, urging him to include the dedication to Alma in the score of the Eighth Symphony. Mahler's precarious state of mind is indicated, not so much in the entreaties themselves, but in the seemingly delirious repetitions and the disintegrating spelling and syntax. Over the second Scherzo's transition to the opening of the finale we find the following:

Du allein weisst was es bedeutet.	You alone know what this means.
Ach! Ach! Gott! [or is it another 'Ach'?]	Ah! Ah! God!
Leb' wol mein Saitenspiel	Fare well my lyre
Leb wol	Fare well
Leb wol	Fare well
Leb wol	Fare well
Ach wol	Ah well
Ach Ach.	Ah Ah.

This new form of address, 'mein Saitenspiel' (my lyre) also appears in a letter to Alma – or is it a written prayer? – sent to her from his composing hut: 'I am possessed by dark spirits; they have cast me to the ground. Come and dispel them . . . Here I lie prostrate and await you; and silently I ask whether I may still hope for salvation, or whether I am to be damned.'[6]

Was there an element of conscious calculation in all this? At some stage during the composition of the finale, Mahler changed the ending of the symphony: instead of ending in the key of B flat major, as originally planned, Mahler conceived the heart-stopping modulation that takes the music back to the symphony's original home key of F sharp major. This necessitated copying out the last ninety-five bars again in the new key, and in doing so, Mahler carefully reproduced some of these 'spontaneous' implorations to Alma at the equivalent points in the score: 'Für dich leben, für dich sterben' (To live for you, to die for you) and, over the symphony's last great cry, his favourite pet name for her, 'Almschi!' Evidently Alma was meant to see these, or maybe somebody was – posterity perhaps? Or was it that these annotations were now so crucial to Mahler's conception of the symphony that he simply could not imagine the music without them?

The question remains however whether this represents a new kind of crisis in Mahler's mental life, or whether – as possibly with the states of mind conveyed in *Das Lied von der Erde* and the Ninth Symphony – it reveals an intensification, brought about by traumatic events, of something that had always been there. In her classic study of bipolar (or manic depressive) disorder and creativity, *Touched with Fire*, the psychologist Kay Redfield Jamison places Mahler's name high on her list of probable manic-depressive composers. The extreme mood-swings exhibited in both Mahler's music and his personal life are strongly suggestive; but Professor Jamison has other evidence to support her case. As she points out, manic-depressive characteristics tend to 'cluster' in families: Mahler's sister Justi experienced terrifying hallucinations, and we have already noted that his highly volatile brother Otto committed suicide. Mahler's breathtaking productivity during his summer 'holidays' is also potentially indicative: the astonishing speed with which Mahler wrote his Eighth Symphony (just eight weeks) would be consistent with the state psychologists term 'hypomania', literally 'under-mania', in which many bipolar artists and thinkers find they are able to work with what can seem supernatural fluency. It is important to stress though that hypomania is not fully fledged mania, which in most cases (unfortunately I do know what I'm talking about here) tends to be creatively crippling. And there lies the problem, in Mahler's case, with the bipolar diagnosis. Mahler may have experienced emotions and impulses that would have unbalanced other people, he may also have been prone to those typical bipolar 'mixed' emotional states, so tellingly expressed by William Blake in *The Marriage of Heaven and Hell*: 'Excess of sorrow laughs. Excess of joy weeps'; but there are no records of Mahler's ever being seriously incapacitated by his extremes of feeling. True, the summer of 1907 saw virtually no composition, but given the shock (or shocks) Mahler experienced that year that's hardly surprising. There is no need to bring in psychopathology to account for a human being losing the will to work after the death of a child. And even in this extreme crisis of the summer of 1910, Mahler was still able to keep on working on his Tenth Symphony, and to bring it to something like completion. Perhaps the truth is that the writing-table always did for Mahler what Erich Heller argues it did for Kafka: prevented him from losing balance in the welter of threatening emotions. Moreover, for all his adult life, Mahler was a remarkably disciplined man: not only in his composition routine, but also in his work as conductor and opera director, and in his rigorous exercise regimes. 'One must have chaos inside oneself in order to give birth to a dancing star,' wrote Nietzsche in *Also sprach Zarathustra*. Mahler certainly knew that chaos, and from some of his music one might infer that that inner chaos had spilled out directly onto the page, the work a direct reflection of the life; but like Flaubert, it seems, Mahler also understood the need to be 'orderly', obsessively so, in his everyday life, so that the violence and disorder might find full creative focus in his music. The anguished comments written on the sketches of the Tenth Symphony may suggest a mind in a dangerous state of turmoil, but the work's superb formal control – evident even in its not-quite-complete state – testifies to something very different. Mahler's state of mind might suggest a centrifuge, everything whirling out from an emptying, disintegrating centre. But in the Tenth Symphony the centre does ultimately hold, just as it always had.

A Farewell Too Far?

If, then, the Tenth Symphony represents such a crucial stage in Mahler's artistic development – if it is the ultimate documentation in both words and music of how he found meaning and strength of purpose even during what was probably his most profound spiritual crisis – how is it then that its message could have remained largely unheeded for the best part of the twentieth century? A great deal of this is bound up with the shocked reaction to Mahler's premature death in 1911, and to the way this affected responses to his last completed works, *Das Lied von der Erde* and the Ninth Symphony – both premiered after the composer's death. In this climate of grief and bewilderment, rumours spread rapidly. It quickly became known that Mahler had begun a Tenth Symphony. Mahler's biographer Paul Stefan apparently heard from Alma (to whom Mahler had evidently played some, or perhaps even all of the symphony on the piano) that the score contained cryptic messages, and that the music expressed 'gaiety, even exuberance', but concluded that, 'Perhaps – perhaps no one will ever set eyes on it . . .'[7] Very soon, that 'perhaps' was to be transformed into a holy interdict. In a lecture on Mahler given in 1912, Arnold Schoenberg spelt out what was soon (as with many of Schoenberg's pronouncements) to become dogma amongst his followers. It was right, Schoenberg insisted that Mahler's Tenth should remain in shadow, its essence unknown, just as it was in the case of Beethoven's 'Tenth', for which sketches were known to exist. With Mahler, as with Beethoven and Bruckner, it would seem that reaching a Ninth Symphony was a kind of lawful limit. Any composer who tried to go beyond it would find himself straying into the territory of the unsayable, and in the process of trying to say it would naturally have to pass into the beyond himself. If there is a message to be divined there it is one for which mere mortals are not yet ready: 'Those who have written a Ninth stood too near to the hereafter. Perhaps the riddles of this world would be solved, if one of those who knew them were to write a Tenth.'[8]

And that, of course, is out of the question. It is worth considering for a moment how seriously such an argument might be taken at a modern musicological conference. But Schoenberg's decision to avert his eyes with holy dread proved remarkably influential, and for a remarkably long time. In 1973, talking about Mahler in the fifth of his filmed Charles Eliot Norton Lectures, *The Unanswered Question*, Leonard Bernstein reiterated what may be considered the orthodox Schoenbergian line. That 'controversial' unfinished Tenth Symphony, that work in which Mahler tried to take a 'tentative' step into the Schoenbergian (i.e. atonal) future, 'remains for me only the one completed movement, which is yet another heartbreaking Adagio saying Farewell. It was one farewell too many.'[9] Even if Mahler had lived, says Bernstein, he would surely never have been able to finish his Tenth Symphony. He had said all he had to say, all he was capable of saying, in his Ninth.

Bernstein does at least have the honesty to say 'for me'. It is a highly personal interpretation, which was evidently not based on any kind of detailed examination of the sketches for the Tenth Symphony. Had Bernstein looked closely, he would have been able to see that Mahler had known perfectly well, not only how the Tenth Symphony would end, but how it would arrive at that ending from that 'one completed movement', which Bernstein reads as 'yet another heartbreaking Adagio saying Farewell'. He might also have revised his opinion of Mahler's 'tentative' step into the Schoenbergian beyond. In fact the Tenth Symphony had probably arrived at something like the state Mahler's Eighth had by the end of his summer holiday in 1906. Taking issue with a Mahlerian of the stature of Leonard Bernstein is not something to be done lightly, and it could well be argued that Bernstein's understanding of *Das Lied von der Erde* and the Ninth Symphony in the light of Schoenberg's death mysticism was one of the factors that enabled him to give such profoundly moving performances of these two works. But when it comes to the Tenth Symphony, Bernstein was just wrong, and in so many ways. So why did he persist in refusing to consider what at the very least might have been? Indeed why should anyone who cares about Mahler persist in not wanting to know what the composer was trying to say – and very nearly succeeded in saying – in his last work? A possible answer to this is given by Michael Kennedy in his biography of the composer. What one learns from hearing the Tenth Symphony performed complete, in Deryck Cooke's 'performing version', is that it is wrong to conclude that Mahler died in a mood of 'valediction', defeated by fate or simply resigned to the inevitable: the Tenth Symphony as a complete artistic statement 'transcends thoughts of death' and ends with 'a gloriously affirmatory and positive assertion of a man's spiritual victory'. Moreover it establishes beyond question that in his last year Mahler was entering a new phase, creatively and philosophically. In some ways the new kind of language he was forging was simpler than that of the complex, multi-faceted Ninth Symphony, but at the same time it was more forward-looking when it came to tonality and, paradoxically, 'even more insistent upon the Classical-Romantic procedures which had always nurtured him'.[10]

In other words, the Tenth Symphony ruins a lovely story – a story in which, it seems, many mystically, or at least superstitiously inclined Mahlerians have invested a great deal. But what if the story the completed Tenth Symphony tells is better, or at least equally valid? ('Sometimes the opposite is also true.') For years the substance of the Tenth Symphony remained inaccessible to those who could neither read music nor decipher Mahler's sometimes cryptic, often dauntingly untidy sketches. Even some of the more expert readers came to the conclusion, incorrectly, that what Mahler had left was, for the most part, a crazy, tangled mass of fragments – reflective, no doubt, of its composer's tortured, unbalanced psychological state at the time of writing. Now thanks to the efforts of a few dedicated investigators – and to one of them in particular – it can be seen, and more importantly heard, that Michael Kennedy was broadly right. How then did this symphony, effectively pronounced dead by many authoritative Mahler-lovers, come to be exhumed and brought to life? And what does it tell us about this 'new phase' Mahler was entering in 1910? I will deal with each of those two questions in turn.

Rescuing the Tenth

After the catastrophic upheaval of the First World War and the collapse of the Habsburg Empire, it must have seemed to many that the world embraced by Mahler's symphonies – and particularly by the Eighth – was not only gone, but best forgotten. In the words of the title of Stefan's Zweig's monumental cultural memoir, it was 'the world of yesterday'. In the music of Mahler's German-speaking world, progressive thinking was now dominated by the radical atonal thinking of Schoenberg and his 'Second Viennese School', by the jazz-inflected modernism of Ernst Krenek's smash-hit opera *Jonny spielt auf* (1926), and by the pungently anti-romantic *Gebrauchsmusik* ('utility music') of Paul Hindemith, itself influenced by the *Neue Sachlichkeit* ('new objectivity') of artists such as Max Beckmann, Otto Dix and George Grosz. Hindemith certainly thought little of Mahler, at least at this stage in his career; but Schoenberg, Berg and Webern continued to revere him as a pioneer who had in many ways prepared the stage for their twelve-tone revolution. Ironically, if Schoenberg had allowed himself to look more closely at the Tenth Symphony at the time of his first experiments with atonal serialism, he would have found yet more confirmation for that view. But interest in

Mahler continued, thanks largely to the efforts of his protégés Bruno Walter and Otto Klemperer, and to his friend and energetic champion Willem Mengelberg in Amsterdam. Then in 1924, thirteen years after Mahler's death, and four years after her divorce from Walter Gropius, Alma Mahler began to think again about the Tenth Symphony. She approached Ernst Krenek, who that year married her daughter Anna, with a view to completing and orchestrating what Mahler had left. Whatever he thought of the sketches as a whole, Krenek decided that, for the moment at least, two movements were readily salvageable: the substantial opening Adagio (longer than the Ninth's concluding slow movement), and the much shorter third movement, entitled 'Purgatorio'. The Adagio existed as a sketch score – not quite the richly detailed full score Mahler would have sent to the publisher, but detailed enough to be performable with a little judicious editing and, occasionally, reading between the lines. The Purgatorio existed in orchestrated score only as far as the thirtieth bar, but the four- or five-stave short score for the rest of the movement had obviously reached a highly advanced stage, with the leading orchestral colours precisely indicated. These two movements were performed, by Mahler's colleague Franz Schalk in Vienna and by Alexander Zemlinsky in Prague. The Purgatorio made no great impression – more context was need to explain this enigmatic little movement's role in the overall structure – but the Adagio was welcomed, at least by those who weren't too purist to contemplate hearing it at all. Around the same time a facsimile of Mahler's sketches was published. This turned out not to be complete (there were several baffling omissions, notably the draft orchestral score of the second movement); but for those with eyes to see, it was evident that what Mahler had left was neither a fragment nor a sequence

of disconnected sketches, but a full-length draft of the entire symphony. Interest increased, especially after Mahler's biographer
Richard Specht revealed that Mahler had regarded the Tenth
Symphony as complete in sketch, and that he trusted Alma to do
whatever she thought fit to bring the music to life. For this we have
not only Alma's testimony, but that of Mahler's New York doctor,
Josef Fränkel. Emboldened by this, the American Mahler champion Jack Diether approached Dmitri Shostakovich, who revered
Mahler, then Schoenberg – whose thoughts about Mahler's Tenth
had obviously shifted somewhat – to see if either would under-
take a completion. Both turned the offer down, but not because
they felt the sketch scores and sketches were too indefinite or
fragmentary. For a composer with a strong spiritual identity and
stylistic sound-world of his own to enter those of another requires
an extraordinary act of empathy and, to a certain extent, self-
abnegation. It is no criticism of either Shostakovich or Schoenberg to say that neither of them felt capable of that.

There is nothing strange about a composer entrusting another
to add the finishing touches to his or her work, any more than
there is in a medieval or renaissance artist allocating the finishing touches in a painting to one of his apprentices. Gabriel Fauré,
Claude Debussy and, in his later years, Sergei Prokofiev all handed
the orchestration of some of their works over to trusted colleagues.
When Mozart realised that he was unlikely to finish his last great
work, his Requiem, he asked his wife Constanze to find someone
else to do the job for him. The completion commonly heard today,
by Mozart's former pupil Franz Xaver Süssmayr, is so well-known
and loved that it has itself acquired an aura of sanctity, many still
refusing to believe that Süssmayr – not otherwise an outstandingly talented composer – could have had any significant part in

creating it. A legend has grown up that Mozart played the parts of the Requiem that were still to be written down to Süssmayr, also giving him detailed instructions as to how to fill the gaps. But there is no evidence for that story at all, and plenty against. And if Süssmayr knew of the existence of a sketch by Mozart for a substantial 'Amen' double fugue to end the 'Lacrimosa' section of the Requiem, he chose to ignore it. In fact it turns out that Süssmayr wasn't even Mozart's first choice. Some musicologists, for example the Mozart scholar Richard Maunder, have argued that there are technical deficiencies in the passages Süssmayr filled in that betray his lack of expertise.[11] The comparison is particularly pertinent because, whichever of the various realisations of Mahler's complete Tenth Symphony one hears – by Joe Wheeler, Clinton Carpenter, Rudolph Barshai, Remo Mazzetti or, outstandingly, by Deryck Cooke – there is considerably more genuine Mahler in any of them than there is genuine Mozart in Mozart's Requiem. And yet the Requiem continues to be performed all over the world as Mozart, while some still refuse even to contemplate looking at what is in essence Mahler's Tenth Symphony. I vividly remember the furious reaction of the great Mahler conductor Klaus Tennstedt when asked what he thought of Deryck Cooke's version of the Tenth Symphony: 'Gar nichts!' (absolutely nothing!). It was obvious that Tennstedt had rejected the Cooke Mahler Tenth without even listening to it, yet Süssmayr's pastiche Mozart was apparently perfectly acceptable – and this was a conductor who ranked Mozart and Mahler equally as his 'two geniuses'. Perhaps the best answer to such resolute unbelievers would be to compel them to listen to several of the completions or realisations listed above; for one thing is striking when one compares them: these are not five different symphonies; they aren't even five different

takes on the same or similar musical material – they are unquestionably the same symphony. They may reveal Mahler in slightly
different clothing, but the message that Mahler has to convey is
unmistakably the same in each case.

So does it matter which version one chooses? I think that it does.
It is not for nothing that Deryck Cooke's 'Performing Version of
the Draft for the Tenth Symphony' has been the most performed,
the most recorded and the most widely admired. The clue is in
the title. Cooke never intended his 'performing version' to represent a 'completion' of Mahler's Tenth Symphony, rather to offer to
the scholar, and perhaps more importantly the ordinary listener,
an overview of the stage the Tenth Symphony had reached by the
time of Mahler's death in 1911. Even for experienced musicians
and musicologists, musical sketches can be very hard to read. Any
sighted person can look at Leonardo da Vinci's unfinished *The
Adoration of the Magi* and not only marvel at the beauty of what
he did finish, but peer into the sketched or half-coloured outlines
surrounding those details and imaginatively reconstruct the entire
picture in his or her own mind. But with music, it seems, there is
no substitute for hearing. For years, even some of the most sensitive and intelligent Elgar commentators dismissed the piles of
sketch material that composer left for his unfinished Third Symphony as incoherent and weak in inspiration. It wasn't until the
composer and Elgar enthusiast Anthony Payne released his own
completion of the sketches in 1998 that the musical world woke up
to what Payne had realised all along: that what Elgar had actually
left was a substantial and highly suggestive torso of a visionary late
work, composed in what could now be seen to be an extraordinary
Indian summer. Even the experts, it turned out, had got it badly
wrong. Might the same be true in the case of Mahler's Tenth Sym-

phony? Why not? Elgar, like Mozart, had left substantial gaps in his structure, gaps whose content could only be inferred. Mahler had not. There was in effect a complete melodic line for the entire symphony, with harmony, counterpoint, even orchestral colour sometimes indicated precisely, sometimes strongly implied. Judging from the comments Alma Mahler and Josef Fränkel made to Richard Specht, it would appear that Mahler felt he'd left enough clues for someone sensitive, intelligent, and above all familiar with his orchestral style to do the rest.

Deryck Cooke's work in deciphering and ordering the sketches was heroic enough in itself, and it is striking that most of those who have provided alternative completions of the score have relied on the complete short score Cooke set out for the un-orchestrated fourth and fifth movements. At first Cooke wasn't sure that he could make a performable version of the entire Tenth Symphony in full score. But with energetic encouragement from composer and fellow BBC producer Robert Simpson, Cooke arranged to give a radio talk about the symphony in 1960, the centenary of Mahler's birth, with the Philharmonia Orchestra playing the two published movements, large sections of the draft score of the second, and as much as possible of the last two movements, wherever a plausible Mahlerian orchestral sound could be inferred from the sketches. The performance was conducted by the German-Jewish emigré composer Berthold Goldschmidt, who also gave important critical input to Cooke as he prepared his score – or rather, at this stage, scores. Cooke himself provided spoken links wherever the continuity faltered, or the material on the page appeared too thin for direct realisation. Before long, however, it began to look as though Cooke's relatively modest aim could not only be achieved, but surpassed. As Cooke worked on the manuscript, he

felt it yielding up more and more of its secrets. And as the short
scores had so clearly been conceived in orchestral terms, it was
not a question of guessing or working out some suitable instru-
mentation, but of letting the manuscript speak for itself. The more
Cooke probed, the more distinctly it seemed Mahler's orchestral
voice was making itself heard.

With time Cooke realised that all but about five or six minutes
of the Tenth Symphony could be performed – the whole work
would have lasted around seventy-five minutes. Thrillingly, this
meant that the whole of Mahler's Adagio finale could be played
in the radio broadcast. For many of those who heard it, this was
a profoundly moving experience, something of which can still be
recaptured in the recording that is now commercially available on
the Testament label. Cooke was rarely an engaging public speaker,
and his tone in the programme is often flat and script-bound. But
the content is enthralling, and he sets up the music judiciously,
Perhaps he knew that, if he underplayed his own contribution, the
impact of Mahler's music would be all the greater. Whatever the
case, the finale was a revelation – not just to the many listeners,
but soon afterwards to Alma Mahler herself. The American conductor and Mahler enthusiast Harold Byrns took a recording of
Cooke's programme to Alma, along with Cooke's newly completed
performing version of the score. Owing to a misunderstanding,
Alma had suddenly withdrawn her approval from Cooke's project.
But Byrns reported that she was moved to tears, and that afterwards she expressed astonishment at how much genuine Mahler
she had heard in it. About a week later, Cooke received a letter,
in not quite flawless English, with feelings one can well imagine.
She tells Cooke of Harold Byrns's visit to her in New York, how he
read some of Cooke's articles on the Tenth Symphony, which she

found 'excellent'. Together with Byrns, she went through the newly completed 'perfoming version' of the entire symphony, at the end of which she asked to hear the BBC studio recording. Alma tells Cooke that she was so moved by this performance that she immediately asked to hear it all the way through a second time. 'I realised then that the time had come when I must reconsider my previous decision not to permit the performance of this work.' As a result of this experience, Alma reveals, she has decided 'once and for all' to rescind her ban and give full permission to Cooke to go ahead with performances in any part of the world.

What feelings did Alma privately experience as she listened to Cooke's restoration of Mahler's Tenth Symphony? In all probability it was quite a cocktail of emotions. Presuming that she followed the score, what must have been her reaction when she came to those passages where Mahler had written messages to her – 'To live for you, to die for you,' and the final heart-wrenching 'Almschi!'? Before she had only seen these words scrawled on the sketch manuscript; now they were presented to her in association with some of the most moving music Mahler had ever composed, decked out in recognisably Mahlerian orchestral colours. Whatever she felt, the testimony of those present indicates that it was intense. And one thing was now beyond doubt: she regarded the result as worthy of Mahler's name, of the surname she had decided to re-adopt as her own.

*

The score performed today as the Cooke 'performing version' of Mahler's Tenth Symphony is a later, revised version, made with the assistance of two Mahler-loving British composers, the brothers Colin and David Matthews. But it is still absolutely consistent with

Cooke's aim, to 'represent the stage the work had reached when
Mahler died, in a practical performing version'. There is, as Cooke
readily admitted, a certain amount of conjectural filling in, and even
some pastiche composing. Harmonies, and more rarely bass-lines
or contrapuntal counter-melodies, have occasionally been added,
but always based on motifs Mahler himself has already presented
in the sketches or sketch scores. There are passages where Mahler
indicates only the leading melodic line, but these are almost invari-
ably recapitulatory – they have occurred before, in which case
the harmony can be inferred from what Mahler wrote when the
melodic idea was first presented. When there is a significant devi-
ation from the previous pattern in a recapitulatory passage, Mahler
usually indicates it: in other words the omission represents a kind
of shorthand, clear enough to those who know his style well and
who have studied the sketches thoroughly. When it comes to the
notes themselves, most of the time what one hears is what Mahler
actually wrote, or so close to what he wrote that one can take it
as essentially authentic. The orchestral colouring is more conjectural, especially in parts of the last two movements, but in this case
– as with melodies, counter-melodies, bass-lines and harmonies –
nothing has been added that is not at least implied by Mahler's own
notation and written instructions. As Colin Matthews put it, in a
radio interview with me, 'If it doesn't sound like Mahler, it almost
certainly is Mahler.' Cooke would never have sanctioned compos-
itional 'going out on a limb' – the kind of idiosyncratic imaginative
touches Shostakovich or Schoenberg might well have felt inspired
to add. Where the material remains vague, Cooke and his team
have respected that. In such passages (and they are not very common), the listener remains free to imagine a complete picture for
her- or himself, as with the sketch outlines in Leonardo's *Adoration*

of the Magi. There is nothing quite comparable with this in the entire history of completions by another hand – except perhaps Joe Wheeler's highly creditable version. But Wheeler didn't have access to as many of the sketches as Cooke, and he almost certainly misread the tempo at the beginning of the finale as Andante instead of Adagio (or as Cooke marks it in his score, *Langsam*), thus seriously diminishing the impact of the long silences between the ominous muffled bass drum strokes Mahler evidently wanted. That passage is, as we shall shortly see, perhaps the most extraordinary inspiration in the entire symphony. What it might signify, and what its dramatic function might be in the complete argument, we will consider next. It is evident however from Cooke's final version of the score that the Tenth was well on its way to being one of Mahler's greatest symphonies, perhaps even the greatest of them all. It has all the intensity of Symphony no. 9, but with an arguably better formal balance: the arch-like structure (Adagio–Scherzo–Allegretto moderato–[Scherzo]–Adagio) is as roundly satisfying overall as that of the 'classical' Sixth, whilst its emotional narrative is if anything even more gripping. And it is important to remember that for Mahler, that narrative only made sense if heard complete: those who have allowed themselves to hear only the opening Adagio have clearly mistaken his intent. In one of a series of intensely effusive love poems sent to Alma in August 1910, whilst he was both working on Symphony no. 10 and preparing for the premiere of the Eighth, Mahler expressed his desires for her and for his latest symphony in these words, written on manuscript paper:

> Let me condense the tremors of my yearning,
> Th' eternity of bliss divine in your embrace,
> Into one great song . . .[12]

It is time now to consider in detail how that 'one great song' unfolds, and what it tells us about Mahler's spiritual journey during that eventful summer of 1910.

I. Adagio

After experiencing the Ninth Symphony's long-protracted, almost unbearably tender 'dying' ending, many listeners will have asked themselves – as Schoenberg and Bernstein did – what could possibly come next? But then, if Mahler had died before starting the Ninth, the same question could reasonably have been asked of the ending of *Das Lied von der Erde*. The Tenth Symphony answers that question, and the answer it provides when heard in its entirety is emphatically not 'yet another heartbreaking . . . farewell', as Leonard Bernstein claimed. At first it is hard to tell precisely what it is. Unaccompanied violas, *pianissimo*, present a ghostly, groping, tonally rootless theme that would not be out of place in one of Shostakovich's death-haunted late works. After the awe-inspiring slow extinction at the end of the Ninth Symphony, this could almost be heard as a faint, numbed, disbelieving reawakening: 'Am I still here?' But then the violas settle slowly onto a soul-restoringly solid chord of F sharp major, reinforced by trombones; the tempo changes to Adagio, and the violins take up the song, *p. aber sehr warm* (soft but very warm).

A word or two about the tempo change is in order here. A tradition has already grown up of taking the 'introductory' viola theme very slowly indeed, and it is undeniably effective: the shadowy searching for something definite to hold onto becomes undeniably more intense when taken at an agonisingly slow crawl. But Mahler had little time for tradition: he famously dismissed it as *Schlamperei* – 'slovenliness', or even 'sluttishness'. Unless he lived to changed his mind about his initial tempo indication, he would almost certainly have said the same here. The indication is 'Andante', literally 'walking pace', and unquestionably faster than Adagio. So this is not in any way a classical 'slow introduction'. The effect of playing it as an Andante can be clearly heard in the recording of Deryck Cooke's 1960 BBC programme, but it has rarely been done that way since. It isn't simply a matter of emotional effect: the alternation between Andante, Adagio and a slightly faster tempo marked *Fliessend* ('flowing') continues for much of this long first movement, and helps give it its rondo-like circular character.

There is much more to this than tempo: what we have here is in effect three different kinds of music, each apparently with its own emotional agenda. The Andante music, almost always played by unaccompanied violas, remains darkly probing; later there is an element of tormented aspiration, but on its almost final appearance (there is one last echo in the coda) it returns on first and second violins, marked *Etwas zögernd* ('somewhat hesitant'), and now it seems to have despaired of ever finding a satisfying tonal resolution. It is in moments like this that Mahler comes closest to the world of Schoenberg's first atonal works. The Adagio music however is warmly aspiring, striving upwards – always from a chord of F sharp major – despite the melodic line and the harmonies twisting themselves into some astonishing dissonances along the way. Harmonically this is the most modernist music Mahler had produced so far, yet the way it repeatedly launches itself from an unambiguous F sharp major suggests that Mahler was far from done with tonality. As we shall see, the ending of this movement, and of the symphony itself, confirms that interpretation. Alongside the Andante and Adagio music, the dance-like sections marked *Fliessend* reveal something else entirely: a wintry dance music, sometimes dejected, sometimes sour or sarcastic. It is the perfect foil to the Brucknerian aspiration of the Adagio passages, a reminder of how often Mahler built opposition, even self-contradiction, into his musical statements.

The despairing, skeletally scored *Etwas zögernd* is followed by an astonishing surprise. The full orchestra, including four trumpets, four trombones, tuba and swirling harps, delivers a hammer-blow chord of A flat minor. After a kind of horror-struck dissonant brass chorale, the *Fliessend* dance music attempts to recover the previous argument. Instead the first violins freeze on a single note, A, and the orchestra piles up an immense dissonance, with the violins' A now painfully sustained on a high trumpet. The shattering discord is heard again, the trumpet note continues, and both sets of violins scream out a stratospherically high cry of despair or terror, as though torn from the heart. Is this a vision of death, of hell, of insanity? But as the music calms, the warm solid F sharp major is heard again, and a much quieter, increasingly peaceful coda gradually draws together the threads of what we have already heard. Some commentators, understandably overawed by this movement's terrifying dissonant climax, have concluded that Mahler was now ready to follow his friend Schoenberg into the atonal Beyond. But that is to ignore something highly significant that happens at the end of this first movement – and indeed one literally 'key' feature of the climactic dissonance itself. It is piled up in thirds, taking in nine of the twelve available notes of the chromatic scale; but the bass is a firm perfect fifth, C sharp and G sharp, the fundamental notes of a conventional dominant chord in the home key of F sharp – see Ex. 8.1(a). It is at least arguable then that this abysmal dissonance, apparently teetering on the brink of tonal dissolution, could also be read as a hugely expanded dominant chord. Then, just nine bars from the end of the movement, another chord is built up softly in thirds above the same C sharp-G sharp bass, only this time the notes of the chord thus built up all belong to the scale of F sharp major, into which key the final four bars of the movement deftly twist – Ex. 8.1(b). This is not a 'resolution' of the movement's climactic dissonance in the approved textbook meaning of the word, but in another sense it is. The discord has been 'rationalised' in F sharp major, then resolved more or less correctly into that very key.

Symphony No 10, First Movement

There is one other feature of the Adagio's climax that can be drawn, with a little harmonic lateral thinking, into this pattern of

'half-resolution'. If the hammer-blow chord of A flat minor following the violins' softly disintegrating *Etwas zögernd* passage is
reread as G sharp minor (A flat and G sharp are identical on the
piano), then this chord, combined with the climactic dissonance
and its last-minute 'rationalisation' and turn to the home key,
can be seen to form the first stage in a gigantic II–V–I cadence
in F sharp major. This is one of the oldest and most conventional
cadential formulae in Western classical music. Here then is the
first, and by no means the last vindication of Michael Kennedy's
claim that the Tenth Symphony 'establishes beyond doubt that
Mahler was entering a new phase'. On one level this extraordinary
harmonic-dramatic sequence is indeed 'even more prophetic of
the collapse of tonality' than anything in the Ninth Symphony; yet
at the same time, Mahler's outlining of a traditional, tonally secure
pattern in the later stages of the Adagio is 'even more insistent
upon the Classical-Romantic procedures which had always nurtured him.'[13] Mahler looks forwards and backwards at the same
time, and somehow finds a kind of bridge connecting the musical
'world of yesterday' and Schoenberg's vision of the future. But
what else would one expect from a composer whose declared aim
in writing symphonies was to 'embrace everything'?

II. Scherzo

Having stared into the future harmonically in the first movement
of the Tenth Symphony, Mahler now proceeds to outline the shape
of things to come in the dimension of rhythm. Strictly speaking,
the nine-note, borderline atonal dissonance in the first movement
was not in itself prophetic: Schoenberg had already stepped off
the cliff-edge into non-tonality in the finale of his Second String
Quartet, composed in 1907–8 and premiered, with scandalous

effect, in Vienna in December 1908 (Mahler had seen the score). But the innovations in the Tenth Symphony's first Scherzo are without precedent. A year before Igor Stravinsky finished his ballet *Petrushka*, and three years before the Russian modernist released his still more rhythmically ground-breaking *Rite of Spring*, Mahler treads boldly into giddying, eccentric new dance measures. At a time when many post-Wagnerian composers – including Mahler's friend and unofficial mentor Bruckner – tended to adopt a steadying *Lohengrin*-like metrical regularity in their music, Mahler's attitude to rhythm always showed a refreshingly vital freedom. Think of the opening 4/4, 3/4, 2/4, 4/4 pattern that springs so beautifully from the words 'Veni, veni creator spiritus!' at the opening of the Eighth Symphony; or, at the other extreme, the sinister limping 4/8, 3/8 alternations in the trio sections of the Scherzo of the Sixth. But this movement goes way beyond anything he had ever tried before. At the beginning we have a bar of 3/2, two of 2/2, one of 5/4, another 2/2 bar, then a complex alternation of bars of 3/4 and 2/2. The energy in this writing is terrific, while the folk-dancing motifs themselves are transformed into something almost cubist – it can be like watching a high-spirited rural Austrian stomp through rapidly shifting panels of frosted glass.

Some respite is provided by a gentler contrasting *Ländler* theme, now in a reassuringly regular 3/4 pulse, though the flashes of acid orchestral colouring and touches of harmonic distortion remind us that this is still the composer of the opening Adagio. But something else does too: the *Ländler*'s rising four-note motif – G–B flat–G–B flat, in the movement's home key of F sharp – strongly recalls the figure that launched the violins' great song in almost every one of the first movement's Adagio sections. The daring half-resolution at the end of the opening movement has

prepared the way for something unexpected, but in context wonderfully logical: a furious, exhilarating dance, building steadily – a
few more reflective moments notwithstanding – to a great cry of
joy, with the rising four-note *Ländler* motif now shouted out triumphantly by massed horns. If the first movement's Adagio music
expressed aspiration, however tortured at times, this first Scherzo
shows that striving has not been in vain. If Mahler had finished
the symphony at this point, that would have been the end of the
'farewell to life' interpretation of *Das Lied von der Erde* and the
Ninth Symphony – or rather it would have given the unquestion-
able 'Abschied' or 'Le-be-wohl' elements in those two works a new
retrospective colouring. It could now be seen that the confron-
tation with death in those two works was not the culmination,
but an important stage in Mahler's continuing spiritual journey.
Like many a man or woman approaching his or her fiftieth birthday, and at the same time trying to come to terms with irreparable
loss, Mahler had faced mortality square on, but with unusual,
lived-through intensity. But having done so, he was ready for a
'new phase'. The dark utterances of *Das Lied von der Erde* and the
Ninth Symphony may have seemed to make the exuberance and
exultation of the Eighth a thing of the irrecoverable past – but,
as the first Scherzo of the Tenth Symphony shows in its ecstatic
closing moments, they could be recovered. The Eighth Symphony
expressed an essential aspect of Mahler's personality: eclipsed,
certainly, after the crisis of 1907, but in the end irrepressible. It
is tempting to borrow a phrase from Berlioz and call this first
Scherzo 'the return to life'.

But the symphony now takes a very different turn, challenging
the Scherzo's final tumultuous assertion and demanding an even
more profoundly heroic attempt at resolution.

III. Purgatorio

At what stage in the composition of the Tenth Symphony did Mahler find Walter Gropius's letter, and thus learn of Alma's infidelity? It would appear that the first two movements were completed, or nearly completed, in short score before that cataclysmic discovery, in which case any 'return to life' message would now face the ultimate trial by fire. One should always be careful of trying to read the influence of immediate life events into a work in progress: Mahler almost certainly continued to work on the orchestral sketch score of the first Scherzo after Gropius's 'accidental' revelation, but if so it doesn't appear to have made any significant difference to the character of the music – the life-affirming goal remains the same. But there is one sign that the trauma left its mark on the first Adagio. The shattering nine-note climactic dissonance does not appear in the preliminary sketch score: it was inserted later on in the process, almost certainly in response to what Mahler learned, and as a direct expression of the spiritual crisis it precipitated.

There is however evidence in the manuscript that the Purgatorio was composed at least partly after that devastating shock. It is in this movement that we find the first of those desperate comments, half diary entries, half pleas to God, Alma or someone or something less definite. On the second page of the orchestral score occurs the fragmentary exclamation, *Tod! Verk!* ('Death! Annun[-ciation]!') – almost certainly a reference to the chilling passage in Act II of Wagner's *Die Walküre* in which Brünnhilde appears to the doomed Siegmund as the *Todesverkündigung*, 'the annunciation of death'. And on the last page of the sketch short score we find *Erbarmen!!* ('Have mercy!!'), along with an almost exact quotation of Christ's final agonised cry from the cross, *O Gott, O*

Gott! Warum hast du mich verlassen? ('Oh God, oh God! Why hast thou forsaken me?'), and finally an echo of the Lord's Prayer, *Dein Wille geschehe!* ('Thy will be done!'). Then there is the character of the music itself. The opening accompanying figure unmistakably evokes another song from Mahler's *Des Knaben Wunderhorn*: 'Das irdische Leben' ('Earthly life'). The title of the song (seemingly Mahler's own) places it in deliberate opposition to the serene depiction of a child's dreams of paradise in 'Das himmlische Leben' ('Heavenly life'), that became the song-finale of Mahler's Fourth Symphony. This titular opposition suggests that what is depicted in 'Das irdische Leben' is indeed a kind of hell. A child cries out to its mother repeatedly, 'Mother, oh mother, I'm hungry! Give me bread or I shall die!' The mother's replies are apparently meant to be reassuring: just wait, she insists, the grain will be harvested tomorrow, then it is about to be threshed, then it is on the point of being baked. But by the time the bread is baked, the child is already dead. A starving child, whose mother cannot (or perhaps will not) provide what it desperately needs, 'Oh God! Why hast thou forsaken me?', the potential loss of the *Ewig-Weibliche* – it all adds up. And at the heart of this spooky little movement, mostly scored for drastically scaled-down forces, is an anguished full-orchestral trio section, full of heart-rending, lamenting cries that will return, transformed, in the black vision at the opening of the Finale.

At one point Mahler changed the title of this movement from 'Purgatorio' to 'Purgatorio oder Inferno' – 'Purgatory or Hell' – but later crossed out the last two words. The question remains relevant however. For Roman Catholics, Purgatory is the place where redeemed souls go after death to have their sins purged from them by 'sulfurous and tormenting flames', as the Ghost famously describes them in *Hamlet*. For the souls in Hell however there is no hope of final release: the decree of damnation is absolute. It all mirrors the tone and imagery of that letter Mahler sent to Alma from his composing hut: the letter that cries out of possession by 'dark spirits', that begs her to grant him the knowledge of whether he may still 'hope for salvation', or expect to be 'damned'.

The links between the Purgatorio and Mahler's mental crisis only become explicit however when one takes the comments scrawled on the manuscript paper into account. In the next movement, the second Scherzo, the music mostly speaks for itself.

IV [Scherzo]

Mahler did not actually label this movement 'Scherzo' in his sketches, yet its character, and particularly its sustained driving 3/4 dance pulse, make the identification inevitable. Where the first Scherzo subjected its dance rhythms to wild metric mutations, the second keeps up its driven, nightmarish waltz tempo right through to the end. This is in fact the most 'sketchy' of the four movements. Identifying the order of Mahler's sketches, and in some cases the actual musical substance, posed Cooke more problems here than in any of the other four movements, and there are passages that still sound somewhat thin, even after Cooke's brilliant and sympathetic reconstruction work. Without doubt Mahler would have added more contrapuntal and harmonic detail, and plenty of telling orchestral colour, yet even here the melodic continuity is more or less unbroken: the essence of the symphony's 'one great song' is all there on the pages. Strikingly, every rival completion since Cooke's accepts his ordering of the surviving material.

From the very beginning there are strong echoes of the first movement of *Das Lied von der Erde*, 'The Drinking Song of the

Earth's Misery'. As early as the fifth bar the sharp *fortissimo* chord from three low trombones (indicated as such in the sketch) directly recalls the harshly dismissive ending of that anguished, seemingly nihilistic song. This is a vital clue for anyone who wants to add musical flesh to Mahler's sketches. Cooke is, as usual, respectfully restrained in his scoring and filling out (he actually removed some of the extra percussion writing added early on by Berthold Goldschmidt), but so much still comes across in a sympathetic performance. While the resemblance to 'The Drinking Song of the Earth's Misery' is patent, the language is more extreme, with plenty of wide expressionist leaps in the melodic and contrapuntal lines and a greater incidence of dissonance. The contrasting, gentler *Ländler* sections are perhaps the least clearly defined music in the whole symphony, requiring more imaginative participation on the part of the listener than anywhere else in Cooke's final score; even here though the emotional impetus and melodic sweep carries the music forwards. And now the comments scrawled on the manuscript readily connect to the mood and character of the music: *Der Teufel tanzt es mit mir* ('The Devil dances it with me'), *Wahnsinn, fass mich an, Verfluchten* ('Madness, seize me, the accursed one'), *Vernichte mich, dass ich vergesse, dass ich bin, dass ich aufhöre zu sein, dass ich ver . . .* ('Annihilate me, that I may forget that I am, that I may cease to be, that I . . .'). The very incompleteness of some of these comments, and the violence and untidiness of the writing (in marked contrast to most of the musical script) testify to both their urgent sincerity and their spontaneity. Some have accused Mahler of being melodramatic (a still-common complaint from Mahler-sceptics), but to look at these frantically scribbled interjections whilst following the music makes the accusation seem churlish.

The most significant of these comments occurs at the end of the movement. Gradually the Scherzo's fury abates into a sinister, disintegrating coda. The fragmentary look of the music on the page is now eloquent, the music is 'breaking down' before our ears. Ghostly fragments of dance rhythms peter out on timpani, bass drum and cymbals. Without doubt Mahler would have done more with this, perhaps bringing the sound world closer to that of his most demonic Scherzo, the central movement of his Seventh Symphony. But it can still be intensely moving, and the final touch – a sudden low thud on a very large muffled bass drum – can be a heart-stopping shock even when one knows what is coming. This is the point at which Mahler added that remark, obviously addressed to Alma, 'You alone know what this means.' Alma herself provided the explanation in her *Memories and Letters*. It refers to an event that occurred not long after the couple's arrival in New York, either in 1907 or 1908. Alma had just received a visitor in her rooms at the Hotel Majestic, when suddenly something in the street far below caught their attention. There seemed to be some kind of commotion taking place. Alma and her guest leaned out of the hotel window and saw a long procession making its way slowly up the street along the side of Central Park. It turned out to be the funeral cortège of a fireman who had died a heroic death in a blaze in the city – apparently the newspapers were full of the story. It was just as the chief mourners were passing by the hotel that the procession came to a halt, and the master of ceremonies stepped forward to give a short speech – what he actually said was inaudible from the Mahlers' eleventh-floor suite. Then followed something chilling: a brief stroke on a muffled drum, followed by a 'dead silence'. Then the procession began its slow tread once again. Finding herself moved to tears by this spectacle, Alma turned anxiously to look at Mahler's window. Could it be that he hadn't noticed, and if so might that be for the best? 'But he too was leaning out and his face was streaming with tears. The brief drum-stroke impressed him so much that he used it in the Tenth Symphony.'[14] But it isn't just one drum-stroke. The deadly muffled thuds continue, each one followed by a 'dead silence', into the Finale, which now follows without a break.

V. Finale

Mahler is quite specific about the kind of drum stroke he wants. It is marked 'vollstandige gedämpfte' in the sketch, i.e. 'completely muffled'. Did he in fact want the drum to be shrouded? If he had, this would give the drum a sinister appearance even before it had sounded a note. This is the dark heart of the Tenth Symphony. From the silences emerge some of the most sombre sounds Mahler ever created: a subterranean growl on two contrabassoons (precisely indicated in the sketch) and a baleful slowly climbing figure on a deep bass instrument – almost certainly a bass tuba, though Mahler may not have been quite sure about the kind of tone colour he wanted at the time of writing. The British philosopher Bryan Magee, a close friend of Deryck Cooke, tells an extraordinary story about this passage. It occurs in his introduction to the collection of Cooke's writings entitled *Vindications*. It was 27 October 1976, and Cooke was under observation for a suspected brain tumour. Around midnight, Magee was at home talking to a female guest about Mahler, about Deryck Cooke, and about his work on the Tenth Symphony. Magee decided to play her extracts from one of the recordings. When they came to the beginning of the finale, Magee was startled by how powerfully it affected both of them. It suddenly became clear to him that this passage expressed a real existential catastrophe. If it was possible to express the extinction, the absolute end of everything, in music, Mahler had done it here. The next day Magee received a call: Cooke had suffered a stroke the previous day and had been rushed to hospital. He had died some time between midnight and one in the morning.

One doesn't have to believe in extrasensory perception to believe the story, or to acknowledge the aptness of Magee's description of the music. This does feel like the absolute end, the bottom dropping out of everything. It is a deeper catastrophe than even the climactic dissonance in the Tenth Symphony's first Adagio, and this time it is one that seems incapable of even an ambiguous 'half-resolution'. A composer can resolve a discord, but a silence? And yet, astonishingly, that is what actually happens in the finale of Mahler's Tenth Symphony. The fragmentary motifs that emerge from the silences, one strongly reminiscent of the tortured cry in the central section of the Purgatorio, become a little more definite – figures can be made out, even in this abysmal darkness. One of them, a rising minor seventh on the horn (again clearly indicated) is taken up by a solo flute, and from this emerges a long, exquisitely touching melody. Talking on BBC Radio 4's long-running *Desert Island Discs* programme, Berthold Goldschmidt described this flute melody as the one thing above all that justified what Cooke did in rescuing Mahler's Tenth Symphony. It is like Orpheus, almost destroyed by the loss of Eurydice, beginning to sing his way out of his own personal Hell of grief. Somehow the symphony's 'one great song' has survived even this catastrophe. At first it is painfully fragile, but as the violins take up the song it grows in warmth, strength and ardour. But then, just as it seems to be building to a radiant B major climax (for the first time in a long while, we are back on the borders of F sharp major), the muffled drum thuds are heard again, the baleful introductory music returns, and memories of the Purgatorio seem to sink back again into despair.

There now begins a sinister Allegro moderato which, after several glances back at the Purgatorio and second Scherzo, seems to arrive in calmer regions, again in B major, and again with memories of the flute's song. But the Allegro moderato music interrupts this momentary reverie, more urgently this time, and a huge climax is reached, bringing a return of the first movement's climactic dissonance, with the high-held trumpet note that originally sounded through it. This time there is no immediate soothing effect. Horns sound out the violas' ghostly probing unaccompanied theme from the very beginning of the symphony, this time with the trumpet's high A sustained, then falling slowly. (The importance of observing the marked Andante tempo is crucial here, or the trumpeter would run out of breath far too soon.) But by now we should be aware that Mahler's 'one great song' can survive almost anything. It survived this dissonant onslaught once before; it survived even the vision of absolute nothingness at the beginning of the finale; and it survives again now. Mahler did not indicate in the sketch which instrument, or instruments, were to take up the melodic line afresh here. Cooke decided on woodwind, then brass, following implications in the sketches. It could have been strings, always the core of Mahler's orchestral sound palate, but by delaying the entry of the violins until the next modulation, Cooke subtly heightens the effect of the latter, and throws the movement's hymn-like final section into more effective relief. The woodwinds' entry is in B flat major, in which key (as we've already seen) Mahler originally intended to end the symphony. This would have provided a kind of long-term resolution to the B flat *minor* of the Purgatorio, but combined with the change in the leading motivic material from that movement onwards, it might have produced another case of the 'dangerous disparity' Cooke found in the Fifth Symphony. We would have been presented with a Tenth Symphony in two quite distinct (if slightly unequal) halves. But one doesn't have to have perfect pitch to grasp the significance of what Mahler eventually decided. In the space of a single bar, violins lead the music deftly to the home key of the first two movements, F sharp major. The spacing of the chord in the lower voices exactly recalls the beginning of the first movement's Adagio section. We are back where we almost started, on solid ground again.

The radiant hymn, or wordless love-song, that ends the Tenth Symphony is one of its chief glories. Comparison of Cooke's performing version with the notes of the sketch (conscientiously reproduced in the published score) will show that for the most part what Cooke has provided is a highly professional realisation as string writing of what Mahler left, with discreet additions on woodwind and occasionally brass. The notes are almost entirely Mahler's own: even the missing harmonies in the short G major section can be inferred from a comparison with the equivalent passage earlier in the movement – as Mahler almost certainly intended. One thing however is particularly striking about the harmonies in this last section. Tonality may be 'extended', in ways that might have surprised even Wagner, but the sense of rooted-ness – of F sharp as the secure 'home' – persists to the very end. It is one of the things that makes this section so fundamentally serene, despite the impassioned outbursts along the way. After all this symphony's exhilarating and terrifying adventures, the tonal solidity, associated so ecstatically with the *Ewig-Weibliche* at the end of the Eighth, has been regained. Granted, it has also been transformed, enriched, yet the continuity with the musical statement whose premiere Mahler was preparing in the summer of 1910 remains. There are perhaps as many potential readings of Mahler's spiritual progress in the fraught years between the Eighth Symphony's completion and its triumphant premiere as there are ears to hear. There is one however that strikes me forcefully. Mahler has hymned his ideal love, his *Ewig-Weibliche*, ecstatically in Symphony no. 8, while simultaneously allowing us to see just enough of the shadow side of all that heavenly glory, the pain and doubt barely concealed behind the protestations of eternal bliss. Then, in *Das Lied von der Erde* and the Ninth Symphony, he has pitched himself into that shadowy world and confronted his worst fears and deepest griefs with astonishing courage and imaginative intensity. Now, in the Tenth Symphony, under conditions of terrifying duress, he has not only acknowledged the very worst, but begun to edge his way back to something better, more hopeful perhaps, certainly exquisitely beautiful, and musically more secure and integrated than anything Mahler had created since the Eighth Symphony's overwhelming conclusion.

As for the meaning of the strings' great final cry, over which Mahler wrote his last fervent 'Almschi!', inevitably that has been much debated. For Deryck Cooke, this was the music, not of death, but of love – as that last avowal of devotion to Alma made abundantly clear. For Michael Kennedy the ending of the Tenth is gloriously affirmative, an assertion of nothing less than spiritual victory. For Mahler's biographer Henry-Louis de La Grange, however, that last 'Almschi!' could more readily be read as a cry of desperate longing, an entreaty to Mahler's heartless *Ewig-Weibliche* not to desert him in his time of deepest need. Any of these is possible, yet that does not diminish the fact that, for Mahler, surviving the horror of the summer of 1910 and bringing the Tenth Symphony to this state of near-completion was in itself as great a spiritual victory as the following month's sensational premiere of the Eighth. Like the symphony's melodic songline, Mahler's sanity has been tested to breaking point, and yet it has survived. Whatever the ending of the Tenth may or may not tell us about Mahler's feelings for Alma at this late stage of his life, it is surely not wrong to hear the afterglow of that inner victory in the symphony's close.

*

If it is possible to read Mahler's Tenth Symphony as an extraordinarily courageous act of 'holding together' and of re-affirmation, that interpretation can also be applied beyond the personal, psychological dimension. What we now call 'classical' music was entering a period of fascinating diversification in the first decade and a half of the twentieth century. When Mahler was born in 1860, the Austro-German musical world was polarising sharply between the 'progressives', who venerated Wagner and Liszt, and the 'classicists' or 'classical romantics' whose great father figure was Brahms. At the same time nationalism was stirring on the margins of Mitteleuropa: in Bohemia, in Hungary, in Scandinavia and with particular urgency in Russia. In 1868, when Mahler was eight, the Norwegian Edvard Grieg completed the first version of his now world-famous Piano Concerto – Lisztian in some of its stylistic elements, but owing a marked debt to Norway's flavoursome indigenous folk music. By 1910 it was one of the most popular works in the concert repertoire – so much so that only the previous year it had secured the distinction of being the first piano concerto ever to be recorded. But there was more to this concerto's success than a sign that countries outside the German-speaking world could also produce music that was worthy to be heard (however much Schoenberg may have continued to deny it). In 1945, the Hungarian conductor Antal Doráti expressed amused disdain when he found the score of Grieg's concerto in the living room of the nationalist-modernist Béla Bartók. Bartók was indignant: Grieg was hugely important, a crucial figure, he told the still doubtful Doráti. Didn't he realise that Grieg was one of the first to throw away the 'German yoke' and turn back to the music of his own people for inspiration?[15] Back in 1911, the year of Mahler's death, Bartók had composed his groundbreaking *Allegro barbaro* for solo piano, one of his first works to draw on his experience collecting folk music in Eastern Europe and the Balkan peninsula. For Bartók, Mahler embodied the 'German yoke' he was energetically trying to throw off. But what might Bartók have thought if he'd been able to hear Mahler's Tenth Symphony? It would have been fascinating to observe his reaction to the first Scherzo, with its complex rhythmic games, strongly associated with the folk music Mahler himself knew. Might he even have hailed Mahler as an important forerunner?

In time, Bartók's *Allegro barbaro* would be seen as a more significant blow for musical modernism than for nationalism, which for readily understandable reasons plummeted out of fashion in the years immediately after the First World War. The same is true for the ballets Stravinsky composed in 1909–13: *The Firebird* (1909–10), *Petrushka* (1910–11) and *The Rite of Spring* (1911–13), though at the time of the *Firebird*'s premiere in 1910 it was Stravinsky's 'Russianness' that caught Parisian critics' attention, and Stravinsky's increasingly daring rhythmic experimentation – even the convulsively irregular dance patterns of the notorious 'Sacrifical Dance' from *The Rite* – was often explained (and sometimes dismissed) as a manifestation of Russian nationalism. Stravinsky's harmonic experimentation, leading in *The Rite* to his own highly idiosyncratic equivalent of Schoenberg's 'emancipation of the dissonance', was another matter. As we've already seen, a nationalist aim could also be identified lurking behind the works Arnold Schoenberg was producing in 1909–11, though this would have been far less easy for contemporary listeners to make out. Emboldened by his first voyage into the atonal beyond in his Second String Quartet, Schoenberg had composed his Freudian 'monodrama' *Erwartung* (1909), and his first purely orchestral non-tonal experiment, *Five Pieces for Orchestra* (1909). The harmonic world opened up in these works – in which dissonance is indefinitely suspended, never resolved – is far wilder than almost anything in Mahler's Tenth.

In other quarters, however, nationalism was producing very different kinds of musical flowering, some also with far-reaching consequences. When it came to atonal harmony, Schoenberg saw himself as the radical heir to Wagner – and to one work of Wagner's in particular: *Tristan und Isolde*. The Prelude to Wagner's opera famously strikes out from a mysterious discord, not easily rationalised in textbook terms, which remains incompletely resolved at the end of the Prelude. This aching dissonance is only satisfactorily eased into consonance at the end of the opera, some four hours later. But there is another radical prelude by Wagner, one whose innovative nature Schoenberg discounted, presumably because it failed to suit his own 'progressive' agenda. This is the Prelude to *Das Rheingold*, the first instalment of the massive four-part *Ring* cycle. What Wagner offers in this instance is nothing less than the possibility of 'emancipation of the consonance'. A chord of E flat major is sustained for around five minutes, without a single change of harmony, from which fertile music motifs emerge – from the chord itself and from the notes of the E flat major scale. As a young man Sibelius was powerfully impressed by this Prelude, and wrote about it after making his own journey by boat down the River Rhine in 1894. After having taken dissonance and tonal ambiguity as far as he felt capable in his Fourth Symphony (1910–11), Sibelius returned resolutely to tonality in his next symphony, the Fifth (1914–19), which, as we've seen, he compared to a river in his diaries. In the first minute of this symphony we hear only the notes of a major scale – significantly it's the scale of E flat – as the harmony rocks back and forth between two chords, with a motif deriving from both gradually putting out shoots and tendrils like a plant growing from seed. The finale of Sibelius's Fifth similarly opens with a long stretch of music built up above an implied sustained E flat pedal bass. In the second half of the twentieth century Sibelius's move back to rooted consonance was dismissed as regressive; but opinion has shifted considerably in recent times, and in the counter-revolutionary scores of the American minimalists, especially Steve Reich and John Adams, the influence of Sibelius's thought processes and sound-world is patent. Interestingly, it was in 1910 that the English nationalist composer Ralph Vaughan Williams found his voice resonantly for the first time, in his still hugely popular *Fantasia on a Theme by Thomas Tallis*, in which for almost the entire first section (around five and a half minutes of music) *only* consonances are heard. This very different kind of radicalism has cast a long shadow, and can be heard today both in new concert works and in film and TV documentary scores.

Of course nationalism was by no means the only force steering the wild musical experimentation of the early twentieth century. The rise of nationalist ideologies could be seen as one attempt to fill the void after Nietzsche's proclamation of the death of God.

An increasing interest in stranger, less dogmatically defined forms of mysticism was another, as in the case of the Russian composer Alexander Scriabin. Scriabin's construction of non-tonal chords, by piling up intervals such as fourths and fifths in his later piano works and his orchestral *Poem of Ecstasy* (1908), is arguably closer to what Mahler does in his nine-note climactic dissonance than any of Schoenberg's remarkable contrivances. The mystical thinking that lay behind Scriabin's innovations was partly influenced by Nietzsche, but also by the avowedly internationalist attitudes of Theosophy, an occultist religion founded in America in the late nineteenth century, inspired by the writings of Helena Blavatsky, and growing enormously in popularity amongst the artistically inclined middle and upper classes in the early twentieth. Significantly this was the period that also saw the publication of the American philosopher William James's hugely influential *The Varieties of Religious Experience* (1902), in which mystical experiences are examined from a psychological, empiricist point of view. American transcendentalist thinking, with its emphasis on spiritual 'self-reliance', also left its mark on the teeming, kaleidoscopic musical canvases of Charles Ives, whose most famous work, *The Unanswered Question*, was composed in 1908. Like Mahler, Ives saw his role as a composer as that of embracing the world, in all its baffling multiplicity. But *The Unanswered Question* is one of his most clearly focused works, and its attempt to embrace both pure consonance and atonality is particularly striking in the context of these times. Here slow, quiet strings provide a cyclical background of tonal triads (depicting 'The Silence of the Druids', according to Ives's note in the score), against which a solo trumpet repeatedly poses 'The Perennial Question of Existence': a non-tonal phrase that seems to demand some kind of response. Four woodwind instruments attempt to provide an answer, but their replies become increasingly chaotic, finally breaking up in what sounds like frustration or despair. The trumpet sounds the question once more, but this time only the strings are heard, settling for the last time on their final chord of G major. Is the 'question' really unanswered? Or, as Leonard Bernstein put it challengingly, do the 'Druids' have it – tonality is eternal? Whichever interpretation one chooses, *The Unanswered Question* seems to leave many listeners with a sense of a deep split at the heart of being: the eternal-tonal and the world of human, time-bound questioning may coexist, but they remain as fundamentally separate and irreconcilable as parallel universes. It is fascinating to consider that, as Ives was composing *The Unanswered Question*, a young researcher at the Swiss Patent Office named Albert Einstein was developing his Theory of General Relativity, according to which time itself could be said to move at different rates depending on gravitational influence. *The Unanswered Question* could almost have been composed to illustrate Einstein's revolutionary assertions.

This brings us then to another feature of Mahler's Tenth that makes it such an outstandingly original statement for its time, and one that makes resistance to its message all the harder to understand or condone. During the course of this roughly seventy-five-minute symphony all the worlds opened up in the pieces mentioned above are acknowledged in some form or other, however difficult to reconcile they might seem. We are led to consider the possibility of atonality, of chords built up in non-tonal patterns of regular intervals, but also of re-imagined, enhanced tonality, sustained gloriously in the symphony's final section; dizzying new rhythmic possibilities are opened out, but so too is the possibility of utter, deadening silence, in which time itself seems to stop; folk or urban popular music is evoked in both Scherzos and in the *Fliessend* dance music from the opening Adagio, sometimes with intense affection, sometimes with something closer to disgust or fear, but always on the highest level of imagination. The desperate unappeasable longing of *Tristan* finds a twentieth-century echo, but so too does the rooted affirmation of the *Rheingold* Prelude, along with its organically fertile motivic growth. In this Mahler goes far further than even his friend Richard Strauss, in whose opera *Salome* (1905) brilliant shock-horror modernism emerges like a writhing worm from the decaying tendrils of very late, monstrously over-ripe romanticism. In any case, by 1910 Strauss had already stepped back from the expressionist brink with his tender, opulent evocation of the European world of yesterday, *Der Rosenkavalier*. It is important too to stress that Mahler's Tenth Symphony is not a wildly eclectic collage like Ives's *Central Park in the Dark*, composed alongside *The Unanswered Question* in 1908. As with Orpheus in the ancient Greek myth, Mahler's journey takes him through very different worlds in this symphony; and also as with Orpheus, it is singing that enables him to sustain his sense of purpose and direction, even in the depths of Hell. The Tenth Symphony's gigantic songline embraces a whole world of musical possibilities and draws them all into 'one great song'. Some have suggested that if Mahler had lived, he would have followed Schoenberg into a complete rejection of tonality. But the Tenth as a complete statement indicates something very different: that what seemed for much of the twentieth century to be an irreconcilable split, between Schoenbergian modernism and any kind of music with its roots still in tonality, was in fact bridgeable, even if a little 'lateral' thinking was required in the process. In this respect perhaps Dmitri Shostakovich was Mahler's most sympathetic, profoundly understanding successor, though even his achievement does not go far beyond what Mahler accomplished in his Tenth Symphony. Here then is another pressing reason why Mahler's Tenth, even in its not-quite-finished, sometimes audibly un-perfected state, still needs to be heard. Leonard Bernstein was very wrong to call it a 'tentative' step down the Schoenbergian doctrinal path: instead, more than a century after it was written, it holds up before us an image of a more inclusive, more world-embracing musical future, perhaps more relevant to us now than ever.

'A Mysterious Building'

Composing the Tenth Symphony may have been an existential lifeline for Mahler through the Inferno of summer 1910. But to those around him his behaviour was a source of the gravest anxiety. Somehow he either persuaded himself, or allowed himself to be persuaded, that the thing to do was to consult Sigmund Freud. As we've seen, Mahler had previously entertained doubts about Freud, especially his belief that sexuality was at the root of everything – this despite his assertion to Alma that Eros was 'creator of the world'. Whether Mahler had had a change of heart about Freud, or whether he was desperate to show Alma that he was willing to try anything, is hard to gauge. Whatever the case, a relation of Alma, a Viennese neurologist named Richard Nepallek, established contact with Freud, and Mahler cabled him for an appointment. Three times he arranged a meeting, then cancelled at the last minute; but Freud was well accustomed to what he called 'resistance' on the part of prospective patients, and eventually he strong-armed Mahler into a definite commitment by telling him that he would soon be leaving for Sicily, and that the opportunity would therefore be lost. Mahler yielded, and the two men agreed to meet in the Dutch town of Leiden, where Freud was taking a holiday. The date was fixed for 26 August.

It was very unusual for Freud to consent to such an unconventional form of contact. Freud normally insisted on regular hourly sessions in his chosen consulting room; instead he and Mahler went for a four-hour walk around the town, during which Mahler described some of his problems and Freud made observations. Why did Freud agree to this highly irregular 'session'? On one level he was probably flattered at being approached by such an eminent potential client. And Mahler was an artist: Freud was fascinated by creative personalities, and by the deep truths about the human psyche he felt their work often revealed. Mahler's 'best friend' Dostoyevsky was a particular source of interest to him. It is often said that Freud had an aversion to music; in fact, as he later confessed, what troubled him about music was that it *did* have an effect on him, but one that he found impossible to rationalise – and rationalising was crucial for Freud. He was certainly impressed by Mahler. Whether or not he'd taken much opportunity to acquaint himself with his music, it was soon clear to Freud that he was in the company of a genius, one moreover with a remarkable capacity for understanding when it came to psychological matters. At the same time however Freud found it difficult to get near to the core of what he diagnosed as Mahler's obsessional neurosis. It was, he said, 'as if you would dig a single shaft through a mysterious building'. He did however diagnose what he called a 'Holy Mary complex (mother fixation), which will come as no surprise to anyone who knows Part II of the Eighth Symphony'.[16]

According to Alma, Freud made a few other challenging remarks. Mahler, he said, was looking for his mother, his *Ewig-Weibliche*, in every woman. His mother had been fragile, worn down by the cares of tending to a large family, and by the deaths of several children. Unconsciously, Freud had apparently told him, Mahler wanted his wife to be the same. Alma also says that Freud had rebuked him for shackling a young woman to him when he himself was so racked by anxieties and compulsions – though there may have been an element of literary ventriloquism on Alma's part in this. Alma also tells us (and in this she is backed up by Freud's disciple Ernest Jones) that the fact that Alma's middle name was Maria was highly significant for Freud: it was also Mahler's mother's name (really Marie, but possibly pronounced 'Mari-é'), and it was the name of the Virgin Mother of God, the Queen of Heaven, in Catholic tradition, the Eighth Symphony's *Ewig-Weibliche*. Thanks to Ernest Jones we also have a detailed description of one discovery the two men arrived at together during their stroll around Leiden. At one point in their discussion, Jones tells us, Mahler suddenly said that he now understood something that had troubled him for some time. His music, he claimed, had always been mysteriously prevented from reaching the sublimest, noblest heights by something that seemed like a kind of aesthetic self-sabotage: just when something profound was about to be revealed, some scrap of 'commonplace' melody, some piece of trivial everyday musical nonsense, would thrust itself forward and ruin everything. Talking to Freud had brought him to the realisation of what it stemmed from. His father had always treated his mother roughly, and Mahler recalled a particularly painful scene that had occurred when he was a young boy. It had all proved too much for little Gustav, and he had rushed out of the house into the street, where at that very moment a hurdy-gurdy was grinding out the popular Viennese tune 'Ach du lieber Augustin' (Ah, dear Augustin). 'In Mahler's opinion the conjunction of high tragedy and light amusement was from then on inextricably fixed in his mind, and the one mood inevitably brought the other with it.'[17]

This remark has been quoted many times as though it really does explain one very characteristic feature of Mahler's music: the sudden intrusion of unsophisticated or sentimental popular music into moments of great emotional intensity. It may well be that Mahler was marked by such an early traumatic experience. But is Mahler right to claim that his music is 'spoilt' by these sudden changes of tone? Isn't the contrary true – that this very juxtaposition of profundity and seeming banality is one of the facets of his music that makes it so moving and compelling? It should be pointed out that this particular piece of alleged 'light amusement', 'Ach du lieber Augustin', is in fact the grim story of a bagpiper who is accidentally thrown into a plague pit and only just escapes with his life: throughout the song runs a recurring phrase, 'Alles ist hin' (All is lost) – Schoenberg was to make significant use of the motif associated with those words in his crisis work, the Second String Quartet. In any case, the fundamental problem with the Mahler–Freud diagnosis presented here is surely this: if the root cause of this very prominent stylistic feature was in Mahler's individual traumatic experience, why does it clearly make emotional sense to so many Mahler-lovers today, most of whom are unlikely to have had a similarly shocking experience in childhood? In fact quite a few writers over the ages have noted that 'commonplace melody' can be deeply affecting. Remember Noël Coward's famous line, 'Extraordinary how potent cheap music is'; and three centuries earlier, the English writer and physician Sir Thomas Browne, author of the classic *The Anatomy of Melancholy*, wrote words that Mahler himself could have penned himself: 'Even that vulgar and tavern music, which makes one man merry and another mad,

strikes in me a mood of deep devotion.' Mahler's juxtaposition of
the exalted and the 'cheap' in music was new, but it has had many
imitators. As so often, by mining his own 'subjective' experience,
Mahler had discovered something 'objective' – something that
could speak to, and on behalf of, whole hosts of others.

*

There is an element of irony in all this. As Mahler grappled with the
potential break-up of the central relationship in his own life, Freud
seems to have been completely unaware that he was facing something very similar: a rift that was to end one of the most important
intellectual friendships of the twentieth century, and set off a process of fission that would result in the extraordinary proliferation
of psychotherapeutic disciplines in the later twentieth century. In
1910 Freud appointed his former protégé and (for the moment)
cherished collaborator, Carl Gustav Jung, Chairman for Life of
the newly founded International Psychoanalytical Association.
Soon afterwards he would describe Jung glowingly as his adopted
eldest son, his crown prince and his heir. Could it really be that
Freud, who gave the world the concept of the 'Oedipus complex',
was blind to the potentially tragic implications of such a statement? Jung was already beginning to doubt several of Freud's key
assertions. Was sexuality really as central to understanding human
desires and personality development as Freud insisted? Was religion simply reducible to a 'projection' of mother- or father-centred
neuroses onto the heavens? Most of all, didn't the very paternal way
Freud treated his own pupils run the danger of infantilising them?
By the end of 1912 the relationship had reached a crisis point. At a
meeting in November, when Jung publicly laid bare what he saw as
the conflicts within the psychoanalytical movement, Freud fainted.

A month later he received a letter from Jung damning his treatment of his students as slavish sons. If only Freud could rid himself once and for all of his own complexes (physician, heal thyself) and stop playing the father figure to his pupils/offspring, if instead of forever trying to catch them out and expose their weak spots, he could take a good look at himself – then, says Jung, he might be prepared to change his rebellious attitude, and in the process rid himself of the pain of being in two minds about his former teacher. Freud's response, evidently long considered, was to propose that the two men cease to have any kind of private relationship. 'I will lose nothing by it,' he says airily – and almost certainly untruthfully – for he has known for some time that the emotional connection has dwindled to a 'thin thread', the protracted effect of 'past disappointments'.[18] You have disappointed me – one of the worst things a 'father' can say to his 'son'. Despite Freud's claim that he would 'lose nothing' by splitting with Jung, his daughter Anna would later say she never saw her father so depressed as at this time. One can well imagine his feelings when he received Jung's reply, agreeing in the most coldly formal terms to comply with his wishes for a termination of personal relations. Underneath the ink script of the letter, Jung adds by typewriter the last words spoken by Shakespeare's Hamlet: 'The rest is silence.' If one were to imagine a musical soundtrack to that epitaph for a once-great, hugely influential friendship, it would have to be the beginning of the finale of Mahler's Tenth Symphony.

Imagine for a moment though if, by means of some kind of historical time-shift, Mahler had been able to consult Jung instead of Freud. Would Freud's apostate pupil have been able to penetrate any deeper into the 'mysterious building' of Mahler's mind? It's hard to say, but there are features in Jung's teaching that might have led him to a deeper understanding of his own obsessions, and perhaps even offered a kind of therapeutic help. Jung would probably have arrived at a similar conclusion to Freud about Mahler's 'Holy Mary' complex, but it is also possible that his notion of the 'Anima' – the female component in the male psyche often projected onto others, and in artists frequently reinvented as a creative muse – may have helped Mahler to appreciate the real significance of the *Ewig-Weibliche* in his own work. More importantly for his own well-being, it might have enabled Mahler to, as Jung would have put it, 'take back' his projection of his Anima from Alma, in the process learning to distinguish the real woman from the 'Virgin, Mother, Queen' he had hymned so ecstatically in the Eighth Symphony. Such a discovery could have significantly eased the strain on their marital relationship – always presuming that Mahler would continue to love Alma once he had discovered that she wasn't the mother-goddess he took her to be. Jung might also have been able to enlighten Mahler as to what he called the 'gift of the wound'. For Jung, artists, thinkers and psychological healers like himself were often wounded souls, but the wound itself could also be a tremendous source of creative power and drive. Pater Profundus's agonised, Amfortas-like outpourings in the Eighth Symphony's second part show how much energy Mahler could release creatively when he engaged with the wound in his own psyche.

But it was another post-Freudian psychoanalyst, John Bowlby, whose ideas throw the most light on the significance of Mahler's relationship with his mother. Bowlby rejected Freud's theory, much developed by the former Freudian Melanie Klein, that a child's early development was strongly influenced by infantile fantasies about its mother. Bowlby insisted that there was no need to bring in fantasy: what the child was responding to was real enough, and the crucial determining factor was the 'security' of the child's relationship with its mother. Accounts of Mahler's relationship with his own mother seem to indicate that she was loving, but that she was also prone to illness, and much distracted by pregnancy, childbirth and care of infants, to say nothing of the grief she must have felt at the loss of several of her own children. How much attention was she able to give to her highly sensitive son? It is quite possible that Mahler idealised her, at the expense of her allegedly brutish husband. Children with what Bowlby called 'secure attachments' to the mother do not normally develop mother fixations, nor do they spend the rest of their lives trying to find some figure to adore in place of their mothers. One thing on which many twentieth-century psychotherapeutic schools agree is that what Freud called the 'Mother Complex' is actually a massive over-compensation for something unconsciously felt to be lacking. It is one of the paradoxes of parenting that children with secure bonds to their mothers usually find it much easier to leave home emotionally and develop mature relationships with others than do children with 'insecure attachments'. Mahler's intense love of and absorption in 'mother nature' is another possible symptom of such an insecure attachment. Strikingly, the same claim could be made for Mahler's contemporary Jean Sibelius, whose relationship with his mother also appears to have been problematic.

Mahler's suffocating, almost frightening veneration for Alma, his oceanic, but also emotionally complicated outpouring of adoration for her (or for some impossible fantasy Mother-Goddess) in the Eighth Symphony, his near-mental collapse at the prospect of losing her – are these products of a deep psychological wound of the kind explored by Jung, and later by Bowlby? If so, that could be one of the reasons his music speaks so powerfully and directly to some listeners. As Jung and Bowlby both came to realise, there are in all probability a great many wounded souls in this world. But Mahler does not simply lay bare his own wounds before us, as if the act of artistic creation were no different from opening up one's soul in a psychoanalytic session. In composing he gives form to his feelings, shapes them into something that can be both experienced intensely and contemplated objectively: thus for some listeners his music is able to articulate feelings that may have been previously experienced as disordered and therefore threatening, and in doing so, as Shakespeare put it, give 'to airy nothing a local habitation and a name'. In the process of artistically objectifying his feelings, Mahler takes potentially painful emotions and transforms them into something beautiful, magnificent – perhaps the most affirmative function art can perform for us. We behold an image of our suffering, striving selves, not as we feel we are, but as we might be. There is dignity and beauty even in our pain. At the same time, in the Eighth Symphony's wild, at times almost insane exultation, its mixture of sophistication and naivety, of profundity and borderline 'commonplace' sentimentality, we can sense the glory of simply being alive, wounds and all. In such moments Mahler's music can perhaps help us, as Nietzsche put it in *The Birth of Tragedy*, to face existence in all its wonder and horror and 'say Yes to life'.

Writing of Mahler's literary hero Dostoyevsky, Virginia Woolf made the following wonderful observation. It could apply just as readily to Mahler himself. Woolf has been talking of the restraining social value judgements and standards of 'good taste' under which she felt some of Dostoyevsky's contemporaries laboured:

No such restraints were laid on Dostoyevsky. It is all the same to him whether you are noble or simple, a tramp or a great lady.

*Whoever you are, you are the vessel of this perplexed liquid, this
cloudy, yeasty, precious stuff, the soul. The soul is not restrained by
barriers. It overflows, it floods, it mingles with the souls of others
... for nothing is outside Dostoyevsky's province; and when he
is tired, he does not stop, he goes on. He cannot restrain himself.
Out it tumbles upon us, hot, scalding, mixed, marvellous, terrible,
oppressive – the human soul.*[19]

*

Whatever the truth of Freud's insights, Mahler's reaction to them
seems to have wavered considerably. One moment he was telegraphing Alma to inform her that he was now effectively cured;
the next he was muttering about mountains made out of molehills.
But in any case, there were other pressing matters to be attended
to now, above all the premiere of the Eighth Symphony. Mahler
returned from Leiden to Altschluderbach on 28 August, and only
six days later he was setting off for his full week of rehearsals in
Munich. In all probability work on the Tenth Symphony was put
to one side, but the evidence is that Mahler now considered it
complete as an overall conception, and once he had that in mind,
he rarely made significant changes. What was left to be done was
more a matter of cosmetic enhancement than of creating the living being itself.

The rest we have already seen. Mahler threw himself into the
rehearsals: his energy impressed some, but others, like Lotte Lehmann, were alarmed by his physical appearance and feared the
worst. The two performances were sensationally successful: as
Jonathan Carr observes, this was one of the last great Central European premieres before the old Europe began its own catastrophic
slide into the abyss in the First World War. For Mahler himself it

was an artistic and personal triumph. It seems that around this time Mahler and Alma resumed sexual relations, and as the letter Gropius sketched to Alma shows, for a moment at least it looked as though Mahler might have won the contest and won back the heart of his wife. Or was it really the other way round – in attempting to win back Alma, Mahler had pushed himself too far, and in doing so effectively condemned himself to death, thus opening the door for Gropius to reclaim her? That complex question provided an important stimulus for another major musical work of art. One of those present at the Munich premiere was Alma's former lover Alexander Zemlinsky. In 1916, at the height of the war, Zemlinsky completed his operatic masterpiece *Eine florentinische Tragödie* ('A Florentine Tragedy'). The opera's plot, based on an unfinished verse drama by Oscar Wilde, tells of a rich sixteenth-century Florentine merchant, Simone, who returns home to find his much younger wife Bianca alone with the handsome Guido. Simone is wealthy and powerful, but ugly, and unsurprisingly the beautiful Bianca has turned her attentions elsewhere. Simone rightly suspects the couple are having an affair, but as he hasn't actually caught the lovers *in flagrante*, and as Guido is moreover the son of the Duke of Florence, the laws of gentlemanly etiquette prevent Simone from challenging him to a duel on the spot. Instead Simone pretends to treat Guido as a potential customer, displaying ever more fabulous fabrics and ornaments, while the cornered Guido is forced to feign interest. Provoked by Simone's tactics, and egged on by Bianca, Guido accepts the challenge to duel, but surprisingly Simone proves the stronger: discarding his sword, he strangles Guido. Then comes a breathtaking emotional reversal. Ignoring the body of her lover, Bianca turns in admiration to her husband: 'Why didn't you tell me you were so strong?' 'Why didn't you tell me you were so beautiful?' Simone replies, and the curtain falls with husband and wife reconciled – and on one of the most perverse, disturbing, weirdly beautiful 'happy endings' in musical theatre.

Profoundly hurt by his own rejection by Alma, Zemlinsky was still looking for opportunities to get back at her, a decade and a half after she discarded him and married Mahler. In all probability that was the deciding factor in Zemlinsky's choice of Wilde's text. Alma herself certainly thought so. When she saw the Viennese premiere of *Eine florentinische Tragödie* in 1917 she saw herself, Gropius and Mahler in the opera's love triangle, but this time with Mahler fully avenged. If vindicating his former love-rival caused any pain to Zemlinsky, it was worth enduring it for the opportunity to indict his betrayer on the public stage – and didn't he, Zemlinsky, know perfectly well what it felt like to be written off in favour of a stronger rival? Alma wrote to Zemlinsky in fury; Zemlinsky's reply rammed home the connection with her own perfidy. Fate, he tells her, has driven two people apart. They have retreated into their individual dream-worlds. To bring them back to reality and awareness of each other a crisis, a terrible catastrophe is called for: another life has to be sacrificed to save two others: 'And you, of all people, have failed to understand that?!'And with a deft one-word tweak to the opera's penultimate line, Zemlinsky delivered the *coup de grâce*: 'Why did you not tell me you were so – weak?'[20]

Coda:

14 September 1910 – 18 May 1911

In the event, the love triangle continued. Alma seems to have come to the decision that she had to return to New York with Mahler. But that certainly did not mean breaking completely with Walter Gropius. As we have seen, Gropius sketched a letter giving up Alma to Mahler, but apparently it was never sent. Alma told him that Mahler would die if she left him, and Gropius appears to have been unwilling to shoulder that responsibility. But for Alma the prospect of having a famous husband, increasingly venerated as a composer as well as a conductor, while at the same time keeping up the contact with an adoring and virile young lover, even if at a long distance, clearly had its attractions. Mahler's biographer Henry-Louis de La Grange was convinced that Mahler himself knew that Alma was still corresponding with Gropius, but decided to turn a blind eye on condition she continue to stay with him and support him – which suggests a much more balanced, emotionally pragmatic state of mind on Mahler's part than would have been possible the previous summer. Had the Eighth Symphony's sensational success been in some important way cathartic, or was it simply resignation? In all probability Mahler did know that Alma had continued to correspond with Gropius, but whether he knew how much communication had taken place is another matter – Alma was picking up Gropius's replies at a post office in Vienna. It also seems very likely that the lovers had successfully concealed from Mahler the fact that they were still meeting. Secrecy was vital – and no doubt it added to the excitement. Knowingly or not,

Mahler agreed to let Alma set off by train from Vienna two days before him, ostensibly so that she could visit Paris before joining him for the sea voyage to America. Alma's next letter to Gropius, from Vienna, bears the hallmarks of the excitement of a delicious intrigue. She will board the Orient Express on Friday 14 October at 11.55 a.m. Gropius would also board the train in Vienna but, in keeping with the cloak-and-dagger nature of the escapade, he had his ticket made out in the name of Walter Grote from Berlin, and waited till the train arrived at Munich before joining Alma in her compartment. There is no evidence that the irony of reuniting at the location of Mahler's greatest triumph perturbed either of them. Indeed Alma recalled spending 'hours of bliss' with Gropius in Paris, while Mahler made his way to board the *Kaiser Wilhelm II* at Bremerhaven.

Back in New York, Mahler set about his duties energetically. He also carried on his campaign to win Alma's favour, sending her expensive presents and yet more adoring notes. He radically revised his attitude to her composing, now encouraging her efforts with lavish praise and attempting on her behalf to interest publishers and potential performers. For the moment he seems to have been keen to stay put in New York. The New York Philharmonic might not compare with Viennese musicians in artistic quality, but the conditions of his contract, and the time he was able to spend rehearsing them, made it easier for him to impose his will on them. Critical reactions to his performances in New York were somewhat mixed, though there was genuine enthusiasm in some quarters, and when he took the orchestra on a hugely demanding pre-Christmas tour, taking in the cities of Pittsburgh, Cleveland, Buffalo, Rochester, Syracuse and Utica, audiences and critics were ecstatic. Had Mahler survived the crisis of summer 1910 after all?

Gropius was now worried by what he felt were mixed messages from Alma. Sometimes she seemed ardent enough, at others she was more distant, and there were too many signs that she was adjusting well to life in New York with her husband. A performance of Mahler's Seventh Symphony in Berlin, in January 1911, shook Gropius's confidence still further. Could he really compete with such a Titan? But the Titan was weaker than he knew. Mahler's sore throat, previously linked to his heart defect, returned just before Christmas, but this time he seemed able to power through it, working determinedly with the orchestra and finding time to go snowballing in Central Park with his little daughter Anna, 'Gucki'.

But by February the septic throat returned, this time with a high fever. The family doctor, Joseph Fränkel, recognised the seriousness of the situation and ordered tests to be carried out immediately. This time the diagnosis was genuinely serious: sub-acute bacterial endocarditis, a dangerous infection for anyone with a heart defect, however 'compensated'. Today penicillin, if administered in time, would probably have saved Mahler, but Alexander Fleming's discovery of that drug would not take place until 1928, seventeen years later. Mahler was now in serious danger. Alma was keen to lay the blame on New York, publicly citing the lack of respect he allegedly experienced, bullying by the orchestra's ruling guarantors' committee (as though Mahler had ever caved in to bullies!) and the incomprehension of obtuse critics.

Once again however there may have been an element of deflection going on here. Mahler's determination to plunge himself into a hugely demanding work schedule no doubt contributed to his decline, but even that could be seen as symptomatic of a desire to escape the inner torment caused by Alma's affair with Gropius. If he rightly suspected that it was still going on, that too would have added to the stress on his heart. Dr Fränkel advised Mahler to consult an eminent bacteriologist in Paris, though whether he really entertained much hope from this is hard to judge. Apparently when Mahler learned that the prognosis was bad, he stated that if he were to die soon, then it had to be in Vienna. And so, on 8 April, Mahler and his family boarded the SS *Amerika*, destination Cherbourg.

Two other artistic celebrities were also on board. Mahler's friend, the composer-pianist Ferruccio Busoni, attempted to distract Mahler with demonstrations of invertible atonal counterpoint – kindly meant, at least. Stefan Zweig remembered seeing Mahler silhouetted against the vast grey sky and sea, and claims to have seen both 'boundless sorrow' and 'something resounding into the sublime, like music' in his appearance, but how much that characteristically lyrical memory was influenced by hindsight is hard to say. Alma tells us that 'the beauty of his black shining eyes, his white face, his black hair and blood-red mouth struck terror into my heart'.[1] But on arrival in the hotel in Paris, an almost miraculous transformation took place. Alma woke up to find Mahler fully dressed and shaved, and apparently his old energetic self again. Hadn't he always said that would recover as soon as he set foot in Europe again, he asked her? He was going out for a drive, and as soon as they'd both got over the voyage they would set off together for a holiday in Egypt! Mahler ordered a car, and set out as a man fully restored to health. An hour later he returned, pale and desperately weak. The miracle had been a delusion.

A Viennese blood specialist, Dr Franz Chvostek, was summoned. In Mahler's presence he was heartily optimistic: they would go to Vienna that evening and, given a decent rest, he'd be able to go back to work again. Alone with Alma, however, Chvostek insisted they move him at once: any delay and it would be too late. Mahler arrived at the sanatorium in the Mariangasse on the morning of 12 May to find Vienna already in mourning. Crowds assembled outside, bouquets of flowers were delivered, the papers went into ecstasies of anticipated grief, but Mahler was probably too ill to notice. What would he have made of this belated demonstration on the part of his 'hated, beloved Vienna'? A few were indignant on his behalf. It was all crocodile tears, according to Berta Zuckerkandl, while Karl Kraus was characteristically acerbic: now the Viennese were trying to purge themselves of the effects of bad conscience by deluging him with expressions of sympathy. Even the *Neues Wiener Journal*, which had once led the Mahler witch-hunt, was now proclaiming him as the city's beloved son, and preparing to go into full mourning overdrive.

While Mahler was still lucid he expressed the wish to be buried beside Putzi in Vienna's Grinzing Cemetery. The wish was carried out, and a ghost memory of that eerily silent ceremony, and of the distantly tolling bells, endures in the last of Schoenberg's *Sechs kleine Stücke*, op. 19. Schoenberg, still impoverished, and the victim of another of philistine Vienna's persecution campaigns, had been another of Mahler's last concerns: once he was gone, who would be left to support Schoenberg? Alma, together with her stepfather Carl Moll, duly promised to support him. Another last act was the consigning of the sketches for the Tenth Symphony to Alma – clearly he meant them to survive, and perhaps also to be heard. According to Alma, Mahler – like Beethoven – died in the middle of a violent thunderstorm. But where Beethoven (at least according to one witness) died shaking his fist at the heavens, Mahler passed into unconsciousness with the word 'Mozarte' on his lips – or was that 'Mozartl', a typically Viennese affectionate diminutive? If so, then Mahler was received into the next world, not by the *Ewig-Weibliche*, but by the composer revered by many in his time as the 'divine child', and hymned as such at the opening of Mahler's Fourth Symphony, the work that culminates in 'a child's view of Paradise'. The death rattle then began, and within a matter of hours Mahler was dead. After having told us that Mahler breathed his last breath with the elements raging around him, Alma then tells that when 'his beloved and beautiful soul had fled . . . the silence was more deathly than all else'. Another contradiction incriminating the witness? Perhaps not. Sometimes the opposite is also true.

Notes

Introduction: The Arrival of the Queen of Heaven

1 Alma Mahler, *Gustav Mahler: Memories and Letters*, place/date of publication, p. 178.
2 Ibid., p. 178.
3 The original of this letter is in the possession of the author's piano teacher, Graham Lloyd, and his partner, the composer Ian Venables. It is reproduced with their permission.
4 Alma Mahler, op. cit., p. 335.
5 Ibid., p. 179.

1: Setting the Stage

1 Stefan Zweig, *Die Welt von Gestern* ('The World of Yesterday'), Stockholm, 1942, author's translation.
2 Ethel Smyth, *Impressions that Remained*, Vol. 2, London, 1923, p. 174.
3 Mahler's remarks are found in Henry-Louis De La Grange, *Gustav Mahler*, Vol. 4, *A New Life Cut Short*, Oxford, 2008, pp. 959–63.
4 Peter Heyworth, *Otto Klemperer: His Life and Times*, Vol. 1, Cambridge, 1983, p. 48.
5 Kurt and Herta Blaukopf, *Gustav Mahler*, London, 1974, p. 211.

2: 'Arise, Light of the Senses'

1 Alma Mahler, op. cit., p. 102.
2 'Gustav Mahler: In Memoriam', 1912, included in Arnold Schoenberg, *Style and Idea*, London, 1975, p. 447.
3 Quoted in Lebrecht, *Mahler Remembered*, London, 1987, p. 253.
4 Acts of the Apostles, Chapter 2, vv. 5–11, Authorised Version (King James Version), 1611.
5 Quoted in Lebrecht, op. cit., p. 91.

6 Richard Specht, *Gustav Mahler*, Berlin, 1913, p. 38.

7 Letter to Alma, 22 (?) June 1909, *Gustav Mahler: Letters to his Wife*, ed. De La Grange and Günther Weiss, rev. and trans, by Antony Beaumont, London, 1985, pp. 326–7.

8 Letter to Johann Peter Eckermann, 6 June 1831 (author's translation).

9 Letter to Alma Mahler, 18 October 1910, quoted in De La Grange and Weiss, op. cit., pp. 362–3.

10 Percy Bysshe Shelley, *Essays, Letters from Abroad*, 1845, pp. 33–6.

3: Why Symphony?

1 Karl Eckman, *Jean Sibelius: The Life and Personality of an Artist*, trans. Edward Birse, Helsingfors, 1935, p. 190.

2 Letter to Axel Carpelan, 20 July 1909, in Erik Tawaststjerna, *Jean Sibelius*, Vol. 4, Helsinki, 1988, p. 175.

3 Ibid., Vol. 4, p. 103.

4 See for instance Ian Watt's seminal study, *The Rise of the Novel*, London, 1957.

5 See the booklet notes for the Archiv recorded set of the complete Beethoven Symphonies, Archiv 439 900 2.

6 Richard Wagner, 'Beethoven's Choral Symphony in Dresden: Programme', in *Richard Wagner's Prose Works*, trans. William Ashton Ellis, London, 1898, Vol. 7, pp 247–52.

7 Richard Wagner, 'The Art Work of the Future', in *Richard Wagner's Prose Works*, trans. William Ashton Ellis, London, 1898, Vol. 6, p. 89.

8 Ibid., p. 155.

9 Extracts from Mahler's programme notes for his Second Symphony reproduced in Deryck Cooke, *Gustav Mahler: An Introduction to his Music*, London, 1980, pp. 53–4.

10 Ibid.

11 Ludwig Scheidermair, *Gustav Mahler*, Leipzig, 1901, p. 14.

12 Romain Rolland, *Musicians of Today*, trans. Mary Blaiklock, London, 1915, p. 225.

Interlude: Behind the Scenes

1 Trans. in De La Grange, op. cit., pp. 925–6.

2 Ibid., pp. 926–7.

3 Ibid., pp. 1027–8.

4: God or Demon?

1 Alma Mahler, op. cit., p. 180.

2 Emil Gutmann, *Gustav Mahler als Organisator*, quoted in De La Grange, op. cit., p. 968.

3 Lilli Lehmann, *Mein Weg Leipzig 1913*, quoted in Blaukopf, op. cit., pp. 239–40.

4 Letter of 12 September 1910, in Moldenauer, *Anton von Webern: A Chronicle of His Life and Work*, London, 1978, p. 135.

5 Stefan Zweig, *The World of Yesterday*, Stockholm, 1942, p. 201.

6 Thomas Mann, letter to Wolfgang Born, 17 March 1921, in *The Letters of Thomas Mann, 1889–1955*, trans. Richard and Clara Winston, New York, 1960, p. 110.

7 Thomas Mann, 'Coming to Terms with Richard Wagner', in *Thomas Mann: Pro and Contra Wagner*, trans. Allan Blunden, London, 1985, pp. 45–8.

8 Letter to Anna von Mildenburg, quoted in Cooke, op. cit., p. 63.

5: Approaching the Inexpressible

1 Quoted in Constantin Floros, *Gustav Mahler: The Symphonies*, trans. Vernon and Jutta Wicker, Singapore, 1993, p. 213.

6: Questions of Identity

1 Alma Mahler, op. cit., p. 109.

2 Guido Adler, *Gustav Mahler*, Vienna and Leipzig, 1916, author's translation.

3 Alma Mahler, op. cit., p. 26.

4 Ibid, p. 101.

5 Quoted in Richard Specht, *Gustav Mahlers VIII. Symphonie: Thematische Analyse*, Leipzig, 1910, p. 6.

6 Stefan Zweig, op. cit., Chapter VI, author's translation.

7   Richard Specht, *Gustav Mahler*, 1913, quoted in Lebrecht, op. cit.,
    p. 186.

8   Nietzsche, *Der Fall Wagner* (The Case of Wagner), Section 3, author's
    translation.

9   Nietzsche, *Ecce Homo*, Chapter VII ('Human, all too Human'),
    Section 2, author's translation.

10 Quoted in Joseph Auner, *A Schoenberg Reader*, Yale, 2008, p. 159.

11 Ibid, p. 160.

12 Quoted in Hans Heinz Stuckenschmidt, *Schoenberg*, Richmond,
    2018, p. 277.

13 Quoted in Adler, op. cit., author's translation.

14 Alma Mahler op. cit., p. 170.

15 Quoted in De La Grange, op. cit., p. 950.

16 Rolland, op. cit., p. 225.

17 Golo Mann, *The History of Germany Since 1789*, trans. Marian
    Jackson, London, 1974.

18 Eric Hobsbawm, *The Age of Empire: 1875–1914*, London, 1987, p. 314.

19 Golo Mann, op. cit., p. 429.

20 Goethe, *Faust* Part I, author's translation.

21 Niekerk, 'Mahler's Goethe', *Musical Quarterly*, 2006, No. 2–3, p. 265.

22 Max Reger, letter to Duke George II of Saxen-Meiningen, 14 June
    1912, quoted in De La Grange, op. cit., pp. 976–7.

23 Arnold Schoenberg, letter to Gustav Mahler, 5 July 1910, in Blaukopf,
    op. cit., p. 265.

24 Hans Gál, *The Golden Age of Vienna*, London, 1948, p. 70.

25 Quoted in Peter Vergo, *Art in Vienna: 1898–1918*, London, 1975, p. 33.

26 Ibid., p. 32.

27 Gustav Mahler, programme note for Symphony no. 2, quoted in
    Cooke, op. cit., p. 53.

28 Stefan Zweig, op. cit., Chapter II.

29 Ibid.

30 *Vereignigung bildender Künstler Österreichs*, Katalog, Vienna, 1902.

31 Vergo, op. cit., p. 34.

32 Quoted in Kurt and Herta Blaukopf, op. cit., p. 194.

33 Stefan George, *Entrückung* ('Rapture' or 'Ecstatic Transport').

34 Florian Illies, *1913: The Year before the Storm*, trans. Shaun Whiteside and Jamie Lee Searle, London, 2013.

35 Zweig, op. cit., Chapter III.

36 Simon Winder, *Danubia: A Personal History of Habsburg Europe*, London, 2013, pp. 425–6.

37 Ellis Dye, 'Figurations of the Feminine in Goethe's Faust', in *Goethe's Faust: A Companion to Parts I and II*, New York, 2006, pp. 116–17.

38 Karl Pringsheim, *Erinnerungen an Gustav Mahler*, quoted in Lebrecht, op. cit., p. 195.

39 Alfred Einstein, *Schubert: The Man and His Music*, London, 1951, p. 321.

40 Theodor Adorno, *Mahler: A Musical Physiognomy*, trans. Edmund Jephcott, Chicago, 1992, p. 141.

41 Raymond Hingley, *Dostoyevsky: His Life and Work*, London, 1978, pp. 143–4.

42 Deryck Cooke, op. cit., London, 1980, pp. 82–3.

43 Alma Mahler, op. cit., pp. 47–8.

7: The Shadow Falls

1 Alma Mahler, op. cit., p. 70.

2 Ibid, p. 122.

3 Bruno Walter, op. cit., pp. 206–7.

4 Letter to Bruno Walter, quoted in Michael Kennedy, *Mahler (The Master Musicians)*, London, 1974, p. 67.

5 Letter to Bruno Walter, quoted in Constantin Floros, op. cit., p. 243.

6 Deryck Cooke, op. cit., p. 104.

7 Alban Berg, letter to his wife, quoted in *The Mahler Companion*, ed. Donald Mitchell and Andre Nicholson, Oxford, 1999, p. 470.

8: 'To Live for You, To Die for You'

1 Letter to Alma Mahler, 19 December 1901, in De La Grange and Weiss, op. cit., p. 83.

2 Alma Mahler, *And the Bridge is Love*, London, 1959, p. 128.

3 Alma Mahler, *Gustav Mahler: Memories and Letters*, p. 172.

4 Ibid., pp. 172–3.

5 Erich Heller, *Kafka*, London, 1974, p. 96.

6 De La Grange and Weiss, op. cit., p. 375.

7 Quoted in Deryck Cooke, 'The History of Mahler's Tenth Symphony', printed in the score, *Gustav Mahler: A Performing Version of the Draft for the Tenth Symphony*, London, 1976, p. xiii.

8 Arnold Schoenberg, 'Gustav Mahler', in *Style and Idea: Selected Writings of Arnold Schoenberg*, trans. Leo Black, London, 1975, p. 470.

9 Leonard Bernstein, *The Unanswered Question: Six Talks at Harvard*, London, 1976, p. 317.

10 Kennedy, op. cit., p. 155.

11 See Richard Maunder, *Mozart's Requiem: On Preparing a New Edition*, Oxford, 1988.

12 De La Grange and Weiss, op. cit., p. 378.

13 Kennedy, op. cit., p. 155.

14 Alma Mahler, op. cit., p. 135.

15 Quoted in Malcolm Gillies, *Bartók Remembered*, London, 1990, p. 188.

16 Quoted in Theodore Reik, *The Haunting Melody: Psychoanalytic Experiences in Life and Music*, New York, 1953, p. 343.

17 Ernest Jones, *The Life and Work of Sigmund Freud*, London, 1953–7, Vol. 2, p. 89.

18 Ibid., p. 295.

19 Virginia Woolf, 'The Russian Point of View', in *The Common Reader*, London, 1925, p. 180.

20 Quoted in Antony Beaumont, *Zemlinsky*, London, 2000, p. 245.

Coda: 14 September 1910–18 May 1911

1 Alma Mahler, *Gustav Mahler: Memories and Letters*, p. 195.

Acknowledgements

Over the years, so many people have contributed to the formation of the ideas in this book that to attempt a fully comprehensive list would be a nightmare. Some names however have to be singled out. When it comes to Mahler and his music, I must thank the composers Colin and David Matthews and Robert Simpson, the musicologists Paul Banks, Julian Johnson and Michael Kennedy, and the conductors Riccardo Chailly, Sir Simon Rattle and Klaus Tennstedt. For enriching my knowledge of Mahler's Jewish cultural background I am also grateful to Rabbi Julia Neuberger and to Mahler biographer Norman Lebrecht, whose book *Mahler Remembered* was a particularly valuable source.

When it came to the history of the German-speaking world in which Mahler grew up and prospered, I probably wouldn't have had the confidence to tackle such an immense subject without the inspiration and encouragement of historians Giles McDonogh, Tim Blanning and Sir Richard Evans. Thanks too to my friend Ben Attwood, consultant anaesthetist, for one particularly telling piece of information about the state of anaesthetic medicine in Mahler's lifetime.

When it comes to the literature and philosophy in which Mahler was steeped from early in his life I am especially indebted to the poet and Goethe translator David Constantine, to Professor Rudiger Görner, to the translator and Schopenhauer expert John Harrison, and to the philosopher Raymond Tallis.

For information and insight into psychology, and especially

into Freudian psychoanalysis (and not least into Freud's alleged aversion to music), I must thank Dr Elizabeth Arno, Dr Jeanne Wolff Bernstein, Michelle Duncan, Andrew Jamieson, Darian Leader, Brigitte Mauthner, Julie Jaffee Nagel, David Nice, William Meredith Owen, Josep Marco Pallares, Michael Trimble, and the director of the Freud Museum in Vienna, Monika Pessler. On the subject of Vienna I can't fail to thank Wittigo Keller, curator of the Museum at Vienna's Central Cemetery, for the fascinating and enjoyably macabre personal tour he gave me and my producer Elizabeth Arno during the making of our BBC Radio 3 documentary *Beautiful Death*. Also very illuminating on the subject of Viennese attitudes to death were Dr Isabella Ackerl and Dr Edmund Winter.

Finally, special thanks to Colin Matthews for reading the first version of this book and offering many valuable suggestions, and in a couple of cases, corrections. Thanks, of course, to my editor at Faber, Belinda Matthews, for her insights and for much-needed encouragement when the task ahead seemed just too mountainous. I also much appreciated the sympathetic editorial work of Michael Downes and of Kate Ward, also at Faber. And thanks to my wife Kate, a therapist and mental health practitioner, for support during the writing of the book and for her own highly characterful insights into Mahler and his *Ewig-Weibliche* obsession. What would I have thought had I known, listening to Klaus Tennstedt's heaven-storming performance of the Eighth in London's Royal Festival Hall in 1991, that my future wife was in the alto section of the chorus, having one of the most intense musical experiences of her life. Nearly thirty years later, I'm not sure I could have written this book without her.

Index